"This is a lovely book—rooted in a love for Scripture, and love for all _____ ___ ____ the God who reveals himself in Christ and through the biblical Word. Kurtz has managed to unite faith, scholarship, profundity, and readability on a crucial topic. We need more books like this one!"

Matthew Levering, James N. Jr. and Mary D. Perry Chair of Theology at Mundelein Seminary

"With its negative prefix, divine incomprehensibility appears to say that knowledge of God is impossible, thereby leading some people to become agnostic. Like appearances, however, prefixes too can be deceiving. By retrieving the classical formulation of the doctrine of divine incomprehensibility together with the all-important Creator-creature distinction, Ronni Kurtz ably demonstrates why divine incomprehensibility need not lead to agnosticism. Unlike God, *Light Unapproachable* is far from being incomprehensible. It is a clearly written, cogently argued, and readily comprehensible account of how theology can apprehend what the accommodating God has chosen to reveal about himself."

Kevin Vanhoozer, research professor of systematic theology at Trinity Evangelical Divinity School

"If man's chief end is to glorify God and enjoy him forever, as one catechism puts it, it would seem that knowledge of God should be possible. Yet, all the historic Christian traditions affirm the incomprehensibility of God. How is this possible? Ronni Kurtz has provided for us a masterful demonstration of how incomprehensibility must be accepted as a divine perfection and therefore as something extolling God's glory. This volume shows the implications of this attribute for the practice of theology itself, showing that the knowledge of God does not imply conceptual mastery."

Adonis Vidu, Andrew Mutch Distinguished Professor of Theology at Gordon-Conwell Theological Seminary

"It is nothing short of amazing that so few theologians today have written on God's incomprehensibility. Perhaps this is not surprising. After all, the title wave of modern theology has left us with a domesticated God, vanquishing the beauty of the infinite. In the wake of this wasteland, Ronni Kurtz is planting new seeds with deep roots in sacred Scripture and the Great Tradition. With a clarity that matches the accessibility of his research, Kurtz demonstrates that the incomprehensibility of God is foundational to the recovery of classical theism today. More still, God's incomprehensibility is like a rich garden in which each vine is connected to the next as God's incomprehensibility connects everything from divine simplicity to the analogy of being to our participation in the beatific vision. Truly, Kurtz has planted the seeds for a great harvest to come."

Matthew Barrett, professor of Christian theology at Midwestern Baptist Theological Seminary and author of *None Greater* and *Simply Trinity*

"With the grace of an experienced teacher, Ronni Kurtz shows why the confession of God's ultimate incomprehensibility has formed the heart of Christian theology since at least the fourth century. His book draws the reader into the depths of the God revealed as mystery."

Andrew Radde-Gallwitz, professor in the Program of Liberal Studies at the University of Notre Dame

"Kurtz's *Light Unapproachable* starts out with solid Christian common sense about how God accommodates revelation to us, then elaborates it with biblical analysis, fortifies it with historical witnesses, and applies it to a project in theological method with great promise for a wide range of readers."

Fred Sanders, systematic theologian and professor at the Torrey Honors College at Biola University

LIGHT
UNAPPROACHABLE

DIVINE INCOMPREHENSIBILITY

AND THE TASK OF THEOLOGY

RONNI KURTZ

ivp Academic

An imprint of InterVarsity Press
Downers Grove, Illinois

InterVarsity Press
P.O. Box 1400 | Downers Grove, IL 60515-1426
ivpress.com | email@ivpress.com

InterVarsity Press® is the publishing division of InterVarsity Christian Fellowship/USA®. For more information,
visit intervarsity.org.

Scripture quotations, unless otherwise noted, are from The Holy Bible, English Standard Version, copyright © 2001 by
Crossway Bibles, a division of Good News Publishers. Used by permission. All rights reserved.

The publisher cannot verify the accuracy or functionality of website URLs used in this book beyond the date of publication.

Cover design: David Fassett
Interior design: Jeanna Wiggins

ISBN 978-1-5140-0710-5 (print) | ISBN 978-1-5140-0711-2 (digital)

Printed in the United States of America ∞

Library of Congress Cataloging-in-Publication Data
Names: Kurtz, Ronni, author.
Title: Light unapproachable : divine incomprehensibility and the task of
   theology / Ronni Kurtz.
Description: Downers Grove, IL : IVP Academic, [2024] | Includes
   bibliographical references.
Identifiers: LCCN 2024006603 (print) | LCCN 2024006604 (ebook) | ISBN
   9781514007105 (paperback) | ISBN 9781514007112 (ebook)
Subjects: LCSH: God (Christianity)–Knowableness–History of doctrines. |
   Theology, Doctrinal–History.
Classification: LCC BT98 .K75 2024 (print) | LCC BT98 (ebook) | DDC
   231/.4–dc23/eng/20240513
LC record available at https://lccn.loc.gov/2024006603
LC ebook record available at https://lccn.loc.gov/2024006604

31 30 29 28 27 26 25 24 | 13 12 11 10 9 8 7 6 5 4 3 2 1

TO JOSHUA THOMAS BROWN,

the greatest of gifts and the dearest of brothers.

Forever grateful that in turning his thousand gears of grace

the incomprehensible God made our days align.

Which he will display at the proper time—he who is the blessed and only Sovereign, the King of kings and Lord of lords, who alone has immortality, who dwells in unapproachable light, whom no one has ever seen or can see. To him be honor and eternal dominion. Amen.

1 Timothy 6:15-16

Men of good sense who focus their minds' eyes sharply on the attributes of the ineffable Godhead, see it as existing beyond every created thing, transcending all acuity of intellect, being wholly outside bodily appearance and, as all-wise Paul says, "dwelling in light unapproachable."

Cyril of Alexandria

CONTENTS

ACKNOWLEDGMENTS

IN 2018, I WAS SITTING in a coffee shop in Kansas City, Missouri, working on a manuscript about the doctrine of divine immutability. While developing that manuscript I consistently bumped up against the doctrine of divine incomprehensibility. Each time divine incomprehensibility came up in my research I felt conflicting emotions of frustration and awe. I felt frustration that theological inquiry about an incomprehensible God can be so cumbersome and, at the same time, felt awe in that God's incomprehensibility means the pilgrimage into theological wisdom is a never-ending journey into beauty. In that coffee shop, I felt captivated enough by the thought of God's incomprehensibility that I decided to just take out a sheet of paper and jot my thoughts on the subject down so I could get them out of my head and return to considering immutability. The notes on that sheet of paper became the seed planted that would eventually sprout into this volume.

Not five feet from me that day, sitting at a table next to mine, was Joshua Brown. For any reader who has found in a family member not only a familial relationship but also a best friend, you might know what a gift someone like that can be. While a blood relative, Josh is also a best friend. He is the most consistent of companions, the dearest of friends, and he has spent untold hours listening to more theological musings from me than any one person ought to be subjected. He is of the most stable, generous, kind, and honorable men I know. With much joy, I dedicate this book to him. His wife, Meagan, is worthy of many thanks as well, as she is dear to my wife and me and provides consistent friendship in our lives.

There are others I'd like to acknowledge who stand behind this volume. First is the wonderful and capable team at IVP Academic. David McNutt acquired this book and worked with me in the early stages of development. He took a shot on a young writer, and I will be ever grateful to him for that. Colton Bernasol served as the primary editor of the manuscript, and his editorial insights will surely prove to be a gift to the reader. He made arguments tighter and prose stronger, and the book is much the better for his time in the text.

I'd also like to thank a few academic administrators. First, my dean, Trent Rogers, is more gracious and thoughtful than any faculty member could deserve. Dr. Rogers made sure that my lecture schedule and teaching load was strategic so that I had the bandwidth to bring this volume to completion. As many faculty know, academic administrators who are supportive of your writing and research are a tremendous gift. Second, I'd also like to thank our university's provost, Dr. Thomas Mach. Like Dr. Rogers, Dr. Mach is more supportive and thoughtful than I could say. Moreover, while writing this manuscript, the provost's office was gracious in subsidizing my enrolling in a course in theological Latin at the University of Dayton, which benefited the research for this book. My colleagues in the School of Biblical and Theological studies are also deserving of acknowledgment. Over many lunches, coffees, and class breaks, they have endured with my insistence on talking about what we can and cannot know about the triune God. Special thanks to J. R. Gilhooly, who was the consistent reminder I needed to get the book out of my head and onto paper.

I'd also like to extend thanks and appreciation to my local church—Trinity Church in Dayton, Ohio. The proper location for Christian theology is the church, where other believers have covenanted to pilgrim with you, watching both your life and your doctrine. The pastors and members of Trinity Church made sure I loved the incomprehensible God more than I loved the incomprehensibility of God.

Finally, I'd like to thank my family. My daughter, Finley Jane, had her second and third birthday in the time I was working on this manuscript. If I was not already convinced of God's incomprehensibility before constructing this manuscript, I would have become so due to the incomprehensible gift she is to me. My wife, Kristen Kurtz, is more supportive than I deserve. There are days when writing can feel like the deepest of delights and others when it feels close to torture; when I came home from either experience, she was always what I needed—herself. Moreover, during my writing this book, Kristen was pregnant with our son, Cohen Haddon. Even while persevering through the ups and downs of pregnancy, Kristen was in my corner. There is no acknowledgment section sufficient in length to capture my appreciation for her. Also, to Cohen, thanks for taking it easy on your mom while I was writing. By God's grace, you will come into the world before this book does. I pray that you and your sister grow to love the incomprehensible God and see his otherness not as a reason for despair but an invitation to marvel.

My prayer for the readers of this book is that you would find an impetus for delight and a well of joy in contemplating the incomprehensibility of God. May we be conformed from one degree of glory to another as behold the incomprehensible beauty of the triune God (2 Cor 3:18).

ABBREVIATIONS

AE   Basil of Caesarea. *Against Eunomius*. Translated by Mark DelCogliano and Andrew Radde-Gallwitz. Washington, DC: Catholic University of America Press, 2011.

CE I-III   Gregory of Nyssa. *Contra Eunomius I–III*. Edited by Miguel Brugarolas. Supplements to Vigiliae Christianae. Leiden: Brill, 2018.

CRS   Wilhelmus à Brakel. *The Christian's Reasonable Service*. 4 vols. Edited by Joel R. Beeke. Translated by Bartel Elshout. Grand Rapids, MI: Reformation Heritage, 1992.

CT   Benedict Pictet. *Christian Theology*. Translated by Frederick Reyoux. London: Seeley and Sons, 1834.

DN   Pseudo-Dionysius. *Divine Names*. In *The Complete Works*, translated by Colm Luibheid. New York: Paulist Press, 1987.

GWM   John Webster. *God Without Measure: Working Papers in Christian Theology*. 2 vols. London: T&T Clark, 2018.

Hom.   John Chrysostom. *On the Incomprehensible Nature of God*. Fathers of the Church 72. Translated by Paul Harkins. Washington, DC: Catholic University of America Press, 1982.

ICR   John Calvin. *Institutes of the Christian Religion*. Translated by Henry Beveridge. Peabody, MA: Hendrickson, 2008.

IET   Francis Turretin. *Institutes of Elenctic Theology*. 3 vols. Edited by James T. Dennison. Translated by George Musgrave Giger. Phillipsburg, NJ: P&R, 1992.

IJST   *International Journal of Systematic Theology*

MT   Pseudo-Dionysius. *Mystical Theology*. In *The Complete Works*, translated by Colm Luibheid. New York: Paulist Press, 1987.

NPNF[1] *Nicene and Post-Nicene Fathers*. First Series. 14 vols. Edited by Phillip Schaff. Peabody, MA: Hendrickson, 2012

NPNF[2] *Nicene and Post-Nicene Fathers*. Second Series. 14 vols. Edited by Phillip Schaff and Henry Wace. Peabody, MA: Hendrickson, 2012.

OR   Frederick W. Norris, ed. *Faith Gives Fullness to Reason: The Five Theological Orations of Gregory Nazianzen.* Translated by Williams Lionel Wickham. Supplements to Vigiliae Christianae. Leiden: Brill, 1991.

PRRD   Richard A. Muller. *Post-Reformation Reformed Dogmatics.* 4 vols. Grand Rapids, MI: Baker Academic, 2003.

RD   Herman Bavinck. *Reformed Dogmatics.* 4 vols. Edited by John Bolt. Translated by John Vriend. Grand Rapids, MI: Baker Academic, 2003.

SBD   Edward Leigh. *A Systeme or Body of Divinity: Consisting of Ten Books.* London: William Lee, 1654.

SCG   Thomas Aquinas. *Summa contra gentiles.* 5 vols. Translated by Anton C. Pegis. Notre Dame, IN: University of Notre Dame Press, 1975.

ST   Thomas Aquinas. *The Summa Theologica of St. Thomas Aquinas.* 5 vols. Translated by Fathers of the English Dominican Province. New York: Christian Classics, 1948.

TFC   *The Fathers of the Church.* 127 vols. Washington, DC: Catholic University of America Press, 1947.

TPT   Petrus van Mastricht. *Theoretical-Practical Theology.* 3 vols. Edited by Joel R. Beeke. Translated by Todd M. Rester. Grand Rapids, MI: Reformation Heritage, 2018.

TTT   Franciscus Junius. *A Treatise on True Theology: With the Life of Franciscus Junius.* Translated by David C. Noe. Grand Rapids, MI: Reformation Heritage, 2014.

PART ONE

INTRODUCTION, ANTIQUITY, AND THE BIBLICAL DATA

Introducing the Doctrine of Divine Incomprehensibility

Men of good sense who focus their minds' eyes sharply

on the attributes of the ineffable Godhead, see it as existing

beyond every created thing, transcending all acuity of intellect,

being wholly outside bodily appearance and, as all-wise

Paul says, "dwelling in light unapproachable."

Cyril of Alexandria

THEOLOGY FROM THE CLEFT

"Please show me your glory." These five words make up one of the more audacious requests in the unfolding drama of Scripture. Recorded in Exodus 33, Moses converses with God in hopes to intercede on behalf of Israel following their construction of the golden calf. As a prophet who has "found favor" in the Lord's sight, he turns to make his bold request of God—*show me your glory*.

The audacity of Moses' request is not only matched but raised by the majesty of the Lord's reply. The Lord responded to Moses' request, "I will make all my goodness pass before you and will proclaim my name 'the LORD.' And I will be gracious to whom I will be gracious, and I will show mercy on whom I show mercy." The Lord concludes his proclamation with a mysterious claim, "But, you cannot see my face, *for man shall not see me and live*" (Ex 33:19-20, emphasis added).

As the narrative progresses, instead of leaving Moses ensnared by his limitation of faculties, God provides a remedy to the problem of Moses' inability to physically gaze at the Lord without perishing. The Lord accommodates Moses' weakness through shelter: "Behold, there is a place by me where you shall stand on the rock, and while my glory passes by I will put you in a cleft of the rock, and I will cover you with my hand until I have passed by. Then I will take away my hand, and you shall see my back, *but my face shall not be seen*" (Ex 33:18-23, emphasis added). From the safety of the cleft in the rock, the fullness of God's goodness passes before Moses until he can safely emerge from his shelter to catch a glimpse of the back of the Lord.

There are several theological threads woven into this scene; indeed, from the act upon Sinai one could find the impetus for variegated biblical and theological themes and lanes of worthy exploration. Of these variegated theological lanes, the one most pertinent for our purpose is what seems to be the demonstration of an incomprehensible God. The God of Exodus 33 is goodness and majesty of essence such that he will not even be *seen* by his creatures, let alone comprehended by them. While the doctrine of incomprehensibility is not the primary exegetical focus of Exodus 33, this passage does *demonstrate* that the God of Abraham, Isaac, and Jacob is out of the intellectual jurisdiction of humankind.

What will become clear from both biblical reasoning on passages like Exodus 33 and from theological reasoning given what we see in the biblical data is that from the waters of God's incomprehensibility flows the double stream of blessing and curse in Christian theology. There is the curse of the task's difficulty; as we seek to name God in Christian theology, the theologian's entire enterprise will be frustrated by how this

God seems to be always just out of theological and linguistic reach. On the other hand, there is a profound blessing flowing from incomprehensibility as well since the *otherness* of this God means the glorious well of Christian theology will never run dry; contemplating God's beauty will never be exhausted. Those glorious realities that cause us creatures to marvel at our God are incomprehensibly endless. The theological enterprise of knowing and naming God will not come to full fruition until the church lays hold of her glorious gift of eschatological sight and beholds God with the new vision of the blessed. But until that great day when we move from knowing in part to knowing fully (1 Cor 13:12), the incomprehensibility of God will always be something of an exasperation and thrill for the Christian theologian.

The frustration of knowing and naming the incomprehensible God comes even more into focus as we define the task of Christian theology. If the theological task is the study of God and all things in relation to God, then God's incomprehensibility will bring about a myriad of consequences.[1] Putting the pieces together, it may seem a reason to despair for the student of theology who seeks to know and name the triune God if he is as incomprehensible and altogether different as Exodus 33 depicts him to be. We can hear this despair in the prayer of Anselm as he begins *Proslogion*:

> Come then, Lord my God, teach my heart where and how to seek You, where and how to find You Lord, if You are not present here, where, since You are absent, shall I look for You? On the other hand, if You are everywhere why then, since You are present, do I not see You? But surely you dwell in "light inaccessible" (1 Tim 6:16). And where is this inaccessible light, or how can I approach the inaccessible light? Or who shall lead me and take me into it that I may see You in it? . . . He yearns to see You and Your countenance is too far away from him. He desires

---

[1]This definition of theology comes from many sources, of which the most important for my personal development and the source I pull from here is John Webster, *GWM*, 1:1. Webster enlists Franciscus Junius to reinforce this point. See Junius on God as the principle of theology in *TTT*, 177-79.

to come close to You, and Your dwelling place is inaccessible. . . . I was made in order to see You, and I have not yet accomplished what I was made for.[2]

While at first glance, the doctrine of divine incomprehensibility may seem like reason for the student of theology to despair, when all things are considered, it is instead an invitation to partake in the grace of God. For, as God did for Moses, the Lord has provided shelter for the pilgriming theologian. Like God graciously led Moses to the cleft in the rock as an accommodation for his physical inability to take in an eye-full of God's glory, he has a remedy for our plight as well.

Therefore, like Moses, we will take to the accommodating cleft. From God's providential and gracious accommodation, we will conduct the task of Christian theology *from the cleft*. Like the prophet Moses, from the theological safety of God's accommodation, we will aim to still catch a glimpse of his glory. In the end, instead of an impetus for despair, God's incomprehensibility will be a wellspring of wonder and majesty of which we will never reach the bottom in this life.[3]

TOWARD A DEFINITION OF
DIVINE INCOMPREHENSIBILITY

For any project to succeed, two items are important—defining terms carefully and a clear thesis statement that drives the work. In this section, we will try to arrive at both.

An implication of the Creator-creature distinction is that God is not merely bigger than his creation but altogether different. Consequently, God is incomprehensible in terms of theological knowledge and ineffable in terms of theological language. However, as the Lord wants to be known, God has provided ways for finite creatures to meaningfully

---

[2]Anselm, *Major Works: Monologion, Prologion, and Why God Became Man*, ed. Brian Davies and G. R. Evans (Oxford: Oxford University Press, 1998), 85.

[3]Special thanks to Matthew Barrett for pointing out the role of incomprehensibility in Exodus 33 both many times in person and in Matthew Barrett, *None Greater: The Undomesticated Attributes of God* (Grand Rapids, MI: Baker Books, 2019), 15-19.

know and name him by virtue of divine accommodation. Therefore, as we contemplate God and all things in relation to God, we do theology as receivers of accommodated glory and not creators of intellectual reality. Contemplating God's accommodated glory will impact how we speak and think about the divine nature. We therefore pursue a posture of necessary theological humility and reverence throughout the entirety of the theological task knowing that the possibility of pursuing theological contemplation and application rests upon the grace of the Creator to make himself known to limited creatures.

This book will consequently discuss ideas related to how we know and name the incomprehensible God. We will explore theological method in which the finite creature attempts to contemplate God and all things in relation to God. The limitedness of the creature, combined with the limitlessness of the Creator, will manifest—at least—in ontological, linguistic, epistemological, and temperamental consequences within the theological task. It is these methodological consequences this book explores.

Now that we have the thesis and aim of the book stated, we now move toward a careful definition of terms—most important, defining the doctrine of divine incomprehensibility and one of its corollary doctrines, ineffability. Before arriving at a solid definition, I'd like to establish a few nuances to make sure my claims are clear or not overly rigid or overstated. For the rest of this first chapter, then, we will explore a few nuances and points of clarity that will be helpful as we work toward defining God's incomprehensibility and ineffability. To be specific, we will consider: (1) the tension found in biblical indicatives and imperatives as it relates to knowing God, (2) possible misperceptions about the doctrine of divine incomprehensibility, and (3) two ditches students of theology must avoid while affirming the doctrine of God's incomprehensibility. Considering these three previous points; we will (4) offer a working definition of both incomprehensibility and ineffability.

Tension between indicatives and imperatives. One way to demonstrate the tension found in the doctrine of divine incomprehensibility is to contrast some of the biblical data's indicatives with a few of its imperatives. In other words, there is tension between what the Scripture commands of believers concerning their knowledge of the Lord and what the Scripture says about the creatures' ability to know the Lord. For example, the Scripture demands that God's people know him. In fact, God instructs his people through his prophet, Jeremiah, "let him who boasts boast in this, that he understands and knows me" (Jer 9:24). Moreover, we are told that "this is eternal life, that they know you, the only true God" (Jn 17:3). Maybe the height of the Scripture's imperative calling God's people to know the Lord comes from the lips of Jesus as he states, "You worship what you do not know; we worship what we know, for salvation is from the Jews" (Jn 4:22).

While these passages come together to form what seems to be a clear imperative—know the Lord—it is also important to maintain the indicative force seen throughout Scripture—the essence and ways of the Lord are not fully knowable. As for biblical data on this indicative, we read in Psalms that "Great is the LORD, and greatly to be praised, and his greatness is unsearchable" (Ps 145:3), and "Great is our Lord, and abundant in power; his understanding is beyond measure" (Ps 147:5). The psalmist also says of God's works, "Such knowledge is too wonderful for me; it is high; I cannot attain it" (Ps 139:6). We read elsewhere in the biblical data: "Oh, the depth of the riches and wisdom and knowledge of God! How unsearchable are his judgments and how inscrutable his ways!" (Rom 11:33). Finally, the indicative is seen arguably nowhere clearer than 1 Timothy 6, from which this project takes its title:

> I charge you in the presence of God, who gives life to all things, and of
> Christ Jesus, who in his testimony before Pontius Pilate made the good
> confession, to keep the commandment unstained and free from reproach
> until the appearing of our Lord Jesus Christ, which he will display at the

proper time—he who is the blessed and only Sovereign, the King of kings and Lord of lords, who alone has immortality, *who dwells in unapproachable light, whom no one has ever seen or can see.* To him be honor and eternal dominion. Amen. (1 Tim 6:13-16, emphasis added)

As we will see in the coming chapters, this seeming contradiction has received much attention in theological antiquity. The paradox in which Scripture gives us the imperatival—*know the Lord*—while also giving us the indicative reality—*the Lord is unknowable and unsearchable*—does not lead to the conclusion that the Scriptures are contradictory. Rather, the simultaneous existence of the indicatives and imperatives in tension will produce a number of important theological consequences, especially in the nuances needed to affirm a biblically faithful notion of divine incomprehensibility while allowing a meaningful hope, on the part of the creatures, to know and name God.

Possible misperceptions about the doctrine of divine incomprehensibility. Given that the doctrine of divine incomprehensibility postulates a God that is beyond the reach of creaturely intellect, it ought to come as no surprise there are misperceptions which arise in affirming this doctrine. Identifying possible points of misconception will prove helpful in working toward a definition and in norming some of the claims about the doctrine. So, it is worth outlining a few of these misperceptions in this first chapter as they will provide guiderails for the rest of the book in order that we may not fall prey to an underdeveloped doctrine or an overstated doctrine. While this list is not exhaustive, here are seven possible misperceptions about the doctrine of divine incomprehensibility.[4]

First, divine incomprehensibility is not merely affirming that God is un-comprehended. It is not as if God is a mystery that is yet to be resolved. Or, to put it another way, it is not as if we are on a path toward

---

[4]To see these seven misperceptions and a short answer to each one in a concise form, see table 1.1.

the development of creaturely epistemology such that one day we will comprehend God, but at this point he happens to be un-comprehended by his creation. Rather, the doctrine of divine incomprehensibility, as stated in the thesis of this book, is one of the many implications of the Creator-creature distinction. God is not merely a bigger version of the creature such that with the passing of enough generations and with adequate human intellectual power, the creatures will climb the mystery that is God. On the contrary, God is altogether different from the creature such that all the generations of Earth will come and go and none of them will be any closer to a full comprehension of God than those who came before.

We will make frequent visits to the golden tongue of Christian homiletics throughout this book: John Chrysostom, and for good reason. Chrysostom's dealings with the fourth-century Anomoeanism led to the preacher writing a collection of twelve homilies now titled *On the Incomprehensible Nature of God*. Discussing the severity of Paul's adjective choice of "unapproachable" light, in the third homily of his collection, Chrysostom makes the point we are after here well, saying:

> However, he did not say: "Who dwells in incomprehensible light," but: "in unapproachable light," and this is much stronger than "incomprehensible." A thing is said to be incomprehensible when those who seek after it fail to comprehend it, even after they have searched and sought to understand it. A thing is unapproachable which, from the start, cannot be investigated nor can anyone come near to it. We call the sea incomprehensible because, even when divers lower themselves into its waters and go down to a great depth, they cannot find the bottom. We call that thing unapproachable which, from the start, cannot be searched out or investigated.[5]

The unapproachableness of God's nature renders him incomprehensible, not merely un-comprehended. This side of the beatific vision, we

---

[5] *Hom.* III.12.

will, as Paul says, "know in part" and will not move into the knowing in full (1 Cor 13:9-12).[6]

Second, and related to the first misconception, is that the doctrine of divine incomprehensibility is a product of the noetic effects of the fall. This misconception states that it is only due to the sin of our first parents, Adam and Eve, and the curse they brought about that the mind of the creature is clouded such that we cannot comprehend God. This misconception seems to lack warrant for at least two reasons. First, if this were the case, it seems that other created-yet-unfallen creatures, such as angels, would obtain a full comprehension of the divine nature. We know that angels have ignorance even of God's full work in the economy, let alone his nature *in se*. Peter tells us that "even angels long to look into these things" (1 Pet 1:12 NIV). Second, to assume that angels possess a full comprehension of God would violate the epistemological grounding for the doctrine of divine incomprehensibility in the first place. Again, the grounding for God's incomprehensibility is not merely size, as if God is quantifiable, yet he exists in an infinite quantity which is beyond the reach of finite minds. Instead, a proper understanding of infinitude demonstrates that God is not measurable in terms of quantity but is wholly other from any creature—including the angelic hosts. Again, Chrysostom proves helpful here: "Let us then call him the ineffable, unintelligible God, invisible, incomprehensible, surpassing the power of human language, exceeding the comprehension of mortal mind, unexamined by angels." Chrysostom continues this point: "invisible to the seraphim, unintelligible to the cherubim, undetectable by principalities, dominions and powers—in a word, by the whole creation—known only by the Son and the Holy Spirit."[7] So then, even creatures untouched by sin—like angels—cannot comprehend God, showing that incomprehensibility is not merely a product of sin.

---

[6]This is not to insinuate that a full comprehension of God is coming in the beatific vision but that conversation is for a later portion of this book—chapter five.

[7]*Hom.* III.5.

The third misconception is one that we will treat at length through the following chapters. It is a misconception, and one that has been utilized in theological antiquity, that an affirmation of the incomprehensibility of God means that creatures can have no positive knowledge of God. For the sake of clarity and brevity, allow me to state the point plainly—it is simply not true that an affirmation of God's incomprehensibility necessitates an affirmation that creatures can have no positive knowledge of God. An affirmation that divine incomprehensibility entails a denial of the possibility of positive knowledge would be an injustice to the tradition of negative theology, the role of analogy, and the Lord's efficacy in divine revelation.

Instead of diminishing a possibility of positive knowledge, the doctrine of divine incomprehensibility will cause the theological pilgrim to be careful with truth claims regarding knowledge and language of the divine. This is a far cry from admitting the impossibility of positive theology or a measure of cataphatic predication. Indeed, propositions as rudimentary as triunity and God being love (1 Jn 4:7) are in themselves a kind of cataphasis, a positive knowledge and affirmation of God, and belong to the core of the Christian religion. We will return to the theme of positive theology in chapter six.

The fourth misconception is directly related to the third, and that is the notion that the incarnation of the Son erases the need to affirm divine incomprehensibility. The relationship between the doctrine of divine incomprehensibility and the incarnation of the second person of the Trinity needs to be handled with care, and we will seek to do so in chapter two. Yet, it should be said here that there are two errors to avoid when keeping together incomprehensibility and the incarnation; we must avoid both an idea that the coming of Jesus of Nazareth in the flesh means we can disregard divine incomprehensibility while also avoiding the idea that the incarnation does not really reveal something special, positive, and significant about the Lord. Jesus' words are revolutionary and revelatory when he declares, "Whoever has seen me has seen the Father" (Jn 14:9).

Moreover, the unknown author of Hebrews gets at the revelatory reality of Jesus' incarnation, saying, "Long ago, at many times and in many ways, God spoke to our fathers by the prophets, but in these last days he has spoken to us by his Son" (Heb 1:1-2). The incarnation of the Son of God is the most explicit self-revealing we have from the Lord. In the coming of Jesus Christ, God did not give us more words, propositions, or prophecies about himself; he gave us himself. Yet, while the revelation that is Jesus walking among us is profound beyond words, it nevertheless does not bring to an end the doctrine of divine incomprehensibility.[8]

The fifth misconception of divine incomprehensibility is not only related to the fourth but builds off it. The misconception is that incomprehensibility is nullified by God's work in the economy, or the outward action of God among the creatures. On the contrary, divine incomprehensibility is not nullified by that particular act of the economy we call the incarnation, neither is divine incomprehensibility nullified by the larger concept that is the divine economy in its entirety. While God's economic activity is valuable and even efficacious in God's self-revelation, it does not negate his incomprehensibility. What is more, the biblical data seems to suggest that not only is God's essence incomprehensible, but so too is the fullness of his economic work. It is for this reason that David can say, "You hem me in, behind and before, and lay your hand upon me. Such knowledge is too wonderful for me; it is high; I cannot attain it" (Ps 139:5-6). The subject here of David's not understanding is not the essence of God, but rather the work of God. John also notes the inscrutability of God's economy, saying, "Now there are also many other things Jesus did. Were every one of them to be written, I suppose that the world itself could not contain the books that would be written" (Jn 21:25). To summarize this misconception,

---

[8]In fact, rather than the incarnation rendering incomprehensibility obsolete, it is the incarnation that flows *into* incomprehensibility. As Benedict Pictet says, "Besides, the divine nature dwells in light unapproachable by mortals; it was therefore necessary that the mediator should become man, that we might obtain easier access to the divine nature." *CT*, 279.

not only does the single act of the incarnation not nullify divine incomprehensibility but neither does the entirety of the economy.

The sixth misconception which could possibly arise in dealing with divine incomprehensibility is that an affirmation of the doctrine may take away the zeal Christian's feel toward the task of Christian reasoning on the persons of the triune God. If God is utterly incomprehensible, might this discourage followers of Jesus from doing the hard work of contemplating the deep things of God? Is incomprehensibility an invitation to downplay the need for theological reflection? We ought to earnestly deny this claim. An important point for this book, and an important point for a nuanced and careful doctrine of divine incomprehensibility, is that the doctrine is a revealed doctrine. Revelation plays a central role in the Christian faith as the God who dwells in unapproachable light has not left us in our helpless estate. God has revealed himself in nature, in the apostles and prophets, and ultimately in the person of Jesus Christ. It is through revelation that we come to know God as incomprehensible. Therefore, the doctrine of divine incomprehensibility should be a motivator for thorough Christian reflection; for in no other sphere of our life do we run up against something so majestic to be completely out of bounds in terms of the efficacy of our thoughts and words yet still knowable. God is a revealed incomprehensibility, and in that revelation we learn that it is "in him that we move and live and have our being" (Acts 17:28). A thorough study of the incomprehensibility of God will ultimately lead to the reality that even the love of God is incomprehensible. Instead of finding despair in the doctrine of divine incomprehensibility, Christians will find a bottomless well of wonder. Divine incomprehensibility means that the goodness of God, and all we see as good in him—his love, kindness, justice, mercy, grace—it is all incomprehensibly bottomless, and we will never plumb his depth in our lifetimes—or a thousand lifetimes.

The seventh and final misconception is based on logical argument and is thought to be an internal problem for the doctrine of divine incomprehensibility and divine ineffability. The misconception is that these two doctrines—incomprehensibility and ineffability—are self-defeating. The logic, as it is said to go, is that negative theology, like the denouncement of comprehension or articulation, is in itself a kind of comprehension or articulation. If we describe God as unknowable and unspeakable, then we are making a claim regarding his person and even trying to articulate what his person is like—unknowable.

Some have postulated this self-referentially defeating argument against proponents of divine incomprehensibility. See, for example, Alvin Plantinga, who wrote:

> But if this is so, then, presumably, at least one of our concepts—being such that our concepts don't apply to it—does apply to this being. Either those who attempt to make this claim succeed in making an assertion or not. If they don't succeed, we have nothing to consider; if they do, however, they appear to be predicating a property of a being they have referred to, in which case at least some of our concepts do apply to it, contrary to the claim they make. So if they succeed in making a claim, they make a false claim.[9]

The logic of this claim seems to make sense and is rather straightforward: even a predication of "incomprehensibility" or "ineffability" is a predication pertaining to theological epistemology and theological language, and is therefore self-defeating.

Augustine seemed to feel the tension of this critique too, which suggests that theologians contemplating incomprehensibility today should not merely throw this appraisal aside. Instead, we ought to recognize that an affirmation of real and meaningful incomprehensibility is

---

[9]Alvin Plantinga, *Warranted Christian Belief* (Oxford: Oxford University Press, 2000), 6. For example, Simon Hewitt, *Negative Theology and Philosophical Analysis: Only the Splendour of Light* (London: Palgrave Macmillan, 2020), 21, accredits this view to Plantinga. While Plantinga's line of reasoning is applicable to questioning the validity of *apophaticism*, it is still not entirely obvious that Plantinga deserves to be seen as an enemy of negative theology in its entirety. A charitable reading of Plantinga's work could read him as critiquing a notion of negative theology that would deny *any* possible sort of *cataphasis*. Yet, this objection of incomprehensibility being self-defeating is still worthy of contemplation and answer.

difficult as it is nothing less than the essence of God in consideration. Hear Augustine on this point:

> Have I spoken of God, or uttered His praise, in any worthy way? Nay, I feel that I have done nothing more than desire to speak; and if I have said anything, it is not what I desired to say. How do I know this, except from the fact that God is unspeakable? But what I have said, if it had been unspeakable, could not have been spoken. And so God is not even to be called "unspeakable," because to say even this is to speak of Him. Thus there arises a curious contradiction of words, because if the unspeakable is what cannot be spoken of, it is not unspeakable if it can be called unspeakable. And this opposition of words is rather to be avoided by silence than to be explained away by speech.[10]

Augustine, feeling the tension of predicating ineffability, notes that maybe silence is the best choice of action for the Christian theologian. However, while we ought to listen to the North African theologian in his suggestion of silence, we ought as well to continue hearing him as he concludes, "And yet God, although nothing worthy of his greatness can be said of Him, has condescended to accept the worship of men's mouths, and has desired us through the medium of our own words to rejoice in His praise."[11]

Predicating the apophatic concepts of incomprehensibility and ineffability is not self-defeating because of God's economic activity of self-revelation. God's incomprehensibility is a revealed incomprehensibility. The one who shows up in a burning bush and tells the prophet he is to be called "I Am" has chosen to make himself known. In making himself known, he has revealed that the creature will never fully comprehend his essence or articulate his glories. We have the sturdy epistemological ground of revelation to stand on when we predicate apophatic terms to God. This point will become all the

---

[10] Augustine, *On Christian Doctrine*, NPNF[1] 2:524.
[11] Augustine, *On Christian Doctrine*, NPNF[1] 2:524.

more important as theologians begin to see God's act of self-disclosure as grace. For without such a condescending and accommodating self-revelation, the possibility of a theological endeavor would become fleeting.

These seven possible misconceptions about the doctrine of divine incomprehensibility will be important to keep in mind as we develop a definition of the doctrine and work on variegated nuances and contours of the doctrine. Below is a summary of the seven possible misconceptions, and a quick response, brought together in one place by way of a table.

Table 1.1. Possible Misconceptions about Divine Incomprehensibility

Possible Misconception	Potential Brief Answer
Incomprehensibility is synonymous with God being un-comprehended.	Divine incomprehensibility is not asserting that God is *yet to be comprehended*. It is not the case that with enough theological evolution and contemplation, the creature will arrive one day at a full and complete comprehension of God's essence. God is not only *currently* "un-comprehended"; he is the ever-incomprehensible one who dwells in unapproachable light (1 Tim 6:16).
Incomprehensibility is part of the noetic effects of the fall.	The doctrine of divine incomprehensibility is not rooted in the intellectual capacity of the creature *alone*. Rather, the doctrine is rooted in God's otherness. We cannot comprehend God not *just* because we are fallen, but because we are the creature, and he is the Creator.
Incomprehensibility means that we can have *no* positive knowledge of God.	The doctrine of divine incomprehensibility does not entail *mere apophasis*. Instead, *cataphatic* knowledge of God is possible due to his gracious accommodation. Yet theologians must still be nuanced about the nature of positive names and theology.
The incarnation of Jesus Christ as the fullest revelation of God nullifies the need to affirm divine incomprehensibility.	While the economic act of Jesus' incarnation is a real and even the *best* self-revelation of God, it is nevertheless itself a form of accommodated glory. While we can say, with Jesus, that those who have seen Jesus have seen the Father (Jn 14:9), we must affirm still, also with Jesus, that no one has truly seen the Father but the one begotten Son (Jn 6:46).
While the incarnation might not nullify the doctrine of divine incomprehensibility, the full concept of the economy does.	The church has, throughout its long history, affirmed that God is best known through his works in the economy of redemption. Nevertheless, God *in se* cannot be made synonymous with *what God does* in the economy. Moreover, according to Ps 139:5-6 and John 21:25, even the fullness of the economy is incomprehensible.

Possible Misconception	Potential Brief Answer
Affirming incomprehensibility will diminish Christian's zeal to contemplate their Lord.	The doctrine of divine incomprehensibility is a *revealed* doctrine. Meaning, the God who dwells in unapproachable light (1 Tim 6:16) has *told* us he is incomprehensible and yet still invites us to contemplate his glory through his gracious acts of accommodation. Instead of demotivating the Christian in theological reflection in the lifelong process of Christian contemplation, we are invited to explore the incomprehensible one in whom we move and live and have our being (Acts 17:28).
The doctrine of divine incomprehensibility and divine ineffability is self-defeating because such an affirmation is itself a kind of comprehension and articulation.	Again, a vital point in a healthy understanding of divine incomprehensibility and its corollary doctrine, divine ineffability, is that God has *revealed* himself as such. In affirming the apophatic concepts of incomprehensibility and ineffability we stand on the epistemic ground of God's self-disclosure; from that ground do we draw the authority to affirm these two negations of the divine.

Two ditches to avoid in affirming God's incomprehensibility. When discussing the doctrine of divine incomprehensibility, it is popular to use the illustration of two ditches that must be avoided on either side of the conversation, and for good reason. The repetition this analogy gets is not due to the lack of creativity in theological writers, but for the truthfulness that exists in the reality of both temptations when thinking about divine incomprehensibility.

Steven D. Boyer and Christopher A. Hall state the double temptation well: "While we have good grounds for expecting that reason will be unable to master God the Creator, we also have good grounds for believing that reason should not be abandoned as vain or worthless." They continue:

> This odd juxtaposition of legitimacy and humility challenges us to be on the lookout for two opposite theological errors as we proceed. We will need to avoid *both* an arrogant rationalism that denies the unspeakable greatness of God and thus loses mystery altogether, and an anti-intellectual irrationalism that affirms mystery so quickly and uncritically that reason itself is undermined.[12]

---

[12]Steven D. Boyer and Christopher Hall, *The Mystery of God: Theology for Knowing the Unknowable* (Grand Rapids, MI: Baker, 2012), 14.

The existence of this double temptation—to either make God so explanatory as to lose mystery, or claim mystery so quickly as to lose the privilege and right of theological contemplation—leads Hall and Boyer to the profound conclusion, "Every faculty must approach God as God—and this means that every faculty should expect to be overwhelmed and undone by a supremacy that cannot be mastered. . . . Reason, too, comes before the mystery legitimately, but she comes as a petitioner seeking her Lord's bounty, not as a judge demanding a satisfactory explanation."[13]

These are the two erroneous ditches to avoid when affirming the doctrine of divine incomprehensibility. The language utilized in this book to acknowledge the double error on either side of divine incomprehensibility is that of *theological despair* and *theological idolatry*. On the one side, we must deny that nothing intelligible or truthful can be predicated of God. We, as creatures, due to the revelatory grace of God have hope in knowing and naming God with a measure of confidence trusting that he was not deceptive in his self-revealing. On the other hand, we do not operate within the theological task with such confidence as to name him as he really is. To use the language we will construct in chapter six, while affirming the doctrine of divine incomprehensibility, we ought to avoid the theological despair that all our theology proper is merely equivocation while also avoiding the theological idolatry that in our creaturely mind and words we can know or name God univocally.

To show the consistency of this affirmation throughout theological antiquity, we move from Boyer and Hall writing in 2012 to Gregory of Nyssa, writing some sixteen hundred years earlier in the fourth century. Gregory writes about the tension between mystery and reason in knowing and naming God in his work against Eunomius:

Such then was the thought elaborated by our Teacher. It enables any one, whose vision is not obstructed by the screen of heresy, to perceive

---

[13]Boyer and Hall, *Mystery of God*, 14.

quite clearly that in the manner of existence of the essential nature of the Divinity is intangible, inconceivable, and beyond all rational comprehension. Human thought, investigating and searching by such reasoning as is possible, reaches out and touches the unapproachable and sublime Nature, *neither seeing so clearly as distinctly to glimpse the Invisible, nor so totally debarred from approaching as to be unable to form any impression of what it seeks.*[14]

With Gregory, and the centuries of Christian thinkers who have followed him, we ought to affirm that the divine nature as it really is in itself "intangible, inconceivable, and beyond all rational comprehension." However, at the same time, we affirm—along with the Cappadocians—that we are not so "totally debarred" that we have no ability to "form any impression" of the divine. This is what the tension of avoiding both ditches pertaining to divine incomprehensibility looks like.

Toward a definition of incomprehensible and ineffable. There has been enough groundwork concerning the doctrine of divine incomprehensibility laid that we can move to our working definition of divine incomprehensibility and its corollary doctrine, the ineffability of God. Exodus 33 helped us begin the project by examining the sheer otherness of God and the following nuances helped make sure that we do not overstate the doctrine of incomprehensibility nor its role in the theological task.

Therefore, we will move forward with this working definition of divine incomprehensibility and ineffability, cognizant of nuances laid out thus far. Divine incomprehensibility affirms that God the Creator is wholly other than his creatures and the distinction between the two renders God out of the rational jurisdiction of the creature's theological and intellectual comprehension. In no way can the creaturely imagination comprehend the divine nature as it truly is. As the finite will never

---

[14]*CE* II, 138, 89, emphasis added.

circumscribe the infinite, the creaturely mind will never surround all that is in God. Since God as God is out of reach for the mind of the creature, so too is God as God out of reach for the words and names of the creature. Divine incomprehensibility therefore necessitates divine ineffability as the creaturely limits, combined with the otherness of God, means that we cannot either fully know or name God as he really is *in se*.

While this working definition of the doctrines of incomprehensibility and ineffability is sufficient in talking about these two doctrines, our theologizing about incomprehensibility is not complete until our mind's eye turns toward the nuancing and norming realities of the divine self-disclosure that is God's revelation. While the divine nature is completely outside the rational jurisdiction for the creatures—human and angels alike—God has graciously revealed himself in nature, the Holy Scripture, and the person of Jesus Christ and these three modes of revelation therefore temper what we have to say about divine incomprehensibility. So, while not contradicting the above working definition as it stands, it is not enough to account for a thoroughly Christian doctrine of divine incomprehensibility as the Christian theologian must account for God's work in the economy of redemption as the second person of the Trinity dwells among the creatures before his death, resurrection, and ascension. How exactly revelation norms the utter incomprehensibility and unapproachability of God has yet to be seen and will be the topic of exploration for the chapters to come. For now, we will bring this first chapter to a close with a brief discussion of the theological method and outline for the rest of the book.

METHOD AND OUTLINE: RETRIEVING AND CONSTRUCTING THE DOCTRINE OF DIVINE INCOMPREHENSIBILITY

Retrieving divine incomprehensibility. As the aim of this chapter is to introduce the conversation of God's incomprehensibility and set the stage for the remainder of the book, a word about method and aim is in order. This work aims to be an exercise in both theological retrieval and constructive dogmatic theology.

As a work of retrieval, the primary voices we will interact with throughout this project are from centuries gone by. In part, a posture of retrieval is necessitated by the reality that the early and medieval church had much to say about God's incomprehensibility. The prevalence of the doctrine in the theological literature of these two historical eras renders the lack of such treatments in contemporary theological scholarship surprising.[15] However, as we will see, it is important that we do not here treat the voices of yesteryear as a monolithic unity. As the doctrine of God's incomprehensibility gets at the unsearchable essence of the triune Lord, it ought not be surprising that theologians and theological eras had differing, and sometimes contradictory, emphases in articulating the doctrine. However, while there is indeed diversity throughout theological tradition, there is still enough overlap to work through major voices in hopes of retrieving a working doctrine of incomprehensibility for our day.

Traversing the halls of history reveals a rather consistent affirmation of God's incomprehensibility. Throughout theological antiquity, the doctrine of incomprehensibility has enjoyed a pride of place in theological prolegomena. The cast of theologians whose pen wrote of an incomprehensible God is vast, spanning both continents and centuries. From the theological orations of the Cappadocians and the homilies of Chrysostom to the confession of the post-Reformation, divine incomprehensibility received considerable contemplation and treatment.

---

[15]This is not to say there are no works which give special attention to the doctrine of divine incomprehensibility in modernity. For example, see Tomasz Stępień and Krolina Kochańczyk-Bonińska, *Unknown God, Known in His Activities: Incomprehensibility of God During the Trinitarian Controversy of the 4th Century*, European Studies in Theology, Philosophy and History of Religion 18 (Berlin: Peter Lang, 2018); Gregory P. Rocca, *Speaking the Incomprehensible God: Thomas Aquinas on the Interplay of Positive and Negative Theology* (Washington, DC: Catholic University of America Press, 2004); Paul van Geest, *The Incomprehensibility of God: Augustine as a Negative Theologian in Late Antique History and Religion* (Leuven: Peeters, 2011); and Deirdre Carabine, *The Unknown God: Negative Theology in the Platonic Tradition: Plato to Eriugena* (Leuven: Peeters, 2015).

In the aftermath of Nicaea, the Arian sect known as the Anomoeans grew. Among the theological convictions of the Anomoeans was the heterodox belief that creatures can have a knowledge of God which resembles God's self-understanding. In other words, man "can and does know God as God knows himself."[16] In a series of homilies against the Arian Anomoeans, Chrysostom deals explicitly with the concept of divine incomprehensibility before turning to the consubstantiality of the three persons of the Trinity. In his homilies warning the orthodox against the Anomoean fallacies, Chrysostom calls it "the height of folly" to think that we can achieve a perfect knowledge of God, for God is, in his essence, incomprehensible—both to men and to angels alike.[17] Chrysostom follows this homily with four more like it in which he works through pertinent biblical data to show both the glory of God's incomprehensible essence and folly in men trying to reach a univocal knowledge of that divine essence. These homilies will receive substantial attention in chapter three.

Chrysostom is of course not alone in advocating a strong view of God's incomprehensibility. Moving from the more practical, focused homilies of a fourth-century preacher to the theological work of a seventh-century theologian, Maximus the Confessor had much to say about God's incomprehensible essence. Using the metaphysical triad of substance, potentiality, and actuality, Maximus the Confessor describes the divine essence as being incomprehensible to the creature, at least in a univocal sense. Maximus writes, "God is one, without first principle, incomprehensible, throughout being the total potentiality of being; he excludes absolutely the concept of temporal or qualified existence. . . . [H]e is indefinite, immobile, and infinite, since he is

---

[16]Paul Harkins, introduction in *Hom.*, 23. In his introduction to Chrysostom's volume in the CUA series, Harkins provides a helpful guide to the contours of the conversation around the relationship between divine incomprehensibility and Arianism.
[17]*Hom.*, 59.

infinitely beyond substance, potentiality, and actuality."[18] Maximus employs the categories of substance, potency, and act to help deliver readers to the vital lesson that God is "beyond being." In the end, the oft-quoted line from Nazianzus, pulling from Plato, becomes something of a summary for a considerable portion of theological antiquity: "to know God is hard, to describe him is impossible."[19]

These early voices show to be a first fruits of why the posture of retrieval is appropriate for this project. There is much contemporary thinkers can learn by sitting at the feet of those who have come before us. Moreover, as we turn to develop these historic conversations in greater detail, we see that not only did the early church (along with other eras) have a working category for divine incomprehensibility, but they had also worked through the implications of such an affirmation. So, while Chrysostom is right to call trying to understand God's essence the "height of folly," and Gregory is correct to say describing God is impossible, we can still avoid the temptation of giving into theological despair because the church's doctrine of divine incomprehensibility speaks a better word.

To be clear, any notion of retrieval ought to be heard as a modest claim. There are far too many biblical scholars, theologians, philosophers, and the like doing exceptional work on divine incomprehensibility for this project to serve any "pioneering" purposes. Rather than attempting to pioneer any conversation, my hope here is to turn our collective ear to history in hopes that we might learn from saints gone by and then ask what a nuanced doctrine of divine incomprehensibility might mean for us within modern theological method.

---

[18]Maximus the Confessor, *Two Hundred Chapters on Theology* (Crestwood, NY: St. Vladimir's Seminary Press, 2015), 43. While God is beyond substance, potentiality, and actuality, according to Maximus, he nevertheless is the cause of all three: "He is, however, a substance-causing reality while beyond substance, a potentiality-causing ground while beyond potentiality, and the effecting and unending state of each actuality; so, to speak concisely, he is causative of each substance, potentiality, and actuality, also of each first principle, intermediate state, and end" (45).

[19]*OR* 28.4. Another translation renders it, "It is difficult to conceive God but to define him in words is an impossibility" (*NPNF¹* 7:289).

Constructing divine incomprehensibility. Retrieving a nuanced doctrine of divine incomprehensibility—one that is rooted in the biblical data, historically informed, and dogmatically constructive—will aid in avoiding theological despair on the one hand while also avoiding any theological idolatry on the other. Avoiding this despair-idolatry dichotomy and finding a nuanced way forward to navigate both the indicatives and the imperatives of knowing and naming God throughout Scripture will move us from the activity of historical retrieval to attempts of constructing a dogmatic theology of divine incomprehensibility.

The aim of this project is relatively straightforward. First, I endeavor, even in a small way, to aid in retrieving the doctrine of divine incomprehensibility as a meaningful emphasis in Christian theology. Second, and of stronger emphasis in this project, I hope to move beyond retrieval to construction. After visiting the historic voices and the biblical text concerning God's incomprehensibility, I aim to develop three implications springing from the doctrine for theological methodology. These three implications will each, in their own way, impact the theological method. As we will see, considering divine incomprehensibility, there are (1) ontological implications, (2) linguistic and epistemological implications, and (3) implications of posture for methodology. Constructing these three implications to and from the doctrine of divine incomprehensibility will also provide the book with its outline.

Implications and outline. Working on the relationship of incomprehensibility and these three methodological emphases is the primary aim of the book you hold in your hands. While I am interested in the historical development in hopes to learn from the church's history, the primary aim of this book is tracing the implications of divine incomprehensibility for theological method. This book is a project in asking methodological and dogmatic implications flowing into and out of the doctrine of divine incomprehensibility. For this reason, if readers find themselves less interested in the aspects of retrieving the historic conversation surrounding the doctrine, I advise beginning in chapter five, which will allow readers to jump immediately into my discussion of divine incomprehensibility and theological method; it is in chapters five through seven that I spend a majority of my time describing the import into theological method from the impetus of divine incomprehensibility.

As this project aims to be an exercise in constructive dogmatics, it will pull from exegetical, historical, and philosophical theology. These streams of Christian reasoning will allow us to reach our threefold implications of divine incomprehensibility, and these implications will also provide structure to the book. By way of a roadmap, the outline of the book is as follows. The book is broken into two parts. Part one— "Introduction, Antiquity, and the Biblical Data"—will seek to set the stage and begin the modest work of retrieving a historically and biblically informed doctrine of God's incomprehensibility. Part two— "Divine Incomprehensibility and the Task of Theology"—will work toward the three methodological implications mentioned above.

Following this introduction, chapter two seeks to develop a biblical doctrine of divine incomprehensibility. As we have seen, even in this introductory first chapter, there seem to be passages in Scripture that push on one or another emphases with this doctrine. Working to harmonize tension between passages will take some exegetical work. Furthermore, chapter four hopes to provide a more mature biblical case for the doctrine than a mere proof-texting. I will work to show how the unfolding narrative contained in the Scriptures has a threefold argumentation for the doctrine: some passages (1) declare the doctrine, other passages (2) demonstrate the doctrine, and, finally, other passages (3) demand the doctrine.

Following the chapter focusing on the biblical data, chapters three and four will visit the halls of history in hopes to examine the nuances and development of the doctrine of divine incomprehensibility throughout theological antiquity. While an exhaustive examination of divine incomprehensibility in church history would be a worthwhile project, these chapters will aim to balance brevity and taking the needed space to work through pertinent eras of historical theology. Spending time with thinkers of the past, examining both the confessors and the confessions of the church, will bring to light needed clarification when we confess that God is incomprehensible. The goal of these two chapters, working to bring the doctrine of divine incomprehensibility to bear so that we might turn, in part two, to seeking methodological implications, will be to determine which thinkers of yesteryear we spend time with.

Chapter five begins part two of the book, in which I turn to develop the three methodological implications built on the foundation of the doctrine. The first of the three methodological implications will deal with notions of ontology and seek to root the doctrine of divine incomprehensibility. This chapter will give sustained consideration to the Creator-creature distinction as one of many streams flowing into the ocean of incomprehensibility. We will continue to develop the vital distinction between the Creator and his creatures as a distinction of kind, not merely of degree. In the end, this distinction between God and his creatures will impact how we attempt to know God, the way we talk about God, and our posture in contemplation before God. The conversation will then move toward theological and methodological implications of the Creator-creature distinction, especially what it means for the creature to learn about God in the economy of his divine actions.

Moving on from the ontological implication, chapter six will move into linguistic implications of divine incomprehensibility. The longest of all the chapters in this volume, chapter six will explore the conversation about religious epistemology and religious language in light of God's incomprehensibility. Conversations found in the sixth chapter span from items such as divine accommodation, apophatic/cataphatic predication, archetypal/ectypal theology, equivocal/univocal/analogical language, and more.

For the final of the three implications—the implication of posture—the book will take a slight turn in tone in chapter seven. Since the proper location of theology and the proper culture of theology is the ecclesial body of Christ,[20] this implication will consider the work of the regenerate theologian. Revisiting Gregory of Nazianzus's point that knowing God is difficult but describing God is an impossibility, it would be easy to assume that the theological task is a hopeless endeavor. However, a nuanced understanding of divine incomprehensibility will help show the Christian thinker that while we need not be hopeless in the task of Christian theology, there is a rooted humility flowing from the doctrine. To state the case a touch stronger, because of the divine incomprehensibility, theological humility should not be considered a mere virtue in the theological life. Rather, if God is incomprehensible and our only hope of theologizing rests on his gracious act of accommodation, then we do theology as receivers: those who have received a message from the prophets and apostles in which God is making himself known, and ultimately receivers of the incarnation of Jesus Christ, which is the fullest revelation of God. Therefore, instead of humility as merely a theological virtue, we will see that divine incomprehensibility renders theological humility a necessity. The posture of theological humility is not optional in the life of a theologian; it is demanded by the pride-deflating reality that theology would be a nearly impossible task apart from God's gracious self-disclosure.

The volume will close with ten working theses concerning the doctrine of divine incomprehensibility. In no way are these ten theses meant to be taken as a "final word" on the matter. Rather, these are "working theses" that I put forward in hopes to help fellow theological pilgrims consider as we contemplate the incomprehensible God and all things in relation to God.

---

[20]For this understanding of theology's culture, see John Webster, *The Culture of Theology* (Grand Rapids, MI: Baker Academic, 2019).

2

Divine Incomprehensibility in the Biblical Data

Mystery is the lifeblood of dogmatics. . . . Scripture

is equally far removed from the idea that believers

can grasp the revealed mysteries in a scientific

sense. In truth, the knowledge that God has revealed

of himself in nature and Scripture far surpasses

human imagination and understanding.

Herman Bavinck

GOD AND HIS SELF-REVELATION

The Christian religion is a revealed religion. Reflecting on the dogmatic location of creation, John Webster notes, "In his work of creation, God inaugurates an order of being other than himself, and this work is presupposed in all subsequent ascertains about that order of being, for to create is to bring something into existence, and God's first effect in things is existence itself, which all other effects presuppose, and on which they are founded."[1]

---

[1]*GWM* 1:99.

It is from that very moment when the Lord splits open the sky, calling forth that which was not—from nothing—and establishes the great *oikonomia* that we creatures have progressively been given God's self-disclosure. After the first principle of God in himself, theology seeks to treat the second principle—everything else, including the material world—in relation to him. It is through and in that material world that the Lord has been disclosing his grace and grandeur. Laced in the makeup of the material world is God's revelation. The psalmist tells us that the "heavens declare the glory of God, and the sky above proclaims his handiwork. Day to day pours out speech, and night to night reveals knowledge" (Ps 19:1-2). Moreover, we read in Paul's correspondence with the church in Rome that those who suppress the truth of God will be found unrighteousness as their unbelief is unwarranted, since "what can be known about God is plain to them, because God has shown it to them" (Rom 1:19). Paul can say this since, as he writes, "[God's] invisible attributes, namely, his eternal power and divine nature, have been clearly perceived, ever since the creation of the world" (Rom 1:20). Creation's active role in God's self-revelation is why Webster, building off Aquinas, can refer to creation *ex nihilo* as "divine pedagogy."[2]

God does not leave the important economic act of revelation up to the cosmos alone, however. On the contrary, the Scripture is an unfolding drama in which its main actor, God himself, progressively discloses both his great works and, most important, himself. As the storyline of God's people gradually progresses, we see this God more clearly with each passing epoch. As the Scriptures crescendo in the coming of the Messiah in the person of Jesus Christ of Nazareth, we receive the fullest and final revelation of God this side of glory.

It is the intersection of this progressive revelation and the doctrine of divine incomprehensibility that calls for more consideration and clarity. While there is meaningful efficacy in the revelatory economy

---

[2] *GWM*, 102.

of divine action, at no point in the progression of the biblical storyline do we get a full comprehension of God. Rather, it is quite the contrary, even as Scripture unfolds and we get clearer revelations of who God is and what he is doing, we get clearer attestations of God's incomprehensibility. The question remains, however: in what way or ways does the scriptural data reveal God as incomprehensible?

FOUR BIBLICAL CHALLENGES FOR INCOMPREHENSIBILITY AND THE NEED FOR DOGMATICALLY INFORMED EXEGESIS

To begin, anyone working to suggest a biblical notion of divine incomprehensibility ought to be honest and admit there are passages and pericopes that seem, at least on first exegetical glance, to work contrary to a dogmatic doctrine of divine incomprehensibility. What I mean to say in using a phrase like "problem passages" is to admit that there are passages of the biblical data that seem to cut against the grain of affirming incomprehensibility of the divine; these portions of the text might, in the end, not undermine the doctrine, but they at least call for nuance. For example, there are at least four issues that necessitate extended reflection to do justice to all the biblical data. Moreover, these four issues ought not to be dismissed quickly; rather, those theologians who wish to affirm divine incomprehensibility and divine ineffability ought to spend the needed time reflecting on these four issues and work through the relevant material in search for a convincing response.

The four issues within the biblical data that deserve our attention are (1) the Scriptures seem to provide names for the divine; (2) the phenomenon of biblical figures "seeing" God; (3) the direct biblical commands against ignorance; and finally (4) the revelatory role of the incarnation. While none of these four issues are in themselves reasons to deny the doctrine of divine incomprehensibility, they do—when taken together—call for nuance, especially in the application of divine incomprehensibility in the task of Christian theology. These passages ought to be the impetus for honest questions such as, "If God is nameable, what does that entail for our understanding of ineffability?"; "If God is 'seen' with creaturely eyes, what might that mean for his dwelling in 'unapproachable light?'" These questions, and others like them, will aid the Christian theologian in avoiding either error discussed in the previous chapter—theological despair or theological idolatry. Keeping together God's supreme transcendence and otherness will free us from theological idolatry, while insisting on God's being able to be meaningfully known and named will protect from theological despair. With this nuance in place, we turn to the four issues or tensions in the biblical data.

Naming God in the biblical data. One issue in the exegetical discourse concerning incomprehensibility and ineffability is the concept of "naming" God in the biblical data. On one hand, it would appear that God's self-naming in the tetragrammaton indicates that he is unnameable, as if the closest one could get to a name for this incomprehensible God is a mere affirmation of pure existence, "I AM" (Ex 3:14). On the other hand, it appears that creatures name God throughout the biblical canon, which might seem to undermine any notion of ineffability or God's being un-nameable.

To demonstrate the significant textual evidence that exists for the notion of naming God, it will prove helpful to turn to Pseudo-Dionysius. Arguably the most well-known work of the anonymous mystical theologian was his *Divine Names*, in which Dionysius worked toward the incomprehensibility of God from his inability to be named. However, Dionysius does deal with the exegetical reality of biblical figures naming God throughout Scripture and provides a reasonable and significant list of those names attributed to God in the biblical data. While the quote is long, it is worth quoting at length, and it is worth adding to his quote all the biblical references he alludes to in the quote in hopes of showing just how frequently names are attributed to

God throughout the text. After discussing the ways in which the divine essence is nameless, Dionysius writes:

> And yet on the other hand they give it many names, such as "I am being" [Ex 3:14; Rev 1:4, 8], "life" [Jn 11:25; 14:6], "light" [Jn 8:12], "God" [Gen 28:13; Ex 3:6, 15; Is 40:28], the "truth" [Jn 14:6]. These same wise writers, when praising the Cause of everything that is, use names drawn from all the things caused: good [Mt 19:17; Lk 18:19], beautiful [Song 1:16], wise [Job 9:4; Rom 1:27], beloved [Is 5:1], God of gods [Deut 10:17; Ps 50:1; 136:2], Lord of Lords [Deut 10:17; Ps 136:3; 1 Tim 6:15; Rev 17:14; 19:16], Holy of Holies [Dan 9:24], eternal [Is 40:28], Existent [Ex 3:14], Cause of the ages [Heb 1:2; 1 Tim 1:17]. They call him source of life, wisdom [Prov 8:22-31; 1 Cor 1:30], mind [Is 40:13; Rom 1:34; 1 Cor 2:16], word [Jn 1:1; Heb 4:12], knower, possessor beforehand of all the treasures of knowledge [Col 2:3], power [Rev 19:1; 1 Cor 1:18; Ps 24:8], powerful, and King of Kings [1 Tim 6:15; Rev 17:14; 19:16], ancient of days [Dan 7:9, 13, 22], the unaging and unchanging [Mal 3:6], salvation [Rev 19:1; Mt 1:21], righteousness [1 Cor 1:30], and sanctification [1 Cor 1:30], redemption [1 Cor 1:30], greatest of all and yet the one in the still breeze (1 Kings 19:12).[3]

This Dionysian pericope concludes with him summarizing, "And so it is that as Cause of all and as transcending all, he is rightly nameless and yet has the names of everything that is. Truly he has dominion over all and all things revolve around him, for he is their cause, their source, and their destiny."[4]

Dionysius provides a rather long list of names attributed to God throughout Scripture, and these names could be considered an exegetical discomfort for those wishing to affirm a strong version of incomprehensibility and ineffability, which would propose the creatures' inability to name God. In the end, it is my opinion that the positive

---

[3] *DN* 596A-B. About this Dionysian pericope, Rorem helpfully caveats in his commentary on the *Divine Names*, "The author presents all this material as taken from the scriptures, and it can indeed be documented as such, even if some attributions are debatable." See Rorem, *Pseudo-Dionysius: A Commentary on the Texts and an Introduction to Their Influence* (Oxford: Oxford University Press, 1993), 136.

[4] *DN* 596C.

names of God attributed by biblical figures in the Scriptures is *not* a difficulty for the doctrine; however, the existence of such biblical predications should cause the theologian some reflection and necessitates nuance in the methodological procedures of predication, which will come in chapter six.

Seeing God in the biblical data. Another element of Scripture requires elaboration in light of divine incomprehensibility: the capacity for biblical characters to "see" God. There are passages of Scripture that seem to be at least in exegetical tension with God's response to Moses atop Mount Sinai that man cannot see God and live (Ex 33:20). Throughout the biblical narrative, there are scenes and pericopes in which God seems to manifest his glory in strikingly temporal and personal ways. In Genesis 32, after he crossed the ford of the Jabbok, Jacob was alone, and "a man wrestled with him until the breaking of the day." Genesis 32 continues to say that "when the man saw that he did not prevail against Jacob, he touched his hip socket, and Jacob's hip was put out of joint as he wrestled with him" (Gen 32:24-25). With a dislocated hip, Jacob refuses to let go of the man until the man blesses him. This is exactly what happens as the man changes Jacob's name to Israel and instructs him, saying, "Your name shall no longer be called Jacob, but Israel, for you have striven with God and with men, and have prevailed" (Gen 32:28). This pericope is significant for this project as Jacob, whose name was changed, gives a name to the place of wrestling and renames the place Peniel. The renaming of the site is significant as Jacob explains his choice of name, saying, "So Jacob called the name of the place Peniel, saying, 'For I have seen God face to face, and yet my life has been delivered'" (Gen 32:30).

Along with Genesis 32, Numbers 12 has proven to be another exegetical tension with the doctrine of divine incomprehensibility as expressed through Christian antiquity. The scene in Numbers 12 involves Moses being chastened by Miriam and Aaron. Miriam and Aaron rebuke Moses for marrying a Cushite woman, but their rebuke of Moses provokes a rebuke of their own, this one from the Lord. It is in the Lord's rebuke of Miriam and Aaron that the exegetical difficulty comes into play. The Lord says, "Hear my words: If there is a prophet among you, I the LORD make myself known to him in a vision; I speak with him in a dream." The Lord continues to differentiate this mode of communication with the normal prophets and the exclusive communication with Moses. The Lord continues, "Not so with my servant Moses. He is faithful in all my house. With him I speak mouth to mouth, clearly, and not in riddles, and he beholds the form of the LORD" (Num 12:6-8).

These two passages present not an entire doctrine of divine comprehensibility, yet they are at the very least exegetical difficulties with the doctrine of divine incomprehensibility and what transpires in Exodus 33, in which Moses is told that seeing God would prove fatal for him. It is not my aim in this section to establish an apologetic for the doctrine of divine incomprehensibility in light of these passages. Rather, the point of this section is simply to bring together passages such as Exodus 33 and Numbers 12 in hopes to demonstrate the tension present. The tension felt between these two passages, and other pairings like them, will be what brings balance to definitions and applications in theological methodology concerning divine incomprehensibility in chapters five through seven.

Biblical commands against ignorance. When a biblical reader focuses on the imperatives—know the Lord—and other scriptural variations of that command, the doctrine of divine incomprehensibility can seem to be a liability. For example, the prophet Jeremiah records the Lord as saying, "Let not the wise man boast in his wisdom, let not the mighty man boast in his might, let not the rich man boast in his riches, but let him who boasts boast in this, that he understands and knows me" (Jer 9:23-24). In the New Testament, Jesus rebukes the Samaritan women of multiple husbands as she inquiries about Jesus' identity, saying, "Sir, I perceive that you are a prophet. Our fathers worshiped on this mountain, but you say that in Jerusalem is the place where people ought to worship." This prompts Jesus to reply, "Woman, believe me, the hour is coming when neither on this mountain nor in Jerusalem will you worship the Father. You worship what you do not know; we worship what we know, for salvation is from the Jews" (Jn 4:19-22). Further in John we are told that "this is eternal life, that they know you, the only true God" (Jn 17:3).

Finally, no section on the biblical pericopes and commands against ignorance would be complete without mention of Paul's sermon at the Areopagus. The Epicurean and Stoics approached Paul—the "babbler"—to inquire about the "foreign divinities" he was teaching about with his doctrine of Christ and the resurrection. They brought him to the Areopagus to ask him, "May we know what this new teaching is that you are presenting?" Paul, famously responds:

> Men of Athens, I perceive that in every way you are very religious. For as I passed along and observed the objects of your worship, I found also an altar with this inscription: "To the unknown god." *What therefore you worship as unknown, this I proclaim to you.* The God who made the world and everything in it, being Lord of heaven and earth, does not live in temples made by man, nor is he served by human hands, as though he needed anything, since he himself gives to all mankind life and breath and everything. (Acts 17:22-25, emphasis added)

What the apostle's sermon at the Areopagus and the passages cited before seem to indicate is that God is knowable. In fact, these passages could be rendered as a form of cruelty if taken as a legitimate imperative to *know God*, if he was in fact completely unknowable. At least, these passages come together to suggest that Christians ought to affirm some form of *knowability* of God. In the end, this will call for a careful distinction between *comprehension* and *apprehension*. While God remains ever incomprehensible, due to his gracious accommodation in his self-revealing, he is apprehensible.

The revelatory role of the incarnation. In John's Gospel, Jesus says, "Whoever has seen me, has seen the Father" (Jn 14:9). With considerable clarity, Jesus is here proclaiming the revelatory role of his economic mission. This is a revelatory role the author of Hebrews picks up in opening the book, writing, "Long ago, at many times and in many ways, God spoke to our fathers by the prophets, but in these last days he has spoken to us by his Son" (Heb 1:1-2).

There seems to be a change in the narrative from the time of Moses to the time of Jesus. Maybe we could argue that God was incomprehensible throughout the duration of the old covenant; yet is it not the case that in God's assuming a human nature and walking among us in the incarnation of the second person of the Trinity renders the doctrine obsolete? For example, Paul seems to pick up on this dichotomizing of the times of Moses and the revelatory role of Jesus in his second letter to the Corinthians. Paul writes:

> Since we have such a hope, we are very bold, not like Moses, who would put a veil over his face so that the Israelites might not gaze at the outcome of what was being brought to an end. But their minds were hardened. For to this day, when they read the old covenant, that same veil remains unlifted, because only through Christ is it taken away. Yes, to this day whenever Moses is read a veil lies over their hearts. But when one turns to the Lord, the veil is removed. Now the Lord is Spirit, and where the Spirit of the Lord is, there is freedom. And we all, with unveiled face, beholding the glory of the Lord, are being transformed into the same image from one degree of glory to another. For this comes from the Lord who is Spirit. (2 Cor 3:12-18)

Whereas Moses' request to "see God's glory" was denied in Exodus 33, and whereas when Moses' appearance with the people after seeing the "back" of God's glory rendered his face too terrifying to look at for the Israelites, in the new covenant we will "behold" the glory of the Lord and be transformed from one degree of glory to another. Is it the case that during the old covenant, before the Lord assumed a human nature, he was incomprehensible as he was unable to be seen; but now, in the new covenant, through the incarnation of the second person, the Lord is comprehensible as we see the face of Jesus?

DOGMATICALLY INFORMED EXEGESIS

These four exegetical issues—the notion of naming God in the biblical data, the notion of seeing God in the biblical data, the biblical commands against divine ignorance, and the revelatory realities of the incarnation—all come together and are something of a clarifying call for the theological student. The coexistence of these four biblical realities together with the scriptural proclamation that God dwells in "unapproachable light" calls the student of God's Word to do more than merely point toward individual passages as the deciding factor in the discussion concerning God's knowability.

Rather, the question of the creatures' ability to know the Creator is going to take a more mature theological method than merely proof-texting. The theological reality about affirming either God's incomprehensibility or God's knowability is that the theologian wishing to promote either side has an equally easy job advocating for their position if pointing to individual passages was a sufficient theological method. For example, those wishing to articulate a biblical affirmation for the Lord's knowability might make use of Moses' apparently seeing God "face to face" and God's not speaking to Moses "in riddles" as mentioned from Numbers 12, while those wishing to articulate a biblical affirmation of the Lord's incomprehensibility might remind readers that the psalmists says, "His greatness is unsearchable" (Ps 145:3).

If one seeks to uphold the internal consistency and coherence of the biblical witness and therefore negates the possible explanation of theological inconsistency within the text, any theological method must be robust enough to have explanatory power for both sets of biblical texts. It is my conviction that, when taken together and all things considered, the biblical data affirms that God is incomprehensible. We can see this biblical affirmation by implementing a more robust theological method than mere proof-texting; instead, when we listen to the biblical data as a grand narrative and pursue dogmatically informed exegesis, the biblical reader will see that the Scriptures have something of a threefold witness toward the doctrine of divine incomprehensibility. (1) The Scripture declares incomprehensibility by virtue of individual pericopes and passages which outright affirm the doctrine with considerable explicitness. (2) The Scriptures demonstrate incomprehensibility in passages that show both God's life in himself *in se* and the grandeur of his work in the economy are alike incomprehensible to the creature. While these passages might not explicitly declare the doctrine, they show the doctrine. And finally, (3) the Scriptures demand incomprehensibility through corollary theological and economic affirmations found in the biblical data. For example, while divine perfections such as atemporality, infinitude, simplicity, and others like them are not explicit affirmations of divine incomprehensibility, they demand incomprehensibility implicitly given that the creature is temporal, finite, and complex.

Ultimately, given this threefold method of arguing toward the biblical rational for the doctrine of divine incomprehensibility, my goal is to show the doctrine of divine incomprehensibility is a revealed doctrine. God's self-revelation as incomprehensible will impact much of what we can and cannot say about the doctrine and its theological corollaries.

INCOMPREHENSIBILITY DECLARED

The first leg of the three-legged stool in working toward a dogmatically informed biblical affirmation is to bring forward those passages from the biblical data which seem to declare the doctrine of divine incomprehensibility. Of the three pillars in this proposed threefold biblical method, this step is the most obvious. What I mean to communicate in this first step is that while there are passages that seem to indicate a direct knowability of God (a knowability that a mature doctrine of incomprehensibility can explain), there are passages that directly and explicitly declare that God is incomprehensible. To say that these passages directly and explicitly declare the doctrine, I mean that we need very little to no biblical or theological reasoning to deduce a doctrine based on what is present in the text. Rather, these passages affirm the incomprehensibility of the divine essence outright and are not arrived at by good and necessary consequence nor any kind of hermeneutical deduction.

Given that these passages are so crucial to establishing a positive affirmation of God's incomprehensibility, many of them have either already been alluded to or explicitly mentioned thus far in this project; yet they are worth still mentioning here. We will start in the Psalms in search for those explicit mentions of God's incomprehensibility. For example, in the Davidic Psalm of 139, we read:

> O LORD, you have searched me and known me!
> You know when I sit down and when I rise up;
>   you discern my thoughts from afar.
> You search out my path and my lying down
>   and are acquainted with all my ways.
> Even before a word is on my tongue,
>   behold, O LORD, you know it altogether.
> You hem me in, behind and before,
>   and lay your hand upon me.
> *Such knowledge is too wonderful for me;*
>   *it is high; I cannot attain it.* (Ps 139:1-6, emphasis added)

David admits that even the economic activity of the Lord, such as hemming David in, behind, and before, as well as the Lord's intimidate knowledge and providential plan for David's life, is "too wonderful" for him and something he cannot attain. It is significant to notice that the subject of David's indicative here is not the essence of the Lord, but the activity of the Lord. What David has in view in Psalm 139 is not God *in se*, but rather David confesses the incomprehensibility of God's economic unfolding. This explicit acknowledgment of incomprehensibility concerning God's work *ad extra* will prove significant in chapter six as we work through the role the economic activity plays in the epistemological foundation of religion.

However, suffice it to say here that both God's essence and action are said to be incomprehensible.[5]

Continuing in the Davidic Psalms, in Psalm 145:1-3, David writes:

> I will extol you, my God and King,
>> and bless your name forever and ever.
> Every day I will bless you
>> and praise your name forever and ever.
> Great is the LORD, and greatly to be praised,
>> and his greatness is unsearchable. (Ps 145:1-3)

Two realities confront the biblical reader concerning incomprehensibility in this pericope. First, there is the notion of God's greatness being unsearchable. Within the wording of God's greatness being "unsearchable," readers can see the grandeur of incomprehensibility. It is not the case that God's greatness has been searched and, after all things are considered, the creature cannot make sense or fully grasp God's greatness. Rather, God's greatness is the kind of thing that will not even be searched in the first place. The greatness of God is so other from the creature that the creature cannot begin to search it or investigate it; God's greatness will not come under the scrutiny or examination of humankind. God's greatness, then, more than incomprehensible, is unsearchable. Second, God's greatness being "unsearchable" showcases a bit of the doxological dimension of the doctrine of divine incomprehensibility. Connected to God's incomprehensibility is God's endless impetus of praise. When the student of God's Word lays hold of the Scriptures and finds in them an overwhelming number of reasons to sing God's praise, the reality is that each variegated impetus for God's glory and praise is a bottomless well of adoration. As his essence is unsearchable, it will not be exhausted. Therefore, as Psalm 145 denotes, as his greatness is unsearchable, it will

---

[5]This will, in the end, need nuance; and nuance will come for this statement in both chapters five and six. Chapter five will explore improper dogmatic locations for the doctrine of incomprehensibility, any notion of *size* being one of them. Chapter six will distinguish a difference of divine incomprehensibility between incomprehensibility of essence and incomprehensibility of action. One is of *kind*; one is of *size*.

not be exhausted. The incomprehensibility of God equips the saints with inexhaustible impetus for glorifying God.

Like the above passage, but moving from Wisdom literature to the Prophets, God makes explicit his otherness and his incomprehensibility through Isaiah as the prophet writes:

> Have you not known? Have you not heard?
> The LORD is everlasting God,
>   the Creator of the ends of the earth.
> He does not faint or grow weary;
>   his understanding is unsearchable. (Is 40:28)

The emphasis here, for our purposes, comes with Isaiah's insistence that God's understanding is unsearchable. It is not the case that once searched, the omniscience of God will be found to be too difficult to grasp. Rather, this is a kind of archetypal wisdom that is not even searchable to the creature. The "demonstration" of God's otherness is seen as well in his being "everlasting" and the idea that he does not grow faint or weary; Paul is establishing the distinction between the one who creates and those who are created.

Paul, in the New Testament, picks up on this passage as well, writing, "Oh, the depth of the riches and wisdom and knowledge of God! How unsearchable are his judgments and how inscrutable his ways!" (Rom 11:33). Paul then goes on to quote Isaiah 40:13: "For who has known the mind of the Lord, or who has been his counselor?" This rhetorical question ought to be met with an emphatic, "No one!" The point of Paul's pericope here is that the mind of the Lord is impenetrable. He alone is omniscient, and none can comprehend his perfect and archetypal knowledge.

Or, similarly, returning to Isaiah:

> For my thoughts are not your thoughts,
>   neither are your ways my ways, declares the LORD.
> For as the heavens are higher than the earth,

so are my ways higher than your ways

and my thoughts than your thoughts. (Is 55:8-9)

These two passages give an explicit divine affirmation of not only the distinction between the Creator and the creature but also of the difference between God's "ways and thoughts" and the "ways and thoughts" of humankind. There is an immeasurable "higher than" signified between the thoughts and ways of the divine and the thoughts and ways of the human. "The heavens are higher than the earth," and this immeasurable distance serves as the analogy between God and creatures.

A similar emphasis exists in the New Testament passage of 1 Corinthians 2:9-11. In this passage, Paul utilizes Isaiah 64:4 to demonstrate that the work God is doing on behalf of his covenant people is beyond comprehension. Again, this shows that not only the essence of God but also the action of God is incomprehensible. Furthermore, Paul continues to explicitly affirm that none but God himself comprehend the thoughts of God. Paul writes: "But, as it is written, 'What no eye has seen, nor ear heard, nor the heart of man imagined, what God has prepared for those who love him.'" He continues, "These things God has revealed to us through the Spirit. . . . For who knows a person's thoughts except the spirit of that person, which is in him? So also no one comprehends the thoughts of God except the Spirit of God" (1 Cor 2:9-11).

Our final passage in the list of those that make an explicit declaration that God is incomprehensible is the passage from which this book takes its name—1 Timothy 6:16. In the last chapter of his first epistle to Timothy, Paul writes,

> I charge you in the presence of God, who gives life to all things, and of
> Christ Jesus, who in his testimony before Pontius Pilate made the good
> confession, to keep the commandment unstained and free from re-
> proach until the appearing of our Lord Jesus Christ, which he will
> display at the proper time—he who is the blessed and only Sovereign,

> the King of kings and Lord of lords, who alone has immortality, who dwells in unapproachable light, whom no one has ever seen or can see. To him be honor and eternal dominion. (1 Tim 6:13-16)

Chrysostom makes two important observations about this text. First, the preacher notes that it is the light that is unapproachable, not just God's essence. So, he concludes, "[Paul] did not say: 'who is an unapproachable light,' but: 'Who dwells in unapproachable light.'" Chrysostom gives Paul's reasoning for this word choice, "Why? So that you may learn that if the dwelling is unapproachable, much more so is the God who dwells in it."[6] The second point Chrysostom makes in this sermon was pertinent in the first chapter, so these few sentences from the golden tongue have been quoted before, but they are worth quoting again here. Chrysostom writes, for his second point:

> However, he did not say: "Who dwells in incomprehensible light," but: "in unapproachable light," and this is much stronger than "incomprehensible." A thing is said to be incomprehensible when those who seek after it fail to comprehend it, even after they have searched and sought to understand it. A thing is unapproachable which, from the start, cannot be investigated nor can anyone come near to it. We call the sea incomprehensible because, even when divers lower themselves into its waters and go down to a great depth, they cannot find the bottom. We call that thing unapproachable which, from the start, cannot be searched out or investigated.[7]

Together, these passages become the first of three evidences for a mature biblical notion of divine incomprehensibility. While these passages *declare* that God is incomprehensible—meaning they need not good and necessary exegetical deduction, but rather they affirm incomprehensibility in an explicit way—the following two sections will work through passages that don't explicitly *declare* God's incomprehensibility but *demonstrate* it and *demand* it.

---

[6]*Hom.* III.11.
[7]*Hom.* III.12.

INCOMPREHENSIBILITY DEMONSTRATED

The next step within the outlined threefold hermeneutical method is to consider the biblical passages which demonstrate the doctrine of divine incomprehensibility. Unlike the first section, these passages do not explicitly state that God is incomprehensible. Rather, these biblical pericopes and passages, instead of explicitly stating a doctrine of divine incomprehensibility, nevertheless demonstrate the doctrine. This means that with some deduction, biblical readers can arrive at the doctrine by contemplating what must be true given what the biblical passages depict or affirm. It could be said then that these passages implicitly teach the doctrine of divine incomprehensibility instead of explicitly stating portions or the whole of the doctrine.

These passages describe either an action in the economy or hint at God's essence in ways that finite creatures cannot comprehend. Given this understanding of what it means for a passage to "demonstrate" the doctrine, and given that nearly all of God's actions in the economy are of the scope that creatures cannot attain their fullness of meaning, we will have to focus our attention to a few of the many available pericopes that show this emphasis with considerable force.

We will begin this section by considering a few passages within the Old Testament that could properly be said to demonstrate the doctrine of divine incomprehensibility. First, we return to the passage that began this book—Exodus 33. The scene atop Mount Sinai recorded in Exodus 33 is full of wonder. The prophet Moses request of the Lord, "Please show me your glory" (Ex 33:18), to which the Lord replies, "I will be gracious to whom I will be gracious, and will show mercy on whom I will show mercy." The Lord continues, "You cannot see my face, for man shall not see me and live" (Ex 33:19-20). Few passages demonstrate God's incomprehensibility like this scene with Moses. God's goodness is the kind of thing that proves fatal for the creature if seen. The inability for Moses to gaze upon the essence of the Lord demonstrates that this God will not even be seen, let alone comprehended.

Outside Exodus 33, the climax of Job's narrative becomes quite the demonstration of God's incomprehensible essence and action. After Job's multitude of tragedy opening the book, and after Job's friends attempt to answer and advise Job as to why these things are happening to him and what he ought to do about them, the Lord shows up. As the Lord shows up in Job 38 to answer Job, he does so with magnificence and majesty. Instead of directly answering Job's desire for a kind of theodicy, God expounds his actions in creation and his providence over all things and invites Job to consider his existence compared to God's. The pertinent passages are too many to quote here, but as a sample, consider God's incomprehensibility demonstrated as God says:

> Where were you when I laid the foundation of the earth?
>   Tell me, if you have understanding.
> Who determined its measurements—surely you know!
>   Or who stretched the line upon it?
> On what were its bases sunk,
>   or who laid its cornerstone,
> when the morning stars sang together
>   and all the sons of God shouted for joy? (Job 38:4-7)

The Lord continues with profound questions and questioning. He asks questions like, "Has the rain a father?" (Job 38:28), and "Can you bind the chains of the Pleiades or loose the cords of Orion?" (38:31). He tells Job that it is *him* who the lightening asks where it should strike, and it is *him* to whom the snow and rain must give an account. While creatures play dominion over the Earth, the cosmos largely happens *to* humankind. We have not the power to stop the wind nor make the rains come, yet God commands it all. This God is the one who holds Orion's cords and tells the ocean where to stop; his providence over all creation demonstrates his incomprehensibility. This pericope nowhere explicitly says that God is incomprehensible, but the staggering otherness of God is apparent in his line of questioning toward Job. This is why, while not exegetically explicit, it is a proper reading of the biblical text to insist that this passage *demonstrates* God's incomprehensibility, for who can comprehend the one whom the lightning asks where it ought to strike?

Moving to the New Testament, Paul, writing to the church at Corinth, writes, "For now we see in a mirror dimly, but then face to face. Now I know in part; then I shall know fully, even as I have been fully known" (1 Cor 13:12). For the conversation of divine incomprehensibility, 1 Corinthians 13:12 has proven to be an important one. Here, Paul alludes to a passage we've already seen, Numbers 12:6-8, which reads: "And he said, 'Hear my words: if there is a prophet among you, I the LORD make myself known to him in a vision; I speak with him in a dream. Not so with my servant Moses. He is faithful in all my house. With him I speak mouth to mouth, clearly, and not in riddles, and he beholds the form of the LORD." This passage could be thought of as a "problem passage" for the doctrine of divine incomprehensibility as seen in the opening of this chapter. Moreover, tension arises with it when one considers how Exodus 33 seems to give the exact opposite application; as we have seen, in Exodus 33 (which is quite likely the very passage that Numbers 12 is alluding to), God tells Moses that he *shall not* see him "face to face," as Numbers 12 insists, since "man shall not see me and live."[8]

Commenting on the epistemological tension in these, and other, passages, Paul Macdonald shows how Aquinas handled these pericopes, saying:

> Aquinas points toward a truth and tension that lie at the heart of Christian philosophical theology: whatever knowledge of God we gain in this life remains shrouded in ignorance, given that God surpasses anything that we can think or say about God. And yet, even though our

---

[8]For a comparative study of these two texts, along with Ezekiel 43:3, see Michael Fishbane, "Through the Looking Glass: Reflections on Ezekiel 43:3, Numbers 12:8 and 1 Corinthians 13:8," in *Hebrew Annual Review* 10 (1986): 63-75.

knowledge of God remains shrouded in ignorance—again, we "see" God, at best, "through a glass darkly"—it remains knowledge nonetheless.[9]

It seems if readers are going to maintain a strong consistency of the biblical text, they will be presented with a few options here. It is my opinion that Aquinas points the way forward by acknowledging the tension and emphasizing that whatever the "mouth to mouth" non-riddles that God spoke to Moses in Numbers 12, it could not be that Moses gazed at the essence of God. It seems Exodus 33 provides hermeneutical handrails for this passage, as the scene at Sinai shows that any sight of the Lord's glory would prove fatal for any creature, including Moses. So, while Moses enjoyed a conversing with God that is likely unique to him, it ought not be rendered as any kind of comprehension or sight of essence. Regardless, the 1 Corinthians 13 passage remains: Paul is quite clear that on this side of the beatific vision creatures can only know the Lord in part or as in a mirror dimly.

This interpretation of Numbers 12 and its relationship with Exodus 33 seems vindicated by our last passage of consideration as well when John writes at the opening of his Gospel account of Jesus Christ, "For the law was given through Moses; grace and truth came through Jesus Christ. No one has ever seen God; the only God, who is at the Father's side, he has made him known" (Jn 1:17-18). The incarnation of Jesus Christ, in which the second person of the Trinity takes the form of a servant by assuming flesh, is the first time the creature can rightly say that they've seen God. The tension seen above between Numbers 12 and Exodus 33 is echoed within the incarnation and the book of John. For, on the one hand, John writes in 14:9, "Jesus said to him, 'Have I been with you so long, and you still do not know me, Philip? Whoever has seen me has seen the Father. How can you say, 'Show us the

---

[9]Paul Macdonald, *Knowledge and the Transcendent: An Inquiry into the Mind's Relationship to God* (Washington, DC: Catholic University of America Press, 2009), 173-74.

Father'?" On the other hand, as noted above, John opens his Gospel with the claim that no one has seen the Father. This shows what the revelatory role of the incarnation really affords those who see Jesus Christ. In a way, anyone who has seen Christ can say that they've seen the Father, as Jesus is the "image of the invisible God" (Col 1:15) and the "exact imprint of his nature" (Heb 1:3). At the same time, in its own way, the incarnation is the fullest of God's revelatory accommodations. God accommodates the creature by taking the form of a creature such that those who have weakness of sight and weakness of faith might behold him face to face.

INCOMPREHENSIBILITY DEMANDED

We here move on to the last of our threefold biblical case for the doctrine of divine incomprehensibility. First, we saw that certain passages declare divine incomprehensibility (that is, they explicitly affirm the doctrine). Second, we saw that certain passages demonstrate divine incomprehensibility (that is, the doctrine of divine incomprehensibility can be deduced implicitly from what the passages say). Finally, here we will see that certain passages demand divine incomprehensibility (that is, divine incomprehensibility becomes a necessary corollary based on what these passages affirm).

What becomes apparent in attempting to hold the scriptural teaching concerning God together is that the perfections of God render him incomprehensible. It is for this reason that divine incomprehensibility, speaking properly about predication, is itself not a perfection. Rather, it is an implication of the perfections. When one considers the perfection of God's essence, with both its positive names (holy, good, love, etc.) and its negative names (immutable, impassable, atemporal, etc.), it is difficult to arrive at any other conclusion than divine incomprehensibility. John Owen picks up on the argument toward incomprehensibility rooted in God's perfection. In his work on Christology, Owen writes:

God, in his own essence, being, and existence, is absolutely incomprehensible. His nature being immense, and all his holy properties essentially infinite, no creature can directly or perfectly comprehend them, or any of them. He must be infinite that can perfectly comprehend that which is infinite; wherefore God is perfectly known unto himself only—but as for us, how little a portion is heard of him.[10]

As Owen points out, God is immense and infinite, and those who dwell in finitude will be unable to access that kind of infinitude by either knowledge or language. It is for this reason that those passages that might not seem to be about incomprehensibility but are foundational for an exegetical affirmation of God's perfection become pertinent in this discussion. For example, a passage like Psalm 90:2, "Before the mountains were brought forth, or ever you had formed the earth and the world, from everlasting to everlasting you are God," proves important in this discussion. Inasmuch as Psalm 90:2 declares a God who is atemporal, Psalm 90:2 demands God's incomprehensibility for those who dwell in chronological finitude. Other passages such as Genesis 1:1; Isaiah 40:28; John 1:1; 8:58; Hebrews 13:8; and Revelation 1:8; 22:13, which affirm divine eternality, come together to form such a necessary corollary like divine incomprehensibility.

Another negative name that bears import into the conversation of divine incomprehensibility is divine immutability.[11] While there are numerous passages that affirm God's changelessness, maybe none are as straightforward as Malachi 3:6: "For I the LORD do not change; therefore you, O children of Jacob, are not consumed." As creatures are stuck in chronological succession and moments of time happen to humankind, we are trapped in change. With each passing moment, we creatures get older; we breathe, move, and exist in change. While our

---

[10]John Owen, *On the Person of Christ*, vol. 1, *Works of John Owen* (Edinburgh: Banner of Truth Trust, 2000), 65.

[11]See Ronni Kurtz, *No Shadow of Turning: Divine Immutability and the Economy of Redemption* (Ross-shire, UK: Mentor, 2022).

existence is confined by change, it is not so for the divine life. God's existence is not one made up of ever-changing circumstances, but as this passage and others affirm, God is immutable. God's unchangeable nature renders him, again, out of intellectual comprehension for those who live each moment from one successive change to another. (Again, other passages like Num 23:19; Ps 102:25-27; Heb 6:13-20; 13:8; and Jas 1:17 could be used in a similar manner.)

This pattern seen with atemporality and immutability is replicable with other divine attributes. Readers could turn to doctrines like simplicity, infinitude, incorporeality, aseity, or pure act and see how God's essence and existence is wholly other than the existence of the creatures. It is my contention that even if there were no passages that explicitly affirm the doctrine of divine incomprehensibility, there is a strong enough argument from deductions and necessity that would still render it biblical. Because of these doctrines within theology proper, humankind ought to say, alongside Zophar in the book of Job: "Can you find out the deep things of God? Can you find out the limit of the Almighty? It is higher than heaven—what can you do? Deeper than Sheol—what can you know?"[12]

A final passage that seems to demand the doctrine of divine incomprehensibility from the biblical data is arguably the only instance in Scripture in which God "names himself." We have already seen, from Exodus 33, Moses' willingness to ask audacious things of the Lord; this willingness shows up in Exodus 3 as well when Moses asks God to name himself that he might tell the people of Israel.

---

[12]This method of bringing together the multitude of passages within theology proper to arrive at a conclusion of divine incomprehensibility hopes to be in line with the notion of the "pedagogical context of biblical reasoning." For more on this, see R. B. Jamieson and Tyler R. Wittman, *Biblical Reasoning: Christological and Trinitarian Rules of Exegesis* (Grand Rapids, MI: Baker Academic, 2022). Jamieson and Wittman put forward seven principles and ten rules for biblical exegesis, the second "principle" of biblical reasoning being: "Everything Scripture says about God is part of God's meticulous and wise pedagogy, by which God adapts the form of his wisdom to educate finite and fallen creatures so that we might see his glory. Biblical reasoning fits within this larger context of divine teaching" (23).

Maybe fewer things demonstrate the truthfulness of divine incomprehensibility in our age quite like the profusion of monographs and volumes written on the divine name of Exodus 3:14. Janet Soskice picks up on the uniqueness of Exodus 3, saying, "Exodus 3 marks the high point in a series of names and naming, of people and places." She continues, "While naming and renaming are frequent features of the Hebrew Bible, divine self-naming is extremely rare. God is named, or called upon by name, hundreds of times by others . . . but rarely does God, as it were, name Godself." In fact, Soskice notes that this act of God's naming himself is really a feature reserved for God's interaction with Moses. "This is almost solely in the book of Exodus and to Moses, hence the weight of the encounter of God and Moses at the burning bush. Here God not only gives Moses the Holy Name, YHWH, but glosses it, placing himself as the God of Israel's history."[13] A consequence of the uniqueness of Exodus 3 is substantial ink spilled attempting to explain Exodus 3:14 is the nameless God "names" himself, and even in his self-naming, we receive more mystery than explanation:

> Then Moses said to God, "If I come to the people of Israel and say to them, 'The God of your fathers has sent me to you,' and they ask me, 'What is his name?' what shall I say to them?" God said to Moses, "I AM WHO I AM." And he said, "Say this to the people of Israel: 'I AM has sent me to you.'" God also said to Moses, "Say this to the people of Israel: 'The LORD, the God of your fathers, the God of Abraham, the God of Isaac, and the God of Jacob, has sent me to you.' This is my name forever, and thus I am to be remembered throughout all generations. (Ex 3:13-15)

---

[13]Janet Soskice, *Naming God: Addressing the Divine in Philosophy, Theology and Scripture* (Cambridge: Cambridge University Press, 2023), 20-21. Along with Soskice's chapter "Naming God at Sinai: The Gift of the Name" in this work, see Michael Allen's two chapters on the exegesis and theology of Exodus 3: "Exodus 3 After the Hellenization Thesis" and "The Burning Bush," in Michael Allen, *The Knowledge of God: Essays on God, Christ, and the Church* (London: T&T Clark, 2002), 17-51. See also the insightful exegetical work of Thomas Joseph White on the divine name in Exodus 3 in Thomas Joseph White, *Exodus*, Brazos Theological Commentary on the Bible (Grand Rapids, MI: Brazos, 2016), 35-44.

The scene of Moses before the burning bush demands the doctrine of incomprehensibility and ineffability as readers are greeted with the namelessness of God even in the naming of God. As Soskice points out, there are many who name God throughout the Scriptures, and we will even turn to these analogical names at length come chapter six. Yet, while names play a significant role in the Hebrew Scriptures—as men and women are named and renamed, as Adam even names the creatures of the animal kingdom—this biblical text demands a reverence of incomprehensibility.

Bringing this section of the book to a close, given that there are passages that seem to affirm that we can see, know, and name God, while at the same time there are passages that seem to affirm that God is unseeable, unknowable, and unnamable—at least univocally—any hope to affirm a biblical doctrine of divine incomprehensibility will call for a mature understanding of biblical reasoning. As the reader of Scripture works toward articulating a robust and mature doctrine of incomprehensibility, it will prove helpful to make use of a threefold biblical affirmation of the doctrine: (1) some passages explicitly declare the doctrine; (2) some passages implicitly demonstrate the doctrine; and (3) some passages demand the doctrine from good and necessary consequence.

Table 2.1. Incomprehensibility in the Biblical Data

Declare	These passages can be exegeted to show an *explicit declaration* of God's incomprehensibility.
Psalm 139:1-6	"O LORD, you have searched me and known me! You know when I sit down and when I rise up; you discern my thoughts from afar. You search out my path and my lying down and are acquainted with all my ways. Even before a word is on my tongue, behold, O LORD, you know it altogether. You hem me in, behind and before, and lay your hand upon me. *Such knowledge is too wonderful for me; it is high; I cannot attain it*" (emphasis added).
Psalm 145:1-3	"I will extol you, my God and King, and bless your name forever and ever. Every day I will bless you and praise your name forever and ever. *Great is the LORD, and greatly to be praised, and his greatness is unsearchable*" (emphasis added).
Isaiah 55:8-9	"For my thoughts are not your thoughts, neither are your ways my ways, declares the LORD. For as the heavens are higher than the earth, so are my ways higher than your ways and my thoughts than your thoughts."

Romans 11:33-34	"Oh, the depth of the riches and wisdom and knowledge of God! How unsearchable are his judgments and how inscrutable his ways! For who has known the mind of the Lord, or who has been his counselor."
1 Corinthians 2:9-11	"But, as it is written, 'What no eye has seen, nor ear heard, nor the heart of man imagined, what God has prepared for those who love him'—these things God has revealed to us through the Spirit. . . . For who knows a person's thoughts except the spirit of that person, which is in him? So also no one comprehends the thoughts of God except the Spirit of God."
1 Timothy 6:15b-16	"He who is the blessed and only Sovereign, the King of kings and Lord of lords, who alone has immortality, who dwells in unapproachable light, whom no one has ever seen or can see. To him be honor and eternal dominion. Amen."
Demonstrate	These passages *implicitly demonstrate* God's incomprehensibility by virtue of his majesty and mystery.
Exodus 33:18-20	"Moses said, 'Please show me your glory.' And he said, 'I will make all my goodness pass before you and will proclaim before you my name "the LORD" . . . but,' he said, 'you cannot see my face, for man shall not see me and live.'"
Job 11:7-8	"Can you find out the deep things of God? Can you find out the limit of the Almighty? It is higher than heaven—what can you do? Deeper than Sheol—what can you know?"
Job 38-40	"Where were you when I laid the foundation of the earth? Tell me, if you have understanding. Who determined its measurements—surely you know! Or who stretched the line upon it? On what were its bases sunk, or who laid its cornerstone, when the morning stars sang together and all the sons of God shouted for joy?"
John 1:17-18	"For the law was given through Moses; grace and truth came through Jesus Christ. *No one has ever seen God*; the only God, who is at the Father's side, he has made him known" (emphasis added).
1 Corinthians 13:12	"For now we see in a mirror dimly, but then face to face. Now I know in part; then I shall know fully, even as I have been fully known."
Demand	These passages *demand* the doctrine of God's incomprehensibility by being held together with corollary passages and doctrines in constructive biblical and theological reasoning.
Exodus 3:13-15	"Then Moses said to God, 'If I come to the people of Israel and say to them, "The God of your fathers has sent me to you," and they ask me, "What is his name?" what shall I say to them?' God said to Moses, 'I AM WHO I AM.' And he said, 'Say this to the people of Israel: "I AM has sent me to you."' God also said to Moses, 'Say this to the people of Israel: "The LORD, the God of your fathers, the God of Abraham, the God of Isaac, and the God of Jacob, has sent me to you." This is my name forever, and thus I am to be remembered throughout all generations.'"
Psalm 90:2	"Before the mountains were brought forth, or ever you had formed the earth and the world, from everlasting to everlasting you are God."
Malachi 3:6	"For I the LORD do not change; therefore you, O children of Jacob, are not consumed."

Job 11:7-9	"Can you find out the deep things of God? Can you find out the limit of the Almighty? It is higher than heaven—what can you do? Deeper than Sheol—what can you know."
Passages on negative and positive names of God.	Readers could turn to doctrines within theology proper like simplicity, infinitude, incorporeality, aseity, pure act, and the like to see how God's essence and existence is *wholly other* than the existence of the creatures. These passages, taken together, seem to *demand* the doctrine of divine incomprehensibility.

CONCLUSION: A REVEALED INCOMPREHENSIBILITY

We know that God is incomprehensible precisely because he has revealed himself to be so. The doctrine of divine incomprehensibility, along with the doctrine of divine ineffability, do not suffer a defeating self-referential incoherence because of the revealed status of the doctrine.

The revealed status of divine incomprehensibility will not only protect the doctrine from any notion of self-referential incoherence, but it also impacts theological method. If the doctrine of divine incomprehensibility is a revealed doctrine, and God chose to reveal himself as incomprehensible and ineffable, it follows that there will be significant limitations to how creatures can know and name God.

Furthermore, placing the doctrine of divine incomprehensibility in the category of a "revealed" doctrine ought to help theologians "win back" the doctrine. Instead of the incomprehensibility and ineffability of God's essence leading the theologian to despair or doubt, the Scriptures shift the paradigm and show that the otherness of God is impetus for praise and delight. The scriptural context of divine incomprehensibility is doxological. God's unsearchableness is a matter of praise for the biblical authors. The mystery of God present when we turn our eye Godward is not reason for theological hopelessness but rather theological humility. In humility, we receive the doctrine of divine incomprehensibility as a revealed doctrine and delight in God's not being able to be conquered or subjugated by our language or mind. For these reasons and more, any mature affirmation of God's incomprehensibility will show how the doctrine comes from biblical reasoning and scriptural exegesis. While the doctrine does make sense from a standpoint of philosophical doctrine, first and foremost divine incomprehensibility is not a constructive doctrine of philosophy but a revealed doctrine of Scripture. (Not to pit the two against one another too strongly). In conclusion, readers of the biblical data see the revealed status of the doctrine by looking at those passages that declare the doctrine, demonstrate the doctrine, and demand the doctrine.

3

Divine Incomprehensibility in Theological Antiquity, Part One

The Anomoean Controversy and the Early Church

> *For we do not say as much as needs to be said about*
>
> *God, but as much as human nature can grasp and*
>
> *our weakness can bear. We do not explain what God*
>
> *is; we admit with a good grace that we do not know*
>
> *the exact truth about him. For in what concerns God*
>
> *the height of knowledge is to admit one's ignorance.*
>
> **Cyril of Jerusalem**

CYRIL'S PROFOUND LINE, "In what concerns God the height of knowledge is to admit one's ignorance," is something of a summary of the history of divine incomprehensibility as a doctrine of the church. It is no surprise, to any who have attempted the joyful work of Christian theology, that the finite creaturely mind is met with ignorance when trying to know and name the infinite. Yet the conditions and particulars of this "ignorance" are precisely the material of the conversation surrounding divine incomprehensibility throughout theological antiquity. When Christians confess this informed ignorance of God's nature, what precisely do we mean? Moreover, to what extent does this ignorance prolong? What is the relationship between God's revelation and our ignorance of God? Does ignorance reflect more on the otherness of the Creator or the limits of the creature? Just how informed can our ignorance become? Will we ever overcome this ignorance? These questions, and many like them, are some of the particulars discussed throughout the halls of history in varied Christian traditions.

It is the goal of this chapter and the next to canvas some of these conversations surrounding God's incomprehensibility in theological antiquity. Of course, in the confines of two individual chapters we will not be able to do justice to the entirety of voices and nuances that have built the church's doctrine of incomprehensibility and ineffability. Instead, I plan to cover the major contributions to the conversation over the centuries. At times, this will mean we zoom into an era like the fourth century and work through a number of voices as they dialogue on pertinent matters; other times, this will mean we zoom into particular individuals, like Pseudo-Dionysius, who made individual contributions to the conversation that are worthy of exploration. Giving two chapters to the highlights of the conversation will inevitably mean that some readers will quibble with those who are selected and those left out of these pages; yet, this is not a tracing of historical highlights just for history's sake; this is historical exploration aimed in a particular direction: to help bring to the surface the nuances of God's incomprehensibility that we might make informed decisions about the doctrines' import into theological method.

While this goal will help set the jurisdiction of what is covered in this historical treatment, there is still one more caveat needed for the purpose of filtering the voices and eras covered in this chapter. That caveat is this: the goal of this chapter is not to attempt setting up an apologetic or polemical case for the doctrine of divine incomprehensibility. Theologians like Basil the Great and Gregory of Nyssa had to work diligently to prove the doctrine of divine incomprehensibility; this book assumes their conclusions and works to constructively demonstrate methodological import from the doctrine. This means that a historical treatment, then, will simply trace the historic affirmations of the doctrine as it pertains to an affirmative and constructive definition toward the goal stated above.

We will proceed to work through the historical material starting in the early church in this chapter, giving most attention to fourth century thinkers like Basil, Gregory of Nyssa, Gregory of Nazianzus, and John Chrysostom. If one were to examine church history for the place of disagreement concerning divine incomprehensibility and ineffability, the Anomoean controversy in the fourth century would likely prevail as a leading candidate. Therefore, I will dedicate substantial time to examining the Cappadocians and their work contra Eunomius and other Anomoeans of their day. This chapter will conclude by moving beyond the Cappadocians and spending a number of pages reflecting on the first five homilies from John Chrysostom of his twelve in *On the Incomprehensibility of God*.

DIVINE INCOMPREHENSIBILITY IN
THE FOURTH CENTURY

Though a treatment of the second and third century and its articulation of God's unknowability and ineffability would prove beneficial, this treatment of divine incomprehensibility in the early church will largely take place in the fourth century. As we will see, the fourth century is where the major developments surrounding God's incomprehensibility came from, yet this is not to say that there was no talk of God's unknowability in the centuries before. As Carabine writes in her treatment of negative theology's appropriation in the early church, "The second-century Christian Fathers of Alexandria, Clement and Origen, borrowed from contemporary Middle Platonism the notion of the ineffability and unnameability of God, although even before the second century in the Christian tradition, we find traces of negative definition of God."[1] Therefore, while the bulk of this chronology deals with the controversy surrounding Anomoeanism in the fourth century, it would be incorrect to speculate about the absence of divine incomprehensibility in the first few centuries of the early church.[2]

THE CAPPADOCIANS AND THE EUNOMIAN/ ANOMOEANISM CONTROVERSY

The doctrine of incomprehensibility came into focus, even if secondarily, during the Eunomian controversy. As Stępień and Kochańczyk-Bonińska note, "The incomprehensibility of God was the strongest sign of being Orthodox at that time." Stępień and Kochańczyk-Bonińska conclude their treatment of Gregory of Nazianzus and John Chrysostom with the following observation, showing the doctrine's significant role in conversations of the fourth century. Affirming the doctrine of divine incomprehensibility was vital in defeating the Eunomians, as they mention, because "the best way to reject the doctrine of Eunomians and to weaken their missionary activity was to argue on the impossibility of knowing the essence of God."[3]

While the doctrine of divine incomprehensibility did indeed play a significant role in the debates between theologians such as the Cappadocians and pro-Arian groups such as those in the Anomoeanism controversy, it would be anachronistic and incorrect to argue that it was the primary doctrine under consideration. Instead, under

[1]Deirdre Carabine, *The Unknown God: Negative Theology in the Platonic Tradition: Plato to Eriugena* (Leuven: Peeters, 2015), 223. She goes on to note Philo's significant role in this development, noting, "It was largely Philo's exegesis of Old Testament texts which provided the second-century Fathers with a basis for asserting the ineffable and unnamable nature of God." Carabine herself treats Philo's influence, along with other contemporary figures, see 103-207.
[2]Along with Carabine's treatment in *The Unknown God*, readers can get another account of negative theology in general and incomprehensibility in particular during the second century from D. W. Palmer, "Atheism, Apologetic, and Negative Theology in the Greek Apologists of the Second Century," in *Vigiliae Christianae: A Review of Early Christian Life and Language* 37, no. 3 (1983), 234-59.
[3]Tomasz Stępień and Krolina Kochańczyk-Bonińska, *Unknown God, Known in His Activities: Incomprehensibility of God During the Trinitarian Controversy of the 4th Century*, European Studies in Theology, Philosophy and History of Religion 18 (Berlin: Peter Lang, 2018), 230.

consideration in much of the fourth century were questions of paternity and filiation between the Father and the Son, which brought into focus questions of *ousia* regarding the second person of the Trinity. It was in propagating an extreme form of pro-Arian Christology that Eunomius, and others like him, backed their way into a conversation pertaining to the incomprehensibility and ineffability of God. This is not to downplay the significant role of these two doctrines in the discussion—as we will see, much ink was spilled in the discussion of knowing and naming God—yet this will help us right-size the contours or the dialogue taking place in the Anomoeanism debates.

Simplicity and the "unbegottenness" of the Father. Examining the back-and-forth theological treaties from the hands of both Basil of Caesarea and Gregory of Nyssa's work against Eunomius, along with what remains from Eunomius's own writing, highlights the vital role that both the doctrine of divine simplicity and the concept of the Father's unbegottenness play in the discussion.[4] Working through the Cappadocian responses to Eunomius brings into focus why I say that incomprehensibility, while being a significant portion of the discussion, was a discussion adjacent to what was the real concern—divine simplicity and the Father's being unbegotten.

To state the Eunomian case as clearly as possible as it relates to divine simplicity and the doctrine of unbegottenness, the argument could be understood by the following: the Father's essence is singular in substance, and that simple essence includes his unbegottenness. Eunomius argues that it must be this way, or the predicate of "unbegottenness" might be thought of as an accident that would jeopardize the needed metaphysical notion of divine simplicity. This proves important because when the essence of Jesus comes into focus, anyone should agree that "unbegottenness" is not properly predicated of the Son, and

---

[4]For a thorough treatment of the topic, see Andrew Radde-Gallwitz, *Basil of Caesarea, Gregory of Nyssa, and the Transformation of Divine Simplicity* (Oxford: Oxford University Press, 2009). See especially his chapter "'Truly Repay the Debt': Aetius and Eunomius of Cyzicus," 87-113.

therefore he ought not be thought of as *homoousios* with the Father as he lacks the particularly important predicate of unbegottenness.[5]

It was the relationship between divine simplicity, the Father's unbegottenness, and the implications for the essence of Jesus that was center stage in the Eunomian/Anomoean controversy. As this discussion evolved, the doctrine of incomprehensibility would come to play a major role. Discussing the controversies, Van Geest writes of Eunomius, "Well-versed in philosophy, Eunomius—much more than Arius—had asserted that human beings were capable of grasping God, because words were realities created by God in which the true nature of the object described was really represented." He continues, "According to [Eunomius] this meant that the revealed names of God actually contained God's essence for human beings to grasp."[6] Since Eunomius thought the essence of God could be contained in that particular predicate—unbegotten—he argued that it is through comprehending God as the unbegotten that we can know God and know that he is distinguished from the person of Jesus Christ.

Andrew Radde-Gallwitz provides a helpful summary of Aetius and Eunomius's contention of theological language, saying: "For Aetius and Eunomius, the only way theology can be meaningful is if the ontology of simple divine being is perfectly reflected in our speech about it. Words for God cannot be privative because there is no privation in God. Different names reveal distinct essences. The linguistic realm is a direct map of the ontological."[7] This insistence upon the creaturely ability to comprehend the divine and the linguistic corollary of God's speakability received much pushback from the Cappadocians and others like them.[8]

---

[5]To see Eunomius' argument in syllogism form, see Radde-Gallwitz, who transposes the simplicity and ingenerate argument into a twelve-step syllogism. Radde-Gallwitz, *Transformation of Simplicity*, 106.

[6]Paul van Geest, *The Incomprehensibility of God: Augustine as a Negative Theologian in Late Antique History and Religion* (Leuven: Peeters, 2011), 33.

[7]Radde-Gallwitz, *Transformation of Simplicity*, 114.

[8]For more on the historical aspects of the conversation, along with the sources already mentioned in this chapter, see Mark DelCogliano, *Basil of Caesarea's Anti-Eunomian Theory of Names:*

Take for instance Basil of Caesarea, who claims that it is to deceive his hearers that Eunomius makes such an ordeal about God's essence being comprehended by the predicate of unbegottenness. Basil demonstrates that, using Eunomius' logic of unbegottenness, one could substitute any of the apophatic predicates of the Lord in substitute of unbegottenness, therefore showing Eunomius has an ulterior motive for his highlighting of God's unbegotten nature. Basil argues: "Just as 'incorruptible' signifies that no corruption is present to God, and 'invisible' that he is beyond every comprehension through the eyes, and 'incorporeal' that his substance is not three-dimensional, and 'immortal' that dissolution will never happen to him, so too do we say that 'unbegotten' indicates that no begetting is present to him."[9] Basil continues to show that Eunomius is, at the very least, inconsistent in application of apophatic attributes and is therefore not clear in his use of divine simplicity. Each of these other negative names could be said of the Son, and it is here that Eunomius fails to deal with a fuller understanding of simplicity as it relates to negative theology. Basil demonstrates his logic by use of the term *incorruptible*, saying, "To make his deception plain, do this: take the arguments that he uses for 'unbegotten' (that it is not reasonable to speak about God either 'by human conceptualization' or 'by way of privation'), and notice what happens when you transfer them to some of the other things said about God. You will discover that the arguments he uses are perfectly suited for each term."[10]

He concludes by asking, "Why is it more fitting to give this philosophical account for 'unbegotten' than for 'incorruptible' and in general for each term with the same formation?" He says of Eunomius:

Christian Theology and Late-Antique Philosophy in the Fourth Century Trinitarian Controversy (Leiden: Brill, 2010), and Richard Vaggione, *Aspects of Faith in the Eunomian Controversy: Gregory of Nyssa Against Eunomius* (Oxford: Oxford University Press, 1976).

[9] *AE* 1.9. For a biographical account of Basil of Caesarea, see Philip Rousseau, *Basil of Caesarea* (Berkely: University of California Press, 1994).

[10] *AE* 1.9.

"None of the others assists him in achieving his impiety!"[11] Basil shows
that in missing the theological role of negative theology, Eunomius
instead argues that God's essence *is* unbegottenness, and his "impiety"
is declaring that since Christ does not share in this unbegottenness, he
does not share in the divine essence.

Basil's development of God's unbegottenness in terms of negative
theology is important in understanding his argument and those who
will follow in his footsteps. Basil argues that "just as being 'from
someone' is not the substance when we are talking about human
beings, so too when we are talking about the God of the universe it is
not possible to say that 'unbegotten' (which is equivalent to saying,
'from no one') is the substance."[12] This quotation shows the differing
ways Eunomius and Basil conceive of the concept of God's aseity and
unbegottenness. For Basil, God's unbegottenness acts as an apophatisim that denounces of him any contingency of being. On the contrary, for Eunomius, unbegottenness is the cataphatic predication that
is itself the essence of God. Meaning, the very essence of God is captured in this positive predicate—*unbegotten.* This is precisely where
the doctrine of divine incomprehensibility enters the discussion
during the Anomoean controversy. Eunomius, and his Anomoean
colleagues, opined that comprehension of God's unbegottenness was
an actual possibility, and it is that word *unbegotten*, that contains the
fullness of God's being. Therefore, divine comprehensibility was not
only affirmed but said to have been achieved by the Anomoeans of
the fourth century.

While the exact dates of correspondences between four Cappadocians—Basil of Caesarea, Gregory of Nazianzus, Gregory of Nyssa, and
Eunomius—are not unanimously agreed upon, it is *likely* that Basil

---

[11]*AE* 1.10. To be sure, Basil affirms the Father's unbegottenness, yet he does so as *apophatisim*. He
writes, "As for me, I too would say that the substance of God is unbegotten, but I would not say
that unbegottenness is the substance." *AE* 1.11.
[12]*AE* 1.15.

never had a chance to read Eunomius's follow-up work, *Apology for the Apology*.[13] Basil died in 378, and Eunomius published his second work in five volumes from 378 to 380. Due to Basil's passing before the reception of the *Apology of the Apology*, the church is at a loss for his response. Yet Eunomius is not without his critics after Basil's untimely death; most important, it is after the death of Basil that his younger brother, Gregory of Nyssa, begins to pick up his brother's work against the Eunomians.

Andrew Radde-Gallwitz and Mark DelCogliano note that Gregory "managed to borrow a copy of the first two books for only seventeen days." We read Gregory's work against Eunomius's first two books in his first installment of *Against Eunomius*. Later, in the second and third installment of *Against Eunomius*, Gregory responds to Eunomius's second and third book.[14]

Given that Gregory picks up his pen where his brother laid his down working against the Anomoean misconception of comprehending God, it is not a surprise to read quite a bit of overlap between the brothers. This is not to insinuate that Gregory had nothing to add to Basil's arguments. In fact, Stępień and Kochańczyk-Bonińska pick up on ways in which Gregory advances Basil's notion of God's incomprehensibility. They write:

> However, we can also see certain gradation of the arguments in the answers of Cappadocians. Basil in a more technical way expresses that we can understand that the substance of God exists (καταληψίας ὅτι ἐστὶν ἡ οὐσία), and thus we can have a kind of perception of incomprehensibility (ἡ αἴσθησις αὐτοῦ τῆς ἀκαταληψίας). So, the knowledge of

---

[13]For more on dating of the works, see Andrew Radde-Gallwitz and Mark DelCogliano's introduction in *AE* in *TFC*, esp. 18-39.

[14]Radde-Gallwitz and DelCogliano, introduction to *AE* in *TFC*, 36. Again, Radde-Gallwitz and DelCogliano are helpful here in pointing out that since all we have of Eunomius' *Apology of the Apology* comes from the refutation of Gregory of Nyssa, the fourth and fifth books in the work are lost to history as Gregory did not respond to the last two volumes. For more on the history and reception of both Eunomius' *Liber Apologeticus* and *Apologia Apologiae* see Eunomius, *The Extant Works*, trans. Richael Paul Vaggione (Oxford: Oxford University Press, 2002), 3-34; 79-99.

God, which is sufficient to worship, is the recognition of the existence
of God that man gains from His works. Gregory goes further by saying
that the attributes of God inform us rather about Him being totally
beyond our understanding, and, therefore, to know God means simply
to recognize His total incomprehensibility.[15]

Gregory consistently reminds his readers that the perfection of God is
out of reach of both creaturely knowledge and creaturely articulation.
Moreover, due to the Creator's essence being beyond the creaturely
knowledge and language, two implications become apparent: (1) we
know God best by his economic activity in the world, and (2) we describe God best by use of apophatic predication describing what he is
not rather than what he is.

On the second point, in his book *Gregory of Nyssa and the Grasp of
Faith*, Martin Laird serves readers well by showcasing Gregory of
Nyssa's use of apophatic predication, with or without the alpha privative, or using the alpha as a prefix to negate the attached concept (for
example, "atheist" or, a-theist, means, with the alpha privative, a "non-
theist"), in his articulation of the divine. Readers find in Gregory's
Homily III on the Beatitudes this exposition:

> Yet does not our desire perhaps point us to what is unattainable and
> incomprehensible? What thought of ours is able to investigate the
> nature of that which we seek? What noun or verb can give us a sufficient
> idea of transcendent light? How shall I name the invisible? How [should
> I] describe the immaterial? How [should I] present what has no form?
> How can I deal with what has no size, extent, quality or shape, what is
> not found in space or time, what lies beyond every limitation and every
> definition imaginable, whose function is life and the bringing into
> being of all that is reckoned good, that to which every sublime thought
> and title applies.[16]

---

[15]Stępień and Kochańczyk-Bonińska, *Unknown God*, 114.

[16]Gregory of Nyssa, *Homilies on the Beatitudes*, in *Supplements to Vigiliae Christianae* 52 (Leiden: Brill, 2000), 43.

Using this quote, Laird shows the string of alpha privatives that give testimony to Gregory's reliance on apophasis. In this single quote, Gregory refers to God as invisible, immaterial, that which cannot be seen, that which is without size, that which is without quantity, that which is without form, and that which escapes all limitation and definition.[17]

What Laird points out in Gregory's emphasis on apophatic predication is not unique to his Homilies on the Beatitudes. As expected, this kind of theological construction and emphasis runs throughout his work against Eunomius. Like Basil, Gregory argued that the Anomoean insistence that the divine essence can be captured in that word *unbegotten* is misguided primarily on the basis that God is incomprehensible, and there is no word that can capture his essence. Gregory states that the Eunomians "open their mouths against the ineffable Power" by attempting to "measure the infinite nature with a single title, squeezing the being of God into the word 'unbegottenness.'" Gregory argues that they do so simply to "advance their slander against the Only-begotten."[18] Or, as he says elsewhere in his *Contra Eunomius*, "In this petty and infantile way they toy vainly with the impossible, and with childish hand lock up the incomprehensible nature of God in the few syllables of 'unbegottenness.'" He continues, "They advocate insanity, and think that the divine is of such size and kind that they could by human logic contain it in a single term."[19]

As Gregory spent many pages refuting the Eunomians, there is much that could be said if our goal was simply to rehearse the Cappadocians' arguments for affirming the doctrines of God's incomprehensibility and ineffability. However, since, as has been stated above, this treatment of theological antiquity is working toward a particular goal—dealing with the implications of divine incomprehensibility for

---

[17]Martin Laird, *Gregory of Nyssa and the Grasp of Faith: Union, Knowledge, and Divine Presence* (Oxford: Oxford University Press, 2004), 66.

[18]*CE* II.125.

[19]*CE* II.82.

theological method—I'd like to bring into focus a certain aspect of Gregory's writing. Namely, Gregory, while insisting that a healthy apophasis is the best method for any attempt at describing God, is still nuanced in balancing both God's incomprehensibility together with a nuanced optimism about creatures' ability to know their God.

While Gregory does note that incomprehensibility and ineffability might mean that theologians are simply to remain silence about the essence of God, there is a hope of knowledge and naming. Gregory writes about the safety of silence, saying, "One might argue that safety lies in leaving the divine nature unexplored, as being inexpressible and beyond the reach of human reasoning. . . . Would it not be safer for them all to follow the counsel of Wisdom, and not enquire into things too deep."[20] Yet Gregory does not leave his readers with the false idea that silence is the only option concerning the theological task. On the contrary, Gregory instead articulates a nuanced position that seeks not to know God in a univocal sense but to reach for apprehension, not comprehension. Gregory writes that he is simply advocating his "master's teaching"—that master being his older brother, Basil—that "we have a faint and slight apprehension of the divine Nature through reasoning, but we still gather knowledge enough for our slight capacity through the words which are reverently used of it."[21]

Gregory's vision of using predications and names "reverently" eliminates the notion that the fullness that is the divine essence could be fully described, much less fully described in one word. While the divine essence cannot be fully known or described as it is in itself, there is the hope for the creature to still know their God. Maybe more succinct and clearer than anywhere else, in his second volume of *Contra Eunomius*, Gregory summarizes his, and Basil's, position as it relates to religious epistemology and theological method:

---

[20]*CE* II.97-100.
[21]*CE* II.130.

Such then was the thought elaborated by our Teacher. It enables anyone, whose vision is not obstructed by the screen of heresy, to perceive quite clearly that the manner of existence of the essential nature of the Divinity is intangible, inconceivable, and beyond all rational comprehension. Human thought, investigating and searching by such reasoning as is possible, reaches out and touches the unapproachable and sublime Nature, neither seeing so clearly as distinctly to glimpse the Invisible, not so totally debarred from approaching as to be unable to form any impression of what it seeks.[22]

It is in this tension, where the divine essence is "beyond all rational comprehension" yet where creaturely thought still has a hope which "reaches out and touches" the unapproachable light, that the Cappadocians, and much of the church, would instruct us to operate within the task of theology.

Ineffability and incorporeality in Gregory of Nazianzus. While maybe not as well-known for his work against the Eunomians as his Cappadocian counterparts, Gregory of Nazianzus did spend time in his Orations working against the heterodox group and in so doing contributed to the fourth century conversation concerning divine incomprehensibility. While Gregory speaks directly to the Eunomians in his first theological oration, it is in his second theological oration that he arguably makes his greatest contribution for our discussion here.

Setting the theological and Eunomian context of the theological orations, Christopher Beeley points out how, of the many issues Gregory has with Eunomius, his major concern is that "Eunomius' real error [was] that he selectively, and with no apparent justification, elevates unbegottenness above all other attributes, to the point of making it the very definition of God's essence."[23]

---

[22]*CE* II.138.
[23]Christopher A. Beeley, *Gregory of Nazianzus on the Trinity and the Knowledge of God: In Your Light We Shall See Light* (Oxford: Oxford University Press, 2008), 93.

Against the backdrop of Eunomius' claim that God is properly articulated and comprehended in that word *unbegotten*, Gregory of Nazianzus develops on argument in the opposite direction of Eunomius based on incorporeality and ineffability. Again, Beeley is helpful here: "Gregory analyzes the epistemological dimension of incomprehensibility primarily in terms of human corporeality . . . the human mind conceives things by means of form and order, within the dimensions of time and space and involving the categories of quality, quantity, and relationships that characterize all creatures."[24]

Developing the significance of God's incorporeality, Gregory—with a touch of rhetorical flourish—asks his Eunomian interlocutors,

> To what conclusion will closely scrutinized arguments bring you, you most rational of theologians, who boast over infinity? Is it corporeal? How then can it be boundless, limitless, formless, impalpable, invisible? Can bodies be such? The arrogance of it! This is not the nature of bodies. Or is it corporeal but without these properties? The grossness of it, to say that deity has no properties superior to ours! How could it be worth worship were it bounded? How could it escape elemental composition and disintegration or even total dissolution?[25]

Continuing on this theme, and elaborating on incorporeality's relationship to divine simplicity, Gregory continues and concludes, "But dissolution is utterly alien to God the prime nature. So no dissolution means no division; no division means no conflict; no conflict means no composition, and hence no body involving composition."

In negating any composition and therefore any corporeality in God, Gregory develops a mature doctrine of ineffability. He uses the analogy of his ascending the mountain of divinity in order to better view and articulate God. Yet even in his most ardent attempts to know and name the divine, the theologian comes up rather short of truly naming God's

---

[24]Beeley, *Gregory of Nazianzus*, 99.
[25]*OR* 28.6.

prime essence. This leaves him to conclude that "to know God is hard, to describe him impossible."[26]

In case Gregory's hypothetical ascent up the mountain was not convincing, the Cappadocian moves to consider Paul's being taken up into the third heaven (2 Cor 12:2). Gregory writes of this "rapture" that "had Paul been able to express the experiences gained from the third heaven, and his progress, ascent, or assumption to it, we should, perhaps, have known more about God . . . but since they were ineffable, let them have the tribute of our silence."[27] Gregory brings his twenty-eighth oration to a close by showing why a "tribute of silence" is the path forward for any rational creature. Gregory demonstrates through the rest of this oration that creatures do not have the ability to fully comprehend and name even the "nature of beings on the second level."[28] In other words, creatures have an epistemological limitation when it comes to even knowing other corporeal natures. If we cannot properly know or name fellow corporeal creatures—such as ourselves or others in the animal kingdom—then we ought not attempt to articulate the incorporeal essence of the divine.

To bring our section on Gregory to a close, and in hopes of fully seeing the force of Gregory's argument in this oration, the concept of ascent is vital. Giving attention to the notion of ascent is important in understanding both the emphasis and continuity of Gregory's second theological oration. The following chart attempts to show Gregory's threefold ascent as illustrated in Gregory's affirmation of divine ineffability. Gregory uses this notion of ascent to describe varying creature's movement toward the Lord. What becomes clear in Gregory's use of ascent is that even when ascending toward the divine, the creature never breaks the barrier of ineffability. This point will feature again in later chapters as the proper response to divine

---

[26]*OR 28.4.*
[27]*OR 28.20.*
[28]*OR 28.31.*

incomprehensibility will not be ascent of the creature, but the conde-scension of the Creator through gracious accommodation.

Table 3.1. Ascent and ineffability in *Oration* 28

Person	Ascent as Illustration	Emphasis on Ineffability
First, Gregory himself as a consecrated theologian.	Ascends the mountain of the divine: "I eagerly ascend the mount—or, to speak truer, ascend in eager hope matched with anxiety for my frailty—that I may enter the cloud and company with God" (OR 28.2).	Even atop the mountain as a consecrated theologian: "But when I directed my gaze I scarcely saw the averted figure of God . . . peering in I saw not the nature prime, self-apprehended, the nature as it abides within the first veil and is hidden by the Cherubim . . . but as it reaches us at its furthest removed from God, being, so far as I can understand . . . Thus and thus only can you speak of God" (OR 28.3).
Second, the apostle Paul.	Paul's ascent to the third heaven: "Had Paul been able to express the experienced gained from the third heaven, and his progress, ascent, or assumption to it" (OR 28.20).	Paul doesn't attempt to describe or articulate his experience: "Since they were ineffable, let them have the tribute of our silence" (OR 28.20).
Third, and finally, the hearer of Gregory's oration.	From OR 28.21-28.30, Gregory takes his listeners on their own "ascent" from considering themselves in 28.21 to the highest heaven in 28.30. In order, Gregory calls to mind: 28.22 = Human beings themselves 28.23 = The animal kingdom on land 28.24 = The animal kingdom in the sea 28.25 = The animal kingdom in the air 28.26 = The plants and their fruit 28.27 = All the seas and waters of the earth 28.28 = The air, clouds, and all things in the sky 28.29 = The entire cosmos, planets, and stars 28.30-31 = The angelic hosts of heaven	In considering this hypothetical ascent from humans themselves up to the heavenly hosts: "Even the nature of beings on the second level is too much for our minds, let alone God's primal and unique, not to say all-transcending, nature" (OR 28.31).

Whether it be Gregory himself, the apostle Paul, or any creature God has made: none will pierce the nature of God with comprehension of knowledge or language. No matter how high the creature might ascend, the hope for meaningful language and knowledge of God comes not from creaturely ascending but the Creator's descending. With the correction and warnings of the Cappadocian thinkers in hand, we will here turn to another figure who worked during the Eunomian controversy to develop and defend the doctrine of God's incomprehensibility—John Chrysostom.

CHRYSOSTOM'S FIVE HOMILIES

A well-rounded treatment of divine incomprehensibility in the early church, especially as it developed within the Anomoean controversy, would not be complete without a look at the orations of Gregory of Nazianzus and the homilies of John Chrysostom.[29] While the work of both Gregory of Nazianzus and John Chrysostom both take place after the major works of Basil and Gregory of Nyssa, their work proved important in the continual decline of the extreme pro-Arian views of the Anomoeans. As we have already heard from Gregory of Nazianzus, this section will focus on Chrysostom's homilies against the Anomoeans.

In 385, the first year of Chrysostom's priesthood, the "golden tongue" began to deliver a series of sermons against the Anomoeans, a name describing the followers of Aetius and Eunomius of Cyzicus, who rejected the notion of the Father and the Son being of the same substance on account of the Son's not being begotten.[30] Chrysostom would, all together, deliver twelve homilies dealing with the controversy with the neo-Arian group. Summarizing the content, groupings, and dates of these twelve homilies, Paul Harkin writes,

> So it is that the twelve sermons against the Neo-Arian Anomoeans treat of two themes, the incomprehensibility of God (I-V) and the consubstantiality of Christ with the Father (VII-XII); they fall into two series

---

[29]See Stępień and Kochańczyk-Bonińska, *Unknown God*, 195.

[30]Due to the many chronological references throughout Chrysostom's sermons against the Anomoeans, there is a historical hope of dating them. In fact, see Paul Harkins' introduction in *Hom.*, 19-36.

separated by time and place. Homilies I-X were delivered at Antioch in the years 386-87; Homilies XI and XII belong to 398 and were preached in Constantinople.[31]

While an exposition of all twelve homilies would prove to be time well spent, we will restrict our jurisdiction to the first five homilies of the set as these five directly deal with the Anomoean notion that the creatures can and do know God fully as God knows himself. Moreover, given the ecclesial context of these homilies, the priest is forced to spend time dealing with concerns of those under his care. The homilies suffer from interruptions at certain points as Chrysostom addresses concerns in the congregation, such as warnings about "purse snatchers" stealing from congregants and the concern of following the Jewish feasts in their cultural context. Of course, while we ought to admire Chrysostom for tending to the pastoral concern of those in the fold, we will keep our focus on the content of the homilies in which he addresses the heretical group and therefore the doctrine of incomprehensibility.

Homily One. Stepping in for the bishop Flavion in Antioch, Chrysostom begins his first public treatise against the Anomoeans. He notes that he had been interested in combating the Anomoean heresy that was creeping into the church, but he recognized that the Anomoeans themselves had been coming to hear his preaching. He didn't want to "frighten off [his] prey," so "for a time [he] restrained [his] tongue from engaging in these contests with them."[32] However, Chrysostom says the Anomoeans were themselves "clamoring and challenging me to enter the arena" so he says he "felt confident in my courage, readied my myself for action, and took up the weapons 'to destroy their sophistries and every proud pretension which raises itself against the knowledge of God.'"[33]

Like his other homilies, Chrysostom deals with several biblical texts, yet his primary text in this first sermon comes from 1 Corinthians 13:8-12.

---

[31]Harkin, introduction in *Hom.*, 35.
[32]*Hom.* I.38.
[33]*Hom.* I.39.

The preacher really focuses in on the portion in which the apostle says in 1 Corinthians 13:9-10, "For we know in part and we prophesy in part, but when the perfect comes, the partial will pass away. . . . For now we see in a mirror dimly, but then face to face. Now I know in part; then I shall know fully, even as I have been fully known." Chrysostom explains Paul's use of the three images of (1) a child, (2) a dim mirror, and (3) the indistinct image reflected in the mirror to demonstrate that creatures have a severe limitation to their knowledge of the divine.[34]

To demonstrate his point of how creaturely limitations bring about intellectual limitations, Chrysostom calls his hearers' minds to God's perfections. He shows that due to the distinction between the Creator and the creatures, humans are not capable of even comprehending a single attribute of the divine, let alone his whole essence. Chrysostom writes:

> I know that God is everywhere, and I know that he is everywhere in his whole being. But I do not know how he is everywhere. I know that he is eternal and has no beginning. But I do not know how. My reason fails to grasp how it is possible for an essence to exist when that essence has received its existence neither from itself nor from another. I know that he begot a Son. But do not know how. I know that the Spirit is from him. But I do not know how the Spirit is from him.[35]

With the examples of omnipresence, atemporality, aseity, and the eternal modes of subsistence, Chrysostom shows that it is enough for the creature to say that God exists without attempting to penetrate the incomprehensibility of how God exists. With the intellectual limitations of the creature firmly in the mind of the congregation, Chrysostom then calls out the Anomoeans, saying, "Where are those who say they have attained and possess the fullness of knowledge? The fact is that they have really fallen into the deepest ignorance." He continues, "For people who say that they have attained the totality of knowledge

---

[34]*Hom.* I.18.
[35]*Hom.* I.19.

in the present life are only depriving themselves of a perfect knowledge for the life hereafter."[36]

A feature that is uniquely present in Chrysostom's work against the Anomoeans is his pastoral concern. He demonstrates an ecclesial concern for both the non-Anomoean congregants who might be influenced by the heresy and the Anomoeans themselves. He notes that the Anomoeans are making a similar mistake as Adam in the garden. Adam was not content with the station that the Lord had providentially granted him and wanted to obtain a "higher honor" and therefore "fell from the honor which he had."[37] Likewise, Chrysostom is concerned that the Anomoeans are not content to confess that God exists but want to articulate and pontificate on how God exists and will, in the end, lose both the honor they want to obtain and the honor they could have by living in gratitude for the intellectual honor they do have by virtue of God's self-revelation.

Chrysostom ends his first homily with two final points. First, he notes that even the economic activity of God is incomprehensible, as the prophets confess in admitting "your knowledge is too wondrous for me; it is too lofty, and I cannot attain to it" (Ps 139:6).[38]

Second, Chrysostom writes that not only is God incomprehensible but so too are the rewards that await all saints who rightly believe and obey the Lord (2 Cor 9:15).[39] The preacher asks if, according to Philippians 4:7, God's peace surpasses understanding, then how can we be expected to understand the giver of that peace? He writes:

> What are you heretics saying? His judgements are inscrutable, his ways are unsearchable, his peace surpasses all understanding, his gift is

---

[36]*Hom.* I.20.

[37]*Hom.* I.22.

[38]*Hom.* I.24. Moreover, Chrysostom points out that this is in reference simply to the works of God toward humanity. This passage does not even make mention of his "complete providence, which includes his benevolent care for the angels, archangels, and the powers above. What Paul is here examining is that portion of God's providence by which his benevolent care provides for men on earth." *Hom.* I.28.

[39]*Hom.* I.30.

indescribable, what God has prepared for those who love him has not entered into the heart of man, his greatness has no bound, his understanding is infinite. Are all these incomprehensible while only God himself can be comprehended? What excessive madness would it be to say that?[40]

It appears that the Anomoeans attempted to counter this argument by noting that this is simply in reference to God's economic governance. Chrysostom is convinced that this further establishes his point as it would seem to reason that if his economic activity is incomprehensible, so too would be his essence.[41]

Homily Two. Even more so than in his first homily, Chrysostom ushers in a monumental amount of biblical data to make his argument. However, when taken as a synthesized whole, the second homily is really a comparison of two biblical figures, Zechariah and Abraham, using Luke 1:20 and Romans 4:19-20 and expounding on 1 Chronicles 16:28 and 1 Kings 6:5. In contrasting these two figures, Chrysostom—using many examples—demonstrates that it is the posture of faith to not enter into idle speculation or probing into what God has said, demanded, or promised. Both hearing that they will be receiving offspring, the two examples, according to Chrysostom, have countering reactions: Zechariah questions the messenger by inquiring "How shall I know this?" (Lk 1:18) whereas Abraham, receiving the same news, "did not consider his own body dead nor the dead womb of Sarah. Yet he did not question the promise of God but was strengthened in faith."[42]

Using these two examples, with a plenitude of passages in between, Chrysostom shows that the Anomoeans are the spiritual offspring of Zechariah who attempt to probe where their knowledge ought not

---

[40]*Hom.* I.30.

[41]Chrysostom makes this point saying, "Stop the heretic; do not let him get away . . . the heretic answers that Paul is not talking about God's essence but about his governance of the universe. Very good, then. If he is talking about the governance of the universe, our victory is all the more complete. For if his governance of the universe is incomprehensible, then all the more so is God himself beyond our powers of comprehension." *Hom.* I.31.

[42]*Hom.* II.33.

lead—the essence of God. On the contrary, the orthodox are those who are content to acknowledge that God exists while not inquiring into how God exists. Using this comparison, Chrysostom warns, "Let the Anomoeans hear how vexed God is when he is the subject of curious inquiry. If Zechariah was punished because he refused to believe in the birth of a mortal, how will you Anomoeans escape punishment for your meddlesome inquiries into the ineffable generation from above?"[43] In fact, Chrysostom asks the Anomoean hearers before him, "Do you not think that you deserve to be seared with ten thousand thunderbolts? You are meddlesome and pretending to know that blessed essence which manages all the universe. Is this not a mark of the ultimate madness?"[44]

A major thrust of the second homily is the Creator-creature distinction. Calling upon such texts as Genesis 18:27; Matthew 16:17; Isaiah 40:6; Ecclesiastes 1:2; and more, Chrysostom shows that the biblical narrative refers to humanity in such terms as "dust and ashes, flesh and blood, grass and the flower of grass, a shadow and smoke and vanity, and whatever is weaker and more worthless than these things."[45] His hope is not to bring his hearers to despair but to simply remind them of their station and the limits therein. He then juxtaposes how the Scriptures describe even the actions of God in hopes to demonstrate that based on the distinction of the Creator and the creature, comprehension of the divine essence is simply unthinkable and unattainable.[46]

With the creature in perspective, Chrysostom turns to expounding on two topics in relation to the doctrine of creation—what was created and the ease with which it was created. He writes, "Think how mighty are the masses of mountains, how numerous the nations of people, how tall and countless the trees, how huge the size of buildings, how many

---

[43]*Hom.* II.16.
[44]*Hom.* II.39.
[45]*Hom.* II.19.
[46]See chapter five for a more complete discussion of the Creator-creature distinction.

kinds of four-footed animals, of wild beasts, or reptiles and every sort which the earth carries on its back."[47] Yet it is not just the creation that is Chrysostom's view, but how God brought about that creation, namely, with great ease. He continues, "Despite the fact that the earth is so great and so vast, God made it with such ease that the prophet could find no fitting example. So he said that God made the earth 'as if it were nothing.'"[48] In noting both God's ability to create and the ease with which he creates, Chrysostom demonstrates the otherness of God by demonstrable instances of the divine will and capability.

The juxtaposition of the Creator and the creature leads Chrysostom to conclude, "The distance between the essence of God and the essence of man is so great that no words can express it, nor is the mind capable of measuring it."[49] Reminding the Anomoeans of the smallness of their own selves and the grandeur of God as seen in the creation of nature, nations, and the heavens, Chrysostom concludes by admonishing the congregation to tend to the heretical wounds of the Anomoeans with a soft sponge and treat them as those who have suffered a "mental illness and have lost their wits" that they might be won back to the truth.[50]

Homily Three. The main thrust of Chrysostom's third homily is to consider the knowledge of the angels and principalities. Chrysostom makes an assertion that God is incomprehensible even to the angels and uses a number of Old Testament texts to demonstrate his point. The main point of the third homily is said concisely as Chrysostom writes:

> Let us call upon him, then, as the ineffable God who is beyond our intelligence, invisible, incomprehensible, who transcends the power of mortal words. Let us call on him as God who is inscrutable to the angels, unseen by the Seraphim, inconceivable to the Cherubim, invisible to the principalities, to the powers, and to the virtues, and in fact, to all

---

[47]*Hom.* II.25.
[48]*Hom.* II.25.
[49]*Hom.* II.37
[50]*Hom.* II.51-52.

creatures without qualification, because he is known only by the Son and the Spirit.[51]

The preacher's goal in saying this is to show how absurd is the "extravagant boasting" of the Anomoeans who say that they, "by the weak processes of their own reason, can grasp and define the essence of God who cannot be comprehended by the powers above."[52]

Chrysostom, using Isaiah 6:1-2 and Daniel 6:23 as well as Daniel 10:11, shows that even those creatures—like the angels and men of honor like Daniel—falter in the presence of the divine. In Isaiah's case, even the angels must cover their faces with their wings before the Almighty. In Daniel's case, even the one who stood down the lions could not breathe before mere angelic messengers, let alone the divine presence. Chrysostom uses these examples and others like them to again raise the question about how if even the angels cannot catch a glimpse of God's grandeur and glory, how can the Anomoeans assert that they have comprehended it? Chrysostom concludes the sermon by chastising his listeners about leaving the service before the sacrament is given.

Homily Four. In his fourth homily on the incomprehensible God, Chrysostom begins to develop a more robust doctrine of divine accommodation. This development plays an important role in his hermeneutics—which ought to be instructive for modern biblical readers—and he uses John 1:18 to demonstrate it.

Chrysostom's fourth argument against the Anomoeans is that John writes, rather plainly, that "no one has ever seen God." However, instead of simply quoting the passage as an argument-ender, Chrysostom does the exegetical work to show how John can affirm this along with the Old Testament's testimony of figures interacting with God. Chrysostom, voicing the concern of his interlocutor, writes:

---

[51]*Hom.* III.5.

[52]*Hom.* III.5. Chrysostom continues here, saying, "For the Anomoeans are no better than creatures who crawl on the ground and they are so vastly inferior to the powers above."

Let us see what objection might be urged against what [John] said. Tell me, John, what do you mean when you say: "No one has ever seen God?" What shall we think about the prophets who say that they saw God? Isaiah said: "I saw the Lord sitting on a high and exalted throne." And, again, Daniel said: "I saw until the thrones were set, and the Ancient of days sat." And Micah said: "I saw the God of Israel sitting on his throne." And again, another prophet said: "I saw the Lord standing on the altar, and he said to me: 'Strike the mercy seat.'" And I can gather together many similar passages to show you as witness of what I say.[53]

Chrysostom makes the theological-exegetical decision to define these passages, and others like them, by an affirmation that they are instances of divine accommodation, in which God accommodates the creature's limitations and pursues self-revelation in a manner fitting for the creature.

Chrysostom goes on to articulate the noncomposition of the divine essence, who is without "form or figure." What the prophets saw in each of their own theophanies is something of a form or a figure, and therefore we know it is not the pureness of the divine essence. So, using the progressive nature of revelation, Chrysostom argues that this later "prophet"—John, the beloved disciple—illuminates what it was the former prophets experienced. Namely, the prophets of old who "saw the Lord" saw an accommodated glory that was suitable for their creaturely natures. Chrysostom's exegetical conclusion concerning John 1:18 is, "When you hear that 'no one has ever seen God,' you must understand that the words you hear mean that no one knows God in his essence with complete exactness."[54]

Homily Five. The final homily under examination is the longest in Chrysostom's treatises against the Anomoeans. Chrysostom picks up again with his exposition of John 1:18 and brings it into conversation with John 6:46. Chrysostom focuses on John 6:46 as a continuation of

---

[53]*Hom* IV.18. In this quotation, Chrysostom is referencing Isaiah 6:1, Daniel 7:9, 1 Kings 22:19, and the "another prophet" is Amos, referencing Amos 9:1.
[54]*Hom.* IV.22.

John 1:18: After John instructs his hearers in chapter one that "no one has seen the Father," he continues with an exception in chapter six: "No one has seen the father except him who is from God." Chrysostom here wants to point out that the presence of the word "nobody" or "no one" is to emphatically exclude any creature among those who have "seen the Father." This creaturely exclusion is important because it means that only the Son and the Spirit are of those who have seen God—and to see God is to know God.[55]

Chrysostom spends a good deal of time in this homily developing an argument based on how creatures name God. More specifically, Chrysostom develops a theology of personal properties, and therefore personal names, and common properties. For example, using 1 Corinthians 8:6, Chrysostom shows how Paul names God based on common properties, saying, "One God, the Father from whom are all things, and one Lord, Jesus Christ, through whom are all things." The predicates "Lord" and "God" designating the Son and the Father, respectively, are to be understood as common properties or common predicates that are interchangeable between the persons of the Trinity. However, the personal properties of "Father" and "Son" are not interchangeable between the three persons of the Trinity, as these names are tied to each persons' eternal mode of subsistence, or their personal property.[56]

The distinction of personal and common properties among the Godhead is an important distinction for Chrysostom because he goes on to show that Paul and other biblical writers—especially David—seem to use "God" and "Lord" without reference to hierarchy. Chrysostom, using both exegesis and biblical reasoning, argues therefore that the personal properties ought not signify hierarchy either. In fact, it is in the Son's "sight" of God that we see the denial of hierarchy between the persons. As Chrysostom writes, "The fact that he is from God is a sign and indication that he knows him clearly. For an inferior

[55]*Hom.* V.6.
[56]*Hom.* V.8-17.

essence would not be able to have clear knowledge of a superior essence, even if the difference between them were slight."[57]

Readers should not miss what Chrysostom is attempting against the Anomoeans in this fifth homily, for it is a rather impressive rhetorical and polemical tactic. The Anomoeans give significant weight to the denial of incomprehensibility in order to deny the divinity of Christ. Yet Chrysostom flips the logic on its head and uses an affirmation of divine incomprehensibility in order to affirm Christ's divinity. While the Anomoean logic suggests that God is comprehensible, and his comprehensibility is contingent upon that word *unbegotten*. Chrysostom's logic reverse-engineers the process and argues that God is incomprehensible to creatures, and since Christ has a perfect knowledge of God, he is of the very essence of God as the "only begotten."

The content of these five homilies is not the end of the preacher's battle against the Anomoeans. However, starting in Homily Seven, after a break in subject matter in Homily Six, Chrysostom sets down working against the notion of God's being comprehensible and picks up a constructive case for the Son's unity in power and essence with the Father. However, these first five sermons are instructive for developing the needed nuances of a mature doctrine of divine incomprehensibility. Some of the themes Chrysostom picks up on in these five homilies will make numerous appearances throughout the rest of this volume as I seek to establish methodological implications springing from the doctrine of divine incomprehensibility.

From the Cappadocians and Chrysostom, we receive many needed nuances in both knowing and naming God. Moving forward, the otherness consequential of God's simplicity we see in the Cappadocians along with the implications of God's ontological distinction for the economy of revelation seen in John Chrysostom will both be paramount in establishing methodological guardrails for proper theological wisdom and speech.

---

[57]*Hom*. V.25.

4

Divine Incomprehensibility in Theological Antiquity, Part Two

From Pseudo-Dionysius to Modernity

The mysteries of God's Word

lie simple, absolute and unchangeable

in the brilliant darkness of a hidden silence.

Amid the deepest shadow

they pour overwhelming light

on what is most manifest.

Amid the wholly unsensed and unseen

they completely fill our sightless mind

with treasures beyond beauty.

Pseudo-Dionysius

I HAVE GIVEN THE THEOLOGIANS of the early church substantial attention because their correspondence and controversy with the Eunomians produced much reflection on divine incomprehensibility and divine ineffability. And though there is much to gain from their insights, the early church does not have a monopoly on these two doctrines. On the contrary, both divine incomprehensibility and divine ineffability, in their own way, have enjoyed a rather consistent affirmation throughout much of church history, even into the present age. There have, of course, been tweaks and deviations from the kind of doctrine propagated by the Cappadocians in the variegated eras of church history, but this chapter will not focus on the deviations and denials. Rather, it is the goal of this chapter to pick up and continue with where the previous one left off, namely, to canvas major eras and figures in church history in hopes of highlighting a constructive doctrine of divine incomprehensibility with an eye toward considering the doctrine's methodological implications for the task of Christian theology.

As for the figures and eras considered in this chapter, I will begin with Pseudo-Dionysius as a connection between the early church and that era known as late antiquity. Then, we will continue chronicling through the historic conversation through Aquinas for medieval insights into the doctrine. Also, in the era of medieval thinkers, we will also give extended reflection to the anonymous work *The Cloud of Unknowing*, which has played an important role in the church's doctrine of divine incomprehensibility. After treating some of these medieval figures and works, we will turn our attention to the Reformation and post-Reformation periods. We will end the chapter by examining the modern era and simply ask, Where does the doctrine of divine incomprehensibility stand today? This exploration of the modern doctrine of divine incomprehensibility will use Herman Bavinck as an exemplar of a modern expression of the doctrine. Within modernity, there are other figures one could argue deserve representation in this chapter. I have chosen Bavinck as a modern representation over others due to his positive contributions to the conversation concerning divine incomprehensibility. While many names might come to mind who could be fine interlocutors in demonstrating modern remonstrance *against* the doctrine, the hope with these chapters is not to *defend* the doctrine of divine incomprehensibility from its detractors but to establish a well of voices from which we can draw as we seek to establish methodological implications of the doctrine in coming chapters.

PSEUDO-DIONYSIUS'S *CLOUD OF UNKNOWING*

When a student of theology begins to contemplate the beautiful and tangled realities of theology as it concerns the knowledge of God, it is nearly inevitable that they will sit at the feet of Pseudo-Dionysius the Areopagite. The Dionysian corpus, particularly the *Divine Names* and *Mystical Theology*, carry monumental influence in the history of the church's thought about the names and being of the triune God.[1]

The influence of Dionysius becomes apparent as we see that other figures, such as Thomas Aquinas and the anonymous medieval author of the influential *Cloud of Unknowing*—a Dionysian phrase— rely much on Dionysius's thought. Also, his influence is seen in the fact that contemporary thinkers in the modern era often accredit significant development in the field of negative theology to Dionysius. For example, Paul van Geest writes, "Pseudo-Dionysius was the first to make a systematic distinction between negative (apophatic) theology and positive (cataphatic) theology."[2] Consider Dionysian's translator, Paul Rorem, as he lists the variegated influences of the pseudonymous theologian:

---

[1]It is common, when treating Pseudo-Dionysius, to point out the debates surrounding his identity and dating. Since reflection on the identity and context of the person behind the pseudonym *Pseudo-Dionysius* is not significant in developing the thesis of this chapter, I will simply point readers to works that take on this conversation: see Charles M. Stang, *Apophasis and Pseudonymity in Dionysius the Areopagite: "No Longer I"* (Oxford: Oxford University Press, 2012), and Paul Rorem, *Pseudo-Dionysius: A Commentary on the Texts and an Introduction to Their Influence* (Oxford: Oxford University Press, 1993), as well as the introductory essays from Rene Roques, Jaroslav Pelikan, Jean Leclercq, and Karlfried Froehlich that accompany Colm Luebheid's translation of Dionysius for the Classics of Western Spirituality edition.

[2]Paul van Geest, *The Incomprehensibility of God: Augustine as a Negative Theologian in Late Antique History and Religion* (Leuven: Peeters, 2011), 36.

[The Dionysian] writings are also known to have exerted an important influence on a wide range of topics. . . . For example, this Dionysius *invented* the word *hierarchy*, proposing a hierarchy of angels and a hierarchy in the church. Other significant areas of influence in the Middle Ages include the following: a theological aesthetics, especially with regard to Gothic architecture at the abbey church of Saint-Denis near Paris; Scholastic philosophy and theology, specifically that of Thomas Aquinas; the interpretation of the liturgy as a dramatic allegory; medieval mysticism, including the "cloud of unknowing," another phrase coined by Pseudo-Dionysius; and the entire subject of negative, or apophatic, theology.[3]

Apophasis, cataphasis, and supereminence in Pseudo-Dionysius. While we could dedicate many pages to Pseudo-Dionysius' influence at large in theological discourse, I want to focus on his influence for constructing a doctrine of divine incomprehensibility. In both his works *The Divine Names* and *Mystical Theology* readers are presented with what seems like a chorus of apparent clashing realities—the names of God and his being the nameless one; the revelation of God and his utter transcendence; contemplating the being of God with God's existing beyond being; God's dwelling in the "cloud of unknowing" and that darkness being a ray of *light* itself; the negation of all positive names of God and the hope of meaningful theological dialogue; and so on.

To untangle these Dionysian paradoxes into working theological grammar, it might be helpful to use a phrase coined by Denys Turner— "self-subverting" utterances.[4] Turner defines this phrase as Dionysius'

---

[3]Rorem, *Pseudo-Dionysius*, 3-4.

[4]Denys Turner, *The Darkness of God: Negativity in Christian Mysticism* (Cambridge: Cambridge University Press, 1995), 21. Another Dionysian scholar, Timothy Knepper, has coined a similar phrase—Dionysian "grammatical techniques of ineffability"—that is also helpful in attempting to make sense of what Pseudo-Dionysius is getting at in his theological method. See Timothy D. Knepper, "Pseudo-Dionysius and Paul's Sermon to the Unknown God," in *Ineffability: An Exercise in Comparative Religion* (Dordrecht: Springer, 2017), 30. Knepper works through "six Dionysian techniques of ineffability," which are hypernames, negations, assertions of ineffability, directions toward ineffability, metaphors of darkness, and metaphors of height (31).

theological tendency to bring together "the utterance which first says something and then, in the same image, unsays it."[5] This phrase makes even more sense when one considers another oft-used Dionysian term—*supereminence*. For Dionysius's God stands in a causal relationship with all things created and therefore is *beyond being* itself. Dionysius writes, "Since the unknowing of what is beyond being is something above and beyond speech, mind, or being itself, one should ascribe it an understanding beyond being."[6] He continues this theme:

> Indeed the inscrutable One is out of the reach of every rational process. Nor can any words come up to the inexpressible Good, this One, this Source of all unity, this supra-existent Being. Mind beyond mind, word beyond speech, it is gathered up by no discourse, by no intuition, by no name. It is and it is as no other being is. Cause of all existence, and therefore itself transcending existence, it alone could give an authoritative account of what it really is.[7]

Due to this supereminence of God, the Creator is beyond reach of both the knowledge and the words of the creature. Indeed, the Creator is even beyond being, and that which is trapped in being cannot properly know or name the goodness that exists "supra-existent." It is because of this reality that Dionysius has a theological method that calls the Christian mind to first cataphatically affirm that which is affirmable by virtue of God's economy of creation, in which he stands in causal relationship to all things that exist. Once this is complete, Dionysius calls hearers to then apophatically negate that positive name as inferior to him which is beyond being. As a final step, we are to, according to Dionysius, negate the negation, as God's supereminence is outside the jurisdiction of even negation, or apophatic speech. We can see the first two steps in *Mystical Theology* as Dionysius says, "Since

---

[5]Turner, *Darkness of God*, 21.
[6]*DN* 588A.
[7]*DN* 588B.

[God] is the Cause of all beings, we should posit and ascribe to it all the affirmations we make in regard to beings, and, more appropriately, we should negate all these affirmations since it surpasses all being."[8]

To some, this Dionysian move can seem confusing at best and contradicting at worst. Yet turning once again to Turner could prove helpful in explaining this threefold method of naming. This quote from Turner is longer, but is quite helpful in eliminating caricatures of Dionysius and is therefore worthy of full quotation:

> The natural linguistic medium of his negative, apophatic theology; or, more strictly speaking, they are the natural medium of a theological language which is subjected to the *twin* pressures of affirmation and negation, of the cataphatic and the apophatic. We must both affirm and deny all things of God; and then we must negate the contradiction between the affirmed and the denied. That is why we must say affirmatively that God is "light," and then say, denying this, that God is "darkness"; and finally, we must "negate the negation" between darkness and light, which we do by saying: "God is a brilliant darkness." For the negation of the negation is not a *third* utterance, additional to the affirmative and the negative, in good linguistic order; it is not some intelligible *synthesis* of affirmation and negation; it is rather the collapse of our affirmation and denials into disorder, which we can only express *a fortiori* in bits of collapsed, disordered language, like the babble of Jeremiah. And that is what the "self-subverting" utterance is, a bit of disordered language. . . . Good theology [Dionysius] thinks, has the same outcome, for it leads to that silence which is found only on the other since of general linguistic embarrassment.[9]

This "linguistic embarrassment" comes by way of cataphatic theology in which creatures attempt to name God with knowable names and, in the end, see that even their best efforts do not quite get at explanatory power of him who exist beyond being. Because of this, Turner points

---

[8] *MT* 1000B.
[9] Turner, *Darkness of God*, 22-23.

out, Dionysius is not at all hesitant to show the *vast* list of positive names the biblical writers, whom he calls "the Theologians," enlist to name God. In fact, in *DN* 596A, Dionysius lists fifty-two separate cataphatic identifiers used by the biblical authors to describe God.

Yet it is in the proliferation of positive names that the theologian comes to "linguistic embarrassment" at the realization that even the greatest positive identifiers are insufficient to describe an ineffable God. Dionysius, using the biblical passages of Judges 13:17, Genesis 32:29, and Exodus 3:13, shows that the general response is one of rebuke when man puts God on the dock, asking, "What is your name?" For, according to Ephesians 1:21, the name of God "is above every name that is named either in this age or in that which is to come."[10] So, Dionysius concludes—in a seeming paradox—that God is the "nameless one" who yet has countless names.[11]

However, Dionysius' model of bringing cataphatic and apophatic theology together, then negating any negations, might seem a far too pessimistic way to approach theology for some. And whereas his understanding of the need for the theologian's ascent and eventual union with God might border on being *too* mystical, it should be noted that a key component to Dionysian theology is the nature of revelation and symbols. Van Geest points out that some have difficulty with Dionysius as "negation alone was believed to be unacceptable for a religion based on revelation."[12] While I will address this complaint further in chapter 6, it is worth mentioning here, as Dionysius does have a working category of revelation in his theological method.

As it pertains to revelation, astute readers will see that Dionysius has at least a threefold model of revelation in which the creature comes to know God. The first and most obvious in what has previously been said is that God reveals himself in the economy of creation and stands

---

[10]*DN* 596A.
[11]*DN* 596A-D.
[12]Van Geest, *Incomprehensibility of God*, 37.

in causal relation to all things created. In *DN* 589D Dionysius refers to this model of revelation as the "beneficent processions of God." A less obvious form of revelation are those dramatic movements found in the church's liturgy. Finally, there are those positive names given to God by the biblical writers.

This third model of revelation—the cataphatic names given God by the biblical authors—is an important category for the Syrian theologian. For it is in these names that we come to a significant category in Dionysian theology—the category of symbols. The positive names of God, which derive from cataphatically naming him based on the effects in creation, while not *utterly* true of God (and therefore needing the negation and restriction of apophatic theology) are nonetheless symbols that attempt to get at the thing signified of God. Dionysius writes, "I have discussed analogies of God drawn from what we perceive. I have spoken of the images we have of him, of the forms, figures, and instruments proper to him, of the places in which he lives and of the ornaments he wears." He continues, "I have spoken of his anger, grief, and rage, of how he is said to be drunk and hungover, of his oaths and curses, of his sleeping and waking, and indeed of all those images we have of him, images shaped by the workings of the symbolic representations of God."[13] While this quote comes from *Mystical Theology*, he arguably summarizes his understanding of symbols in theology no place better than in *Divine Names* as he writes:

> But as for now, what happens is this. We use whatever appropriate symbols we can for the things of God. With these analogies we are raised upward toward the truth of the mind's vision, a truth which is simple and one. We leave behind us all our own notions of the divine.

---

[13] *MT* 1033B. While this quote is *technically* true, meaning that Dionysius really has spoken of these items throughout his corpus, it is quite important to point out an oddity with these words: Dionysius here is summarizing what he claims to have said in a work titled *Symbolic Theology*, which is either lost to history or is entirely fictitious. For more on the possible fictitious works of Dionysius see Rorem, *Pseudo-Dionysius*, 134.

We call a halt to the activities of our minds and, to the extent that is proper, we approach the ray which transcends being.[14]

This quote gets at what will be one of the major Dionysian influences on this project: while God is incomprehensible and ineffable, as a grace of his revelation, creatures can still utilize analogical symbols to attempt real and meaningful theological discourse. While I will break from Dionysius on some particularities of what these symbols are and what they can signify, there is still much the modern theologian can learn from spending time in the Dionysian corpus as the theologian shows us significant import into the realm of theological method from God's incomprehensibility and ineffability. Moreover, Dionysius will prove instructive in not only affirming divine incomprehensibility but affirming incomprehensibility as a *revealed doctrine,* as we have seen. An affirmation of incomprehensibility as a revealed doctrine, found *in* the biblical data, has important consequences for any discourse on the doctrine and will protect the doctrine from unjustified criticism.

The* Cloud of Unknowing *and negative theology. While much of this chapter will traverse the material through Christian antiquity chronologically, it is worth breaking from the chronological flow of these two chapters—at least for a moment—and treat the anonymous work *The Cloud of Unknowing.* There is a significant chronological gap between Pseudo-Dionysius and *The Cloud of Unknowing*; the former belongs to that category known as late antiquity, while the latter is dated to the second half of the fourteenth century. Though there is a significant gap in chronology (and language, as the *Cloud* is a work of English prose), there is significant overlap in content. Moreover, the overlap in content, predicated on the impulses of Christian negative and mystical theology, is not one that needs much evidence to support. Readers can see the obvious overlap in content in the reality that while

---

[14]*DN* 592C-D.

we do not know the author of the *Cloud*, we do know that there is substantial use of Pseudo-Dionysius in both the fact that the anonymous author provided his or her own translation of *Mystical Theology* and based the largest work in the anonymous corpus from a phrase coined by Dionysius—"the cloud of unknowing." Furthermore, not only is there a reappropriation of a Dionysian phrase, but there is also a significant emphasis on Dionysian method. The author of the *Cloud* instructs readers, through means often mystical, to move past that "cloud of forgetfulness" upward and into that cloud of unknowing where true contemplation of God takes place.

While not ever named by the author, key to understanding the negative theology in the *Cloud* are the dual concepts of love and light. The author writes that there are two ways creatures can relate to God: one is based on the "faculty of knowledge," and the other is based on the "faculty of love."[15] The author notes that "God . . . is forever beyond the reach of the first of these, the intellectual faculty."[16] But later, the author writes of the hope of attaining communion with God, "He can well be loved, but he cannot be thought."[17]

Therefore, if anyone hopes to participate in that which is considered Christian contemplation,[18] they must first abandon the task of trying to ascend upward to God by virtue of the intellectual life. God lives in an impenetrable cloud of unknowing that the fallible mind of the creature simply cannot break. The author then quite frankly instructs the reader to forfeit the task of intellectual theology, noting, "Do not struggle in your intellect or imagination in any way. For I tell you truly, it cannot be achieved by that kind of struggle; so give it up and do not attempt it."[19]

---

[15]Anonymous, *The Cloud of Unknowing* (London: Penguin, 2001), 23.

[16]*Cloud of Unknowing*, 23.

[17]*Cloud of Unknowing*, 27. He says again, just a few pages later, "For love may reach God in this life, but knowledge may not." *Cloud of Unknowing*, 32.

[18]It is important to note that in both Dionysian literature and in *The Cloud*, *contemplation* is a technical term not to be confused with a mere life of the mind or intellectual exercise.

[19]*Cloud of Unknowing*, 26.

Instead of ascending the mount toward the divine through the intellectual life, the author calls those who wish to contemplate God to "beat continually upon this cloud of unknowing that is between you and your God with a sharp dart of longing love."[20] Using mystical language of "stirring" and "ecstasy," the author suggests that it is in forgetting everything and pushing all intellectual activity below the "cloud of forgetting" that the soul will be raised to the heights of the cloud of unknowing. While *love* is the faculty the author suggests, a paradoxical notion of *light* is the mystical *telos* of the theologians' ascent into the cloud. Explaining the imagery of "cloud" and "darkness," the author clarifies his meaning: "For when I say 'darkness' I mean an absence of knowing, in the sense that everything you do not know, or have forgotten, is dark to you, because you cannot see it with your mind's eye." He continues, "And for this reason it is not called a cloud in the air but a cloud of unknowing that is between you and your God."[21] Paradoxically, then, while words like *cloud* or *darkness* are the author's preferred metaphors for the contemplative life, it is through utilizing the faculty of love that we ascend into the cloud of darkness, which is where the true light of God is to be found.

Bringing our section on the influential *Cloud of Unknowing*[22] to a close, readers can see the pertinence of this medieval mystical work of negative theology for this chapter as the author reveals what becomes clearer throughout the work—the deep reliance on Pseudo-Dionysius. The anonymous author writes:

---

[20]*Cloud of Unknowing*, 35. It is important to note, however, that the author informs readers that even through the "faculty of love," we will fall short of that contemplative life which *truly* knows God as he knows himself. After discussing Mary as the ultimate success of contemplative life, the author writes, "For I tell you one thing, that there never has been and never shall be any living creature, however pure, raised to whatever height of ecstasy in contemplation and love of the Godhead, who does not always have a high and wonderful cloud of unknowing between him and his God" (42).

[21]*Cloud of Unknowing*, 26.

[22]Another anecdote in showcasing the influence of both Dionysius and *The Cloud* is from Jason Baxter, who devotes a chapter to the influence the two had on C. S. Lewis. See "How to Pray to a Medieval God," in Jason Baxter, *The Medieval Mind of C. S. Lewis: How Great Books Shaped a Great Mind* (Downers Grove, IL: IVP Academic, 2022), 99-118.

On a spiritual level, it happens inwardly in the same way with our spiritual senses, when we struggle to gain knowledge of God himself. However much spiritual understanding a person may have in knowing about all created spiritual beings, still by the work of his understanding he can never gain knowledge of an uncreated spiritual being—which is God alone. By the failure of understanding he can do so, because the one thing in which it fails is nothing but God alone. It was for this reason that St. Denis said, "The godliest knowledge of God is that which is known through ignorance."

The anonymous author concludes, "Indeed, anyone who will look into the books of St. Denis will find that his words clearly confirm all that I have said or will say, from the beginning of this treatise to the end."[23] It is important here to return to the thesis of this chapter as the goal of canvasing Pseudo-Dionysius' work and its influence on the anonymous author of the *Cloud of Unknowing* is not simply to rehearse their arguments. Rather, the goal with this chapter, and the one before it, is to work through pertinent figures, works, and eras of theological antiquity all toward the end of establishing a nuanced understanding of divine incomprehensibility and divine ineffability with an eye toward methodological implications. Therefore, it is worth giving an evaluative summary concerning Pseudo-Dionysius and the *Cloud*.

While it is hard to overstate the influence these two authors have had on the discourse and development of negative theology—and for that reason alone, students of theology cannot afford to neglect reading them—it is my belief that they come with a tangled web of both helpful and unhelpful conclusions. Dionysius and those who followed his path of a strict apophasis have, with much precision, demonstrated the sheer impossibility of knowing and naming God as he is in himself. In this way, these thinkers from late antiquity into the medieval era ought to be emulated. Christian thinkers ought to think of God as dwelling

---

[23]*Cloud of Unknowing*, 96.

in a cloud of unknowing—or perhaps, to use a scriptural phrase, dwelling in unapproachable light (1 Tim. 6:16)—and conclude the sheer otherness of God demands a holy silence and ignorance when it comes to attempting to articulate the essence of the triune God.

On the other hand, while Christian thinkers ought to be eager to follow the Dionysian path of confessing an incomprehensible God, we should consider being a touch slower in following the mystical prescription outlined by Dionysius and the author of the *Cloud*. While we should affirm the incomprehensibility of God—and this is an oft-made point in this project—we should affirm that we can know of the incomprehensibility of God because it is a revealed doctrine. God informs creatures that he is incomprehensible and therefore ineffable. Consequently, the goal is not a mystical experience of ecstasy in hopes to penetrate the cloud of unknowing, but the goal is rather to lay hold of God's self-revelation—both special and general—in hopes of analogically knowing and naming the unknowable and nameless God. At the end of the day, while the Dionysian method, with its emphatic use of negation and mystery, gives the contemporary thinker many useful tools in the task of theology, I do not think we need to embrace the dire pessimism embedded in a strict adherence to negative theology. There is an efficacy to divine revelation that equips the student of God with hope of knowing a God who has accommodated himself in hopes that his creatures might meaningfully know him.

This is not to make light of the Dionysian impact and importance of negative theology—which this project will draw on with significant emphasis—but instead a humble attempt to bring what is good about a strict apophatisim into conversation with the consequences of a *revealed* religion.

DIVINE INCOMPREHENSIBILITY IN AQUINAS

Theologians can meaningfully discuss Aquinas as an inheritor of Dionysian thought. Even the most surface level of investigation reveals an obvious Dionysian thread through the angelic doctor's doctrine of incomprehensibility. Given Aquinas's strong utilization of Pseudo-Dionysius in expressing God's knowability and the creature's ability to name him, one might be tempted to conclude that a section on Aquinas might be redundant following a section on the Dionysian influence on the doctrine. However, while Thomas does indeed utilize a number of Dionysian categories and emphases, this is not to affirm that Aquinas did not have his own accents and advancements of the doctrine.

When readers turn toward understanding Aquinas' doctrine of incomprehensibility, they might be surprised to be met with an affirmation of the *knowability* of God early in the *Prima Pars*. Aquinas writes that anything that is actual must be in some ways knowable, and as we would articulate not only the "actuality" of God but the supreme one who is "pure act without any admixture of potentiality," God is therefore knowable as he is actual.[24] However, while God is knowable as he is actual, there are two caveats needed in expressing any notion of knowability in God. First, while God is knowable in a technical sense, the creature runs into an epistemological problem as "what is supremely knowable in itself, may not be knowable to a particular intellect, on account of the excess of the intelligible object above the intellect."[25] Which leads to the second nuance needed in expressing a Thomistic notion of God's knowability: since the essence of God is infinitely above the intellect of the creature, the hope of knowing God is a grace and not something to be achieved by nature. Namely, any concept of knowability of God will ultimate be granted, by grace, to the creature in the blessed beatific vision or a granted intellectual vision.

Key to Thomas's denial that the natural mind cannot climb to the heights of the divine substance is the affirmation of God's incorporeality. The divine nature, incorporeal as it is, stands out of reach for the

---

[24] *ST* Ia12,1.
[25] *ST* Ia12,1.

creature's corporeal senses. Aquinas argues that "act is proportional to the nature which possesses it."[26] Meaning, for creatures who possess corporality, our actions will be within our nature's limitations. Therefore, as those trapped in a corporeal existence, the limits of our agency—even the agency of knowing—will be limited by that very corporal life. As Aquinas states elsewhere:

> For the human intellect is not able to reach a comprehension of the divine substance through its natural power. For, according to its manner of knowing in the present life, the intellect depends on the sense of the origin of knowledge; and so those things that do not fall under the senses cannot be grasped by the human intellect except in so far as the knowledge of them is gathered from sensible things. Now, sensible things cannot lead the human intellect to the point of seeing in them the nature of the divine substance; for sensible things are effects that fall short of the power of their cause.[27]

Like incorporeality, divine infinitude plays a role in a Thomistic expression of divine incomprehensibility. Since all things actual are knowable in accordance with their actuality, we must consider God's actuality in infinitude. Therefore, for any knowledge of God to be exhaustive, the knowledge must comply with the infinitude of the thing known. Aquinas concludes then, "For the created intellect knows the divine essence more or less perfectly in proportion as it receives a greater or lesser light of glory. Since therefore the created light of glory received into any created intellect cannot be infinite, it is clearly impossible for any created intellect to know God in an infinite degree."[28]

---

[26]*ST* Ia12.3. He returns to this theme later and expounds, "It is impossible for any created intellect to see the essence of God by its own natural power. For knowledge is regulated according as the thing known is in the knower. But the thing known is in the knower according to the mode of the knower. Hence the knowledge of every knower is ruled according to its own nature." *ST* Ia12.4.
[27]*SCG* I, 3.3.
[28]*ST* Ia.12.7. Aquinas' use of "light of glory" is a nod to the beatific vision and a nod that will be consequential as this project moves into reflecting on the relationship between incomprehensibility and the beatific vision.

Readers working through Aquinas' affirmation of God's incomprehensibility and ineffability will be sure to hear the echoes of Dionysius. However, there is another sense where readers can differentiate the two on account of Thomas being a touch more optimistic concerning theological epistemology. Or perhaps a better way to say it is that while the two thinkers share a similar formula of diagnosing the doctrine of divine incomprehensibility, their prescription for "overcoming" this intellectual dilemma varies. Whereas the prescription from the Dionysian corpus calls for a mystical ascension into that cloud of unknowing, Aquinas seems to have a bit of a more optimistic view of the efficacy of divine revelation. Of course, much of what Aquinas builds as a constructive approach to theological method in light of God's incomprehensibility uses the tools first developed by Dionysius—showing again that the Italian theologian really is an inheritor of Dionysian thought—there are nuances between the two. It is in the implications and response to the creature's inability to know and name God that readers see the vital role of analogy and negative theology in Aquinas. Both categories—analogy and negative theology—will receive a more substantive reflection in chapter six, but they are important to mention here.

In the *Divine Names* Pseudo-Dionysius laid the groundwork for the important medieval methodology of the *triplex via*. This is a tool Aquinas would pick up time and again in hopes of naming God throughout his work. We can see Aquinas arguing explicitly for this method of naming God in *ST* Ia12.12 as he writes,

> From the knowledge of sensible things the whole power of God cannot be known; nor therefore can His essence be seen. But because they are His effects and depending on their cause, we can be led from them so far as to know of God whether He exists, and to know of Him what must necessarily belong to Him, as the first cause of all things, exceeding all things caused by Him. Hence, we know of His relationship with creatures in so far as He is the cause of them all; also that

creatures differ from Him, inasmuch as He is not in any way part of what is caused by Him; and that creatures are not removed from him by reason of any defect on His part, but because he superexceeds them all.[29]

Thomas concludes his thought in Ia12.13, "In this way therefore [God] can be named by us from creatures, yet not so that the name which signifies Him expresses the divine essence in itself." The utilization of all three—causality, remotion, and eminence—leads Thomas to the conclusion that the creature really does have a hope of meaningfully naming God, although any naming must be done analogically. There is, of course, much more we could say about Aquinas's view of analogical predication. Indeed, readers receive a mature and developed analogical thought in *ST* Ia13. However, chapter six of this project will be dedicated to theological language considering incomprehensibility and ineffability, so we will revisit Aquinas' prescription of analogy in light of negative theology there. For now, we will move on beyond the medieval era into the confessions and confessors of the Reformation in our journey to canvas the historical highlights of this doctrinal conversation with an eye toward theological method.

DIVINE INCOMPREHENSIBILITY IN THE REFORMATION AND POST-REFORMATION

As this canvasing of theological antiquity continues to journey through different eras of church history in hopes of highlighting variegated nuances of divine incomprehensibility, we now move past the medieval era thinkers and into the Reformation and post-Reformation. As has been stated with previous sections, readers might quibble or disagree with the thinkers examined in each section, including this one. Nonetheless, here we will start our conversation with the French Reformer, John

---

[29]*ST* Ia.12.12.

Calvin, in hopes of treating his understanding of natural theology and divine accommodation as it relates to divine incomprehensibility. After Calvin, we will turn to examining a few post-Reformation voices.

Calvin's "lisping" God. In nearly all theological discourse, there are those statements so often quoted that they become nearly ubiquitous with a given doctrinal conversation. So it is with Calvin's quip about God's "lisping" to his children in the conversation of incomprehensibility and divine accommodation.

Refuting the Anthropomorphites—who predicate a corporeal existence in God due to Scripture's ascribing to him variegated body parts—Calvin delivers his oft-quoted phrase. He writes:

> For who even of slight intelligence does not understand that, as nurses commonly do with infants, God is wont in a measure to "lisp" in speaking to us? Thus such forms of speaking do not so much express clearly what God is like as accommodate the knowledge of him to our slight capacity. To do this he must descend far beneath his loftiness.[30]

Before Calvin arrives at his lisping line, he has already laid out important material for getting at his understanding of divine incomprehensibility. Two significant themes that have led up to this quotation in chapter thirteen of his *Institutes* are natural theology and accommodation. Moreover, Calvin has a special interest in how the piety of the Christian thinker plays into these two categories.

Calvin, like many theologians before and after him, views God's craftmanship in creation leaving humankind without an excuse in their knowledge of God. This might be seen nowhere clearer than when Calvin writes:

> The clarity of God's self-disclosure strips us of every excuse. The final goal of the blessed life, moreover, rests in the knowledge of God [cf. John 17:3]. Lest anyone, then, be excluded from access to happiness, he not only sowed in men's minds that seed of religion of which we have

---

[30]*ICR* I.xiii.1.

spoken but revealed himself and daily discloses himself in the whole workmanship of the universe. As a consequence, men cannot open their eyes without being compelled to see him. Indeed, his essence is incomprehensible; hence, his divineness far escapes all human perception. But upon his individual works he has engraved unmistakable marks of his glory, so clear and so prominent that even unlettered and stupid folk cannot plead the excuse of ignorance.[31]

Continuing this theme, Calvin uses the word *insignia* to describe those signposts of creation that clearly communicate God's glory to creatures. Men, seeing all of God's communicative insignia around them in creation are left without excuse and are called to piety before this Creator-God. Indeed, Calvin goes on to utilize the book of Hebrews—Hebrews 11:3 specifically—to call God's "skillful ordering" of the cosmos a "sort of mirror in which we can contemplate God, who is otherwise invisible."[32]

While Calvin has a strong sense of God's general revelation in the role of natural theology, he nevertheless readily admits the limitations of this revelation. The most frequent tool Calvin uses to explain the limitations of natural theology is juxtaposing the knowledge of God as Creator versus knowing God as redeemer.[33] Men, by strength of God's revelatory action in self-disclosing through nature, might come to the former conclusion, while the latter is reserved as a consequence of God's more specific and special revelation.

This point may seem to be rather obvious, however it is too vital for Calvin's system of religious epistemology to miss. For in establishing the limitations of natural theology and proclaiming the special place of a more specific revelation, Calvin establishes the role of piety in Christian theology as students of theology pursue the business of Christian contemplation as receivers of revelation, not creators.

---

[31] *ICR* I.v.1.
[32] *ICR* I.v.1.
[33] See, for example, *ICR* I.ii.1.

The concept of doing theology as radical receivers, not intellectual creators, will become a foundation to a major point of this book in chapter seven. However, for now it is important to note that rooted in this theological starting point is Calvin's point of piety. He writes, "For, to begin with, the pious mind does not dream up for itself any god it pleases, but contemplates the one and only true God." He continues, "And it does not attach to him whatever it please, but is content to hold him to be as he manifests himself."[34]

Finally, this role of piety as the receiver of God's glory and revelatory self-disclosure allows us to arrive at Calvin's doctrine of incomprehensibility. In concluding his thoughts about religious epistemology, the Reformer writes, "What is God? Men who pose this questions are merely toying with idle speculation."[35] Instead of participating in idle speculation, the Christian theologian is to receive God's self-disclosure and what becomes apparent in that self-disclosure is that this God is incomprehensible. While it is a longer quote, it is worth quoting in full as Calvin pulls biblical data from variegated portions of Scripture to show that when brought to proximity with the divine, creatures are compelled to confess their inadequacy before a glorious Creator. Calvin writes:

> Hence that dread and wonder with which Scripture commonly represents the saints as stricken and overcome whenever they felt the presence of God . . . As a consequence, we must infer that man is never sufficiently touched and affected by the awareness of his lowly state until he has compared himself with God's majesty. Moreover, we have numerous examples of this consternation both in The Book of Judges and in the Prophets. So frequent was it that this expression was common among God's people: "We shall die, for the Lord has appeared to us" [Judg. 13:22; Isa. 6:5; Ezek. 2:1; 1:28; Judg. 6:22-23; and elsewhere]. The story of Job, in its description of God's wisdom, power,

---

[34]*ICR* I.ii.2.
[35]*ICR* I.ii.2.

and purity, always expresses a powerful argument that overwhelms men with the realization of their own stupidity, impotence, and corruption [cf. Job 38:1 ff.]. And not without cause: for we see how Abraham recognizes more clearly that he is earth and dust [Gen. 18:27] when once he had come nearer to beholding God's glory; and how Elijah, with uncovered face, cannot bear to await his approach, such is the awesomeness of his appearance [1 Kings 19:13]. And what can man do, who is rottenness itself [Job 13:28] and a worm [Job 7:5; Ps. 22:6], when even the very cherubim must veil their faces out of fear [Isa. 6:2]? It is this indeed of which the prophet Isaiah speaks: "the Sun will blush ad the moon be confounded when the Lord of Hosts shall reign" [Isa. 24:23]; that is, when he shall bring forth his splendor and cause it to draw nearer, the brightest thing will become darkness before it [Isa. 2:10, 19].[36]

It is from this contextual point that Calvin arrives at his famous lisping God. In summary: humanity, due to the strength of God's self-disclosure in general revelation, is without excuse in knowing God. However, to move from knowing God merely as Creator to knowing God salvifically as redeemer necessitates something greater than general revelation. It requires a self-disclosure from God in which the creature can witness that he is brought to nothingness in the presence of this holy God. In his nothingness before God, we finally grasp the deep distinction between the Creator and his creatures such that the Creator is incomprehensible. So then, to accommodate God's furious and deadly holy presence, God—like a nurse to a toddler—lisps to his people, bringing his holy and wholly otherness to their finite minds in accommodated manners that they might try to see the brightness of his glory even amid their existence within darkness.[37]

---

[36]*ICR* I.i.3.

[37]For more on Calvin's doctrine of revelatory accommodation see Paul Helm's chapter "Divine Accomodation," in *John Calvin's Ideas* (Oxford: Oxford University Press, 2004), 184-208. See also the various works by David F. Wright, including "Calvin's Pentateuchal Criticism: Equity, Hardness of Heart, and Divine Accommodation in the Mosaic Harmony Commentary," *Calvin Theological Journal* 21 (1986): 33-50; "Accommodation and Barbarity in John Calvin's Old Testament

For an exegetical example, Calvin utilizes the notion of divine accommodation in his commenting on Hosea. In Hosea 11:8, God states, "My heart recoils within me; my compassion grows warm and tender." Calvin deals with what seems to be a "problem text" for the doctrines of divine impassibility and divine immutability with the text's depiction of God's heart recoiling and his growing in compassion. Calvin writes, "God, we know, is subject to no passions; and we know that no change takes place in him." In light of these commitments to impassibility and immutability in theology proper, Calvin inquires, "What then do these expressions mean, by which he appears to be changeable?" Calvin concludes, "Doubtless he accommodates himself to our ignorance, whenever he puts on a character foreign to himself. And this consideration exposes the folly as well as the impiety of those who bring forward single words to show that God is, as it were, like mortals."[38] Calvin's phrase of God putting "on a character foreign to himself" is a helpful gloss of what divine accommodation teaches—that God's self-revelation considers the weakness of the creature so that humankind mind be able to apprehend God through his written word.

Divine incomprehensibility in Reformation and post-Reformation thought. As the chronicling of history thus far concerning the doctrine of divine incomprehensibility makes obvious, the theologians who make up the post-Reformation era inherited a significant conversation.[39] Doing theology in the Reformation and post-Reformation era gives Christian thinkers the double blessing of having some of the exegetical tools and conclusions of the Reformers while still doing theology just before the Enlightenment begins to strip theology of the supernatural. The consequence is that some of history's best

---

Commentaries," *Understanding Poets and Prophets: Essays in Honour of George Wishart Anderson*, ed. A. G. Auld (Sheffield: Sheffield Academic, 1993), 413-27.

[38]John Calvin, *Daniel 7–12 and Hosea* (Grand Rapids, MI: Baker Books, 2009), 401.

[39]Beyond what I have laid out in these two chapters, readers can examine a helpful historic sketch of the doctrine of incomprehensibility, and some nuances within, by working through Muller's history of the doctrine in its high scholastic thirteenth-century context in *PRRD* 3:46-48, as well as its late medieval context in *PRRD* 3:65-68.

articulations of divine incomprehensibility and divine ineffability come from the writings of the Protestant scholastic theologians.

Moreover, categories that were in use during earlier periods of Christian antiquity become a touch clearer in the hands of the theologians of the Reformation and post-Reformation era. For example, Richard Muller is helpful to point out the Protestant scholastic use of "comprehension" of God verses the notion of "apprehension" of God. Of course, this distinction is not confined to the period of the Protestant scholastics or Reformed orthodox, yet it is a tool often utilized in this era. Muller writes:

> Indeed, a distinction must be made between "comprehension" and "apprehension," inasmuch as we cannot have an "adequate" idea of God in the sense that we know and understand God fully or are able "fully to describe" the divine perfections, but we can have "some imperfect or inadequate ideas of what surpasses our understanding and we can have a 'full conviction that God hath those infinite perfections, which no creature can comprehend.'" Thus language about God proceeds cautiously, frequently according to a negative manner; as when God is called "incomprehensible" or "infinite."[40]

If the notion of comprehension gets at that special ability to wrap around an object such that it can be covered on all sides—the way a hand might comprehend a marble—apprehension instead gets at the notion of grasping at the known material. While the quiddity of the divine essence will not be comprehended, because of God's accommodation through divine revelation, the creature has a hope of apprehension.

Another category that becomes useful in the discussion of God's incomprehensibility in the Reformation and post-Reformation era is that of archetypal and ectypal theology. Again, like comprehension and apprehension, these categories were well in use before this era of

---

[40]*PRRD* 3:165.

antiquity, yet they enjoy the evolved state of becoming more formal categories in theological method. Franciscus Junius is an exemplar in utilizing this distinction, and his usage has implications for theological method in light of divine incomprehensibility.

Working through his category of analogical predication, Junius distinguishes between archetypal and ectypal notions of theological ideation. Of ectypal theology, Junius writes that it is "a certain copy and, rather, shadowy image of the formal, divine, and essential theological image."[41] He continues, distinguishing the two, "More contemporary authorities have designated the former theology [archetypal] as in relation to itself, and the second one [ectypal] as relative." For example, "The one theology [archetypal] is the very same thing as unbounded wisdom, which God possesses concerning His own person and all other things, as they have been set in order with respect to Him necessarily, individually, and by an uninterrupted relation among themselves." Whereas, "The second theology [ectypal] is that wisdom which the creatures have concerning God according to their own manner, and concerning those things that are oriented toward God through His communication of Himself."[42] Building off the "holy fathers" Junius concludes that "God, however, is above every genus" and, as he says, "essence beyond essence." This means that in as much as archetypal theology is God's self-wisdom, it is unattainable and incomprehensible to the creature. This leads Junius to write, in his seventh thesis on true theology, that "archetypal theology is the divine wisdom of divine matters. Indeed, we stand in awe before this and do not seek to trace it out."[43]

As another voice coming from the era of post-Reformation, pointing to Exodus 3:14, Petrus van Mastricht notes that even God's self-naming

---

[41]*TTT*, 104.
[42]*TTT*, 104-5.
[43]*TTT*, 107. We will return to Junius's categorical use of archetypal and ectypal in greater detail in chapter six.

is incomprehensible and ineffable—"I am who I am."[44] The Dutch theologian goes on to give three "proofs" of God's incomprehensibility, or as he prefers, God's imperceptibility. His three proofs, or reasons, for God's imperceptibility are (1) divine simplicity, (2) infinitude, and (3) unity. For Mastricht, and others like him, it is the quiddity that is in question concerning incomprehensibility. Like those before him, Mastricht is happy to concede that creatures have the powers of perception to know that God exists; it is the what-ness of his existence—his essence, attributes, and life in himself—that remains unapproachable to the creature. Mastricht is willing to even negate not only comprehension of quiddity, but even apprehension. He notes, "Concerning this quiddity of the divine essence we declare that it is inaccessible to our intellect . . . we cannot touch it with our knowledge, whether comprehensive or apprehensive."[45] He notes that creatures fail to fully comprehend or name their own quiddity, or that of angels, let alone the divine being.

Mastricht concludes his study of incomprehensibility by turning toward a more apologetic front, working through interlocuters such as the Cartesians, the Socinians, and John Duns Scotus. With these interlocutors, Mastricht's primary concern is whether the creature can hope to positively define the Creator. For, in Mastricht's words, a definition is "a representation of essence"; he negates the possibility of a univocal definition. Instead, Mastricht shows that the Reformed tradition is in line with previous traditions in (1) articulating the perfections of God primarily in the negative.[46] For example, we know "what that essence is not . . . it is not material, not dependent, not mutable, not composite, not finite."[47] Then, Mastricht shows (2) the need for

---

[44] *TPT* 2:74.

[45] *TPT* 2:77.

[46] "The Reformed, although they admit positive concepts of several attributes of God, even so concerning the very essence of God commonly do not acknowledge any but negative concepts, by which we hold concerning the essence what it is not, rather than what it is in itself." *TPT* 2:77.

[47] *TPT* 2:77.

denying univocal predication on the basis of incomprehensibility and ineffability. He writes, "There is not a univocal genus that is appropriate for God and creatures, because he stands infinitely far apart from them all. And there is not a specific difference by which he differs from them, since he stands apart from all of them not in this or that respect, but in all respects."[48] Mastricht has a robust doctrine of divine accommodation that allows him to nuance some of what has been covered, but in this brief historical treatise Mastricht is helpful to show that the pure divine being, who is first above and before all, is simply beyond composition and is beyond defining in terms of genus and difference.[49]

INCOMPREHENSIBILITY IN BAVINCK AND THE MODERN ERA

If it can be said that this book seeks a balanced position on divine incomprehensibility, then that hoped-for balance is exemplified in the Dutch theologian Herman Bavinck.[50] Bavinck brings together a strong affirmation of God's utter incomprehensibility and ineffability together with a nuanced optimism in knowing and naming God analogically thanks to the efficacy of divine self-disclosure. In this way, Bavinck is a strong example of a classically informed understanding of divine incomprehensibility making its way into the modern era.

---

[48] *TPT* 2:78.

[49] *TPT* 2:79.

[50] I recognize the chronological gap between van Mastricht and Bavinck is rather large. However, this two-part historical sketch is not intended to bring every voice to bear concerning divine incomprehensibility. Rather, my hope with these two chapters is to bring attention to *positive* affirmations of the doctrine toward an end. The end to which this historical survey aims is to utilize these articulations and affirmations toward demonstrating the methodological implications of divine incomprehensibility. So, while a history tracing the many voices worthy of exploration in modernity would be worthwhile, it does not fit the particular aim of these chapters. However, readers who are interested in modernity's reception of the doctrine and the ways Enlightenment thinking or the immanentization of God impacted the conversation can see William C. Placher, *The Domestication of Transcendence: How Modern Thinking about God Went Wrong* (Louisville, KY: Westminster John Knox, 1996), 71-128; as well as Stanley Grenz and Roger E. Olsen, *20th Century Theology: God and the World in a Transitional Age* (Downers Grove, IL: IVP Academic, 1993).

To see this nuance at play, let us first hear from Bavinck a full affirmation of a rather strong understanding of incomprehensibility. He writes, opening the second volume of his *Reformed Dogmatics*, that

> Scripture and the church emphatically assert the unsearchable majesty and sovereign highness of God. There is no knowledge of God as he is in himself. We are human and he is the Lord our God. There is no name that fully expresses his being, no definition that captures him. He infinitely transcends our picture of him, our ideas of him, our language concerning him. He is not comparable to any creature. All the nations are accounted by him as less than nothing and vanity. . . . He can be apprehended; he cannot be comprehended.[51]

Or, as he says earlier, "The moment we dare to speak about God the questions arises: How can we?" Bavinck responds to this hypothetical by confessing, "We are human, and he is the Lord our God. Between him and us there seems to be no such kinship or communion as would enable us to name him truthfully. The distance between God and us is the gulf between the Infinite and the finite, between eternity and time, between being and becoming, between the All and the nothing."[52]

Readers might be tempted to affirm that Bavinck would lean toward a strong theological pessimism regarding the possibility of knowing or naming God in meaningful ways. Yet we ought not read this into the Dutch theologian. Instead, Bavinck has a robust doctrine of revelation that protects his understanding of God's unnameability from sheer theological despair. This is why Bavinck could argue that at the heart of this theological conversation is a question of revelation rather than one directly dealing with knowability.[53] In fact, revelation is not an avenue to "overcome" incomprehensibility but is a direct result of revelation. Bavinck argues that "neither in creation nor in re-creation

---

[51]*RD* 2:49.

[52]*RD* 2:30

[53]This is why Bavinck can say, "The question concerning God's knowability has been reduced to another question, namely, whether God has willed and found a way to reveal himself in the domain of creatures." *RD* 2:50.

does God reveal himself exhaustively. He cannot fully impart himself to creatures." This is, of course, not a limitation on the part of the divine as if God wanted to exhaustively reveal himself in some portion, or entirety, of the economy. Rather, as Bavinck notes, "For that to be possible [the creatures] themselves would have to be divine. There is, therefore, no exhaustive knowledge of God. There is no name that makes his essence known to us. There is no concept that fully encompasses him. There is no description that fully defines him."[54]

While God does not reveal himself exhaustively to the creature on the basis of the creaturely limitation, he does, nevertheless, go about self-disclosure in ways that allow for the creature to meaningfully apprehend God while not fully comprehending God. Bavinck points out the variation between *gnōsis* and *katalēpsis*, or apprehension and comprehension, in this regard. Apprehension will allow the creature to make meaningful yet nuanced movements toward knowing and naming God, whereas comprehension gets at the impossibility of the creatures' ability to wrap around—physically, mentally, or otherwise—the object under consideration.

As with the figures seen above, such as Pseudo-Dionysius, Aquinas, Calvin, and others like them, two important features of Bavinck's theological method given his doctrine of divine incomprehensibility are negative theology and analogical theology. In terms of negative theology, Bavinck, in summarizing the contribution of Dionysian negative theology, writes, "negative theology is more excellent than positive theology: it makes God known to us as transcending all creatures. Nevertheless, even negative theology fails to furnish us any knowledge of God's being, for in the final analysis God surpasses both all negation and all affirmation, all assertion, and all denial."[55] While it is not altogether clear in Bavinck's text if he is merely restating the Dionysian position in historical exercise or if he meant to work through

---

[54]*RD* 2:36. Bavinck continues, "That which lies behind revelation is completely unknowable."
[55]*RD* 2:38.

the Dionysian position in affirmation, it is clear that whatever Bavinck thought of Dionysian articulation, he does eventually arrive at the conclusion of the need of analogical theology. Bavinck writes:

> The knowledge we have of God is altogether unique. This knowledge may be called positive insofar as by it we recognize a being infinite and distinct from all finite creatures. On the other hand, it is negative because we cannot ascribe a single predicate to God as we conceive that predicate in relation to creatures. It is therefore an *analogical* knowledge: a knowledge of a being who is unknowable in himself, yet able to make something of himself known in the being he created. . . . It is completely incomprehensible to us how God can reveal himself and to some extent make himself known in created beings: eternity in time, immensity in space, infinity in the finite, immutability in change, being in becoming, the all, as it were, in that which is nothing. This mystery cannot be comprehended; it can only be gratefully acknowledged.[56]

With our two part survey of historical theology now complete, we can now turn toward asking in what ways the doctrine of divine incomprehensibility appears in the biblical data. The voices and eras chosen in this brief excursion down the halls of history will continue to stay relevant for our purposes as we move from documentation to construction. So, while the formal portion covering historical eras and emphases concludes here, the voices of these figures will still play a significant role in developing both the doctrine of divine incomprehensibility and working on the doctrine's methodological import.

---

[56]*RD* 2:48-49.

DIVINE INCOMPREHENSIBILITY AND THE TASK OF THEOLOGY

5

IMPLICATIONS FROM ONTOLOGY

The Creator-creature Distinction

A participatory approach to theology wishes to stress that
God is prior to the world in every way. That underlines our
problem when it comes to speaking about God, cautioning
us to avoid idolatry. However, it also provides the key
to understanding how human language, as used, for
instance, in the Bible, can indeed apply to God after all. The
legitimacy of that endeavor does not rest on God's being
like the world but rather . . . on the world imitating God.

Andrew Davison

THE ARRIVAL OF THIS CHAPTER marks a turn in the book. The previous four chapters sought to set up the biblical and historical contours of the doctrine of divine incomprehensibility. Doing so meant that we needed to spend significant time working through historical development and a biblical articulation of the doctrine. However, now we turn from documenting what *has* been said—whether in history or the biblical witness—toward construction. Namely, I hope here to work toward thinking through the implications the doctrine of divine incomprehensibility brings into Christian theological method. With the historical and biblical treatment of the doctrine in hand, we will work toward three significant implications concerning the doctrine— an ontological implication, some linguistic implications, and finally, an implication of posture in Christian theology.

Given that part two of the project is a turn, it seems that front-loading my thesis will have the double advantage of bringing transparency to the aim of the book while also affording clarity as to where we are heading for the remainder of the project. So, here's what I hope to communicate with these remaining chapters, as a unified thought: the doctrine of divine incomprehensibility finds its proper dogmatic location in the distinction between the Creator and the creature. The Creator-creature distinction means that God is not merely bigger in size than his creatures, but altogether different in kind. This *otherness* of God—which is demonstrated in the divine names and divine perfections—means that full comprehension of the divine essence is out of the intellectual jurisdiction of creatures. However, in his grace, God desires to be known and has revealed his glory in accommodated means such that while creatures may not comprehend, they *can* attempt to apprehend. God's grace in accommodating his glory by the means of revelation does not render him univocally nameable or knowable by the creature, but it does mean that Christians can have *meaningful* knowledge of their triune God. Consequently, while God enjoys archetypal and univocal self-knowledge, the creatures get the grace of participating in this knowing and naming through ectype and analogy thanks to God's accommodation. Finally, since the task of theology would be intermingled with hopelessness had God not revealed himself in a manner appropriate for the creatures' limitations, we pursue theology as radical receivers of accommodated glory. Our position as those who *receive* theology via God's revelation means that we are not theologically hopeless, yet we *must* be theologically humble;

moreover, theological humility is not *merely* an intellectual virtue in the Christian life but rather an ontological necessity due to our limitations and utter reliance on God's revelation and accommodation.

Given the overview of this project summarized here, two things could be easy to miss which are important for this chapter. First, this outline starts by suggesting the proper dogmatic location of the doctrine of divine incomprehensibility is the Creator-creature distinction. I will work toward demonstrating this point in the remaining pages of this chapter. Second, this project seeks to examine three implications for theological method based on divine incomprehensibility:

- An implication from ontology
- An implication of language and knowledge
- An implication of posture

The first, the implication from ontology, which we focus on in this chapter, focuses on the Creator-creature distinction in hopes of giving proper ground and footing to the doctrine of divine incomprehensibility. This is an important point to distinguish because whereas the second and third implication—language, knowledge, and posture—are implications flowing *from* divine incomprehensibility, the first implication—ontology—is an implication flowing *into* divine incomprehensibility. Rooting divine incomprehensibility in the Creator-creature distinction will, in the end, have its own set of consequences for theological method. However, for clarity, it is still important to note that this chapter seeks to dogmatically locate the doctrine of incomprehensibility, while the following chapters seek to ask the "So what?" questions about the methodological import of the doctrine.

THE DOGMATIC LOCATION OF INCOMPREHENSIBILITY

To suggest a dogmatic location of any doctrine, given the systematic nature of the Christian faith, is to not suggest other locations. For example, when I suggest that the proper dogmatic location of the doctrine of divine incomprehensibility is the Creator-creature distinction, I am also suggesting a few places the doctrine should not be located. Namely, while they may contribute to a notion of incomprehensibility, I do not think the proper location of divine incomprehensibility is in sin or size. To put it plainly: God is not incomprehensible to the creature merely due to a noetic effect as a consequence of sin, nor is God incomprehensible to the creature due to his being like them, but grander in size. Likewise, it is improper to view God as merely a bigger version of the creature, as if size or quantity is the primary distinction between God and his people. Rather, the divine is altogether different in kind. Throughout theological antiquity, this has been referred to as the Creator-creature distinction, and it is my contention that it is the proper dogmatic location for the doctrine of divine incomprehensibility.

In his second homily against the Anomoeans, Chrysostom brings to bear the textual evidence that distinguishes the Creator from the creature. He notes that the creature—or humanity—is dust and ashes (Gen 18:27), flesh and blood (Mt 16:17), grass and the flower of grass (Is 40:6; Ps 103:15-16), a shadow (1 Chron 29:15; Ps 102:11), smoke (Ps 102:3), vanity (Eccles 1:2), and "whatever is weaker and more worthless than these."[1] Chrysostom notes that his aim in stating this lowly status of humankind from the Scriptures is not to "heap dishonor on humankind but [the prophets] are trying to check the conceits of the foolish."[2] The conceits of the foolish are to assume they can comprehend God or know him as he is in his essence.

In contrast to the lowliness of the creatures, Chrysostom turns to demonstrate the majesty of God. He asks, "Tell me. Are you meddling with God, who has no beginning, who cannot change, who has no body, who cannot corrupt, who is everywhere present, who surpasses all things, and who is above the whole creation?"[3] In the same way he lists a few biblical statements about humanity, he notes a few biblical

---

[1]*Hom.* II.19.
[2]*Hom.* II.19.
[3]*Hom.* II.22.

statements concerning God. For example, the Bible shows that God "touches the mountain and they smoke" (Ps 104:32); "he shakes the earth under heaven from its foundations, and its pillars totter" (Job 9:6); "he threatens the sea and makes it dry" (Is 51:10); "he says to the deep: 'You shall be dried up'" (Is 44:27); "the sea saw and fled: Jordan was turned back; the mountains skipped like rams, and the hills like lambs" (Ps 114:3-4). Chrysostom carries on in this manner for quite some time; he shows (1) what God has created and (2) the ease with which God has created it in comparison to the lowliness which the Scriptures talk of the creature.[4]

In this homily, the fifth-century preacher shows the drastic difference between the Creator and the creature, but the question remains, How does the distinction between Creator and creature ground the doctrine of divine incomprehensibility? Aquinas will prove helpful. Thomas is consistent to show that the knowledge of a knower must be in line with the essence of the knower, and as the essence of the creature and the Creator has significant distinctions, there will be limits to the creatures' intellectual jurisdiction. In *Summa Theologica*, Thomas writes,

> It is impossible for any created intellect to see the essence of God by its own natural power. For knowledge is regulated according as the thing known is in the knower. But the thing known is in the knower according to the mode of the knower. Hence the knowledge of every knower is ruled according to its own nature. If therefore the mode of anything's being exceeds the mode of the knower, it must result that the knowledge of that object is above the nature of the knower. Now the mode of being of things is manifold. For somethings have being only in this one individual matter; as all bodies. But others are subsisting natures, not residing in matter at all, which, however, are not their own existence, but receive it: and these incorporeal beings, called angels. But to God alone does it belong to be His own subsistent being.[5]

---

[4]*Hom.* II.19-30.
[5]*ST* Ia.12.4.

Thomas contrasts three beings here, two incorporeal and one corporeal. He notes that humankind's nature is confined by bodies. He then moves on to those subsisting natures that do not reside in matter, with the important qualification that their subsistence is a given subsistence and does not exist by on its own, like angelic beings. Finally, he shows that both corporeal beings, like humans, and incorporeal beings whose subsistence is not with matter but still have a received subsistence, like angels, both have a "mode of existence" that is distinct from the one being who could be said to "be His own subsistent being." Thomas's conclusion is that as both humans and angels do not exist in the same mode of existence as God; they inhabit a "different mode of the knower" and therefore are not able to comprehend God as a self-sufficient subsistence. This observation is significant, for it shows that even an incorporeal existence is not enough to broach the God who dwells in unapproachable light. How much more, then, is this light unapproachable for those who dwell in corporeal flesh?

Thomas uses a similar demonstration in *Summa Contra Gentiles*. Using "gradation of intellects," Thomas makes a series of comparisons to show his point. First, he compares two creatures—someone who is unschooled and simple with someone who understands the "subtle speculations of philosophy."[6] Then he compares the creature who understands philosophy with the intellectual capacities of an angelic being. He writes, "But the intellect of an angel surpasses the human intellect much more than the intellect of the greatest philosopher surpasses the intellect of the most uncultivated simple person; for the distance between the best philosopher and a simple person is contained within the limits of the human species, which the angelic intellect surpasses." He continues, "For the angel knows God on the basis of a more noble effect than does man; and this by as much as the

---

[6]*SCG* I, 3.4.

substance of an angel, through which the angel in his natural knowledge is led to the knowledge of God, is nobler than sensible things and even than the soul itself."

After this first comparison, Thomas moves the analogy to contemplate God's knowledge of himself. His conclusion is that while there is a substantial difference in the gradation of intellect between (1) an unschooled simple person, (2) the greatest philosopher, and (3) an angelic being, the gap between any of these three is lesser than the gap between the angelic being and God's knowledge of himself. Thomas concludes, "The divine intellect surpasses the angelic intellect much more than the angelic surpasses the human. For the divine intellect is in its capacity equal to its substance, and therefore it understands fully what it is, including all its intelligible attributes."[7]

The reason the gap between God's self-knowledge and the comprehension of the angelic being is the largest gap in the example is due to the distinction between that which is created and that which creates. God's essence is a self-subsisting essence that is unchanging, simple, infinite, and the like; there is a distinction between that essence which is self-subsisting and the essence of the creature, such that the creature cannot overcome the "mode of knowing" that is contained in the "mode of existence."

NOT SIN OR SIZE: IMPROPER LOCATIONS
OF INCOMPREHENSIBILITY

Sin. To root the doctrine of divine incomprehensibility in the Creator-creature distinction is to not root the doctrine in alternative dogmatic locations. In hopes to illustrate why the distinction between the Creator and the creature serves as the best ground for the doctrine, it is worth taking a moment to reflect on two alternative dogmatic options for locating the doctrine, namely, sin and size.

---

[7]*SCG* I, 3.4.

Beginning with sin, to say it plainly, while the noetic impact of original sin is detrimental to the intellectual life of the creature—especially in theological reflection—sin is not in itself a sufficient location to ground the doctrine of divine incomprehensibility. What I mean to say in negating hamartiology as the proper dogmatic location of incomprehensibility is that it is not because we are sinners that we cannot comprehend God; it is rather that we are creatures that we cannot comprehend God.

Returning to the anonymous author of *The Cloud of Unknowing* gives us a chance to see an attempt to locate the doctrine of divine incomprehensibility within the jurisdiction of sin. The anonymous author writes of the "eternal sweetness" that is proper contemplation of God after working through the proposition of the two faculties of humans—knowing and loving. Considering that faculty of knowing—that is, knowing God—the author writes, "This is the work in which humanity would have continued if we had never sinned, and it is the work for which we were made and everything was made for us to help and further us in it, and by it we shall once more be restored."[8] Or, again later in the work, the author writes,

> Will is the faculty by which we choose good after it has been identified by reason, and by which we love God, desire God, and finally rest in God with complete joy and consent. Before humanity sinned, the will could not be deceived in its choice, its love, or any of its activities, because then it was able by nature to apprehend everything as it was, but now it cannot do so unless it is consecrated by grace. For frequently, through the infection of original sin, it apprehends as good something that is evil and has only the appearance of good. . . . For until the time comes when then imagination is to a great extent controlled by the light of grace in the reason—as it is by continual meditation on spiritual matters, such as their own sinfulness, the Passion, the kindness of our Lord God, and many other similar topics—they are quite unable to set

---

[8] Anonymous, *The Cloud of Unknowing and Other Works* (London: Penguin, 2001), 24.

aside the strange and alien thoughts, delusions and images that are supplied and imprinted in their minds by the light and ingenuity of imagination. All this disobedience is the punishment of original sin.[9]

While the anonymous author would be correct to insist on the intellectual implication of the fall along with all the frustrations and obstacles that might bring for the task of theology, it seems mistaken to locate or root the doctrine of divine incomprehensibility in any hamartiological setting. We have already seen justifiable reasoning for this claim in this very chapter. For above, we saw Aquinas note that the "mode of knowing" is correspondent to any beings' "mode of existence." So, while it is true that the creature now lives an incorporated life that is wrapped up with a sin-riddled nature, it is not a difficult task to think of two varying creatures whose mode of existence is not intermingled with sin—namely, angelic beings and prelapsarian human beings.

We saw in Aquinas that while the mode of existence for angelic beings is not an incorporeal existence, it is nevertheless a received incorporeality, which is the explanation for why the angels—like other creatures—cannot comprehend God. Angelic beings, while not trapped in corporeality, are nevertheless still trapped in finitude. As has been said, that which is finite will never circumscribe that which is infinite. Angels have their existence by the power and say-so of a causal power, and while incorporeal are not *a se*. This distinction of subsistence is the causal explanation for the angelic incomprehensibility of the divine. The reason this point is worth repeating is because the case of the angelic beings shows that attempting to dogmatically locate God's unknowability as a

---

[9]*Cloud of Unknowing*, 90–91. It should be noted that while it appears that original sin is a significant operative category for the anonymous author throughout *The Cloud,* the author does give a few nuances. For example, "For I tell you one thing, that there never has been and never shall be any living creature, however pure, raised to whatever height of ecstasy in contemplation and love of the Godhead, who does not always have a high and wonderful cloud of unknowing between him and his God" (42). This quote seems to make it hard to argue that the anonymous rooted the doctrine of incomprehensibility in hamartiology *only*; yet, my point in this section is to argue that any notion of original sin is insufficient to ground the doctrine, and the anonymous author gives a touch more credence to original sin as the explanatory cause of the cloud of unknowing than I would be comfortable with.

mere consequence of sin will not have the explanatory power for all possible examples. Like angels, prelapsarian human beings prove to be another test case for which rooting incomprehensibility in the doctrine of sin will not do. While the biblical data is limited on the intellectual life of Adam and Eve, it is not an unreasonable proposal to insist that Adam and Eve did not know God as he knows himself.

Consequently, while theologians ought to affirm the intellectual import from hamartiology given that sin has infected not just the material world of the creature's but also the thought life of humankind, it is, nevertheless, not a sufficient dogmatic ground for the doctrine of incomprehensibility. The Creator-creature distinction is still a preferable location over any notion of sin.

Size. Locating the doctrine of divine incomprehensibility in the Creator-creature distinction is not only a more fitting location than the doctrine of sin but also a more fitting location than any predication of size within the divine essence. While this location—one of size—is admittedly a touch more abstract than the first improper location—one due to sin—the attempt of location would go something like this: God is so infinitely bigger than the creature that the creature does not stand a chance of comprehending God. Readers should see the change in emphasis from this proposed location and my proposal of the Creator-creature distinction: whereas the Creator-creature distinction roots the doctrine of divine incomprehensibility in God's being altogether different in kind, locating the doctrine of divine incomprehensibility in God's grandeur attempts to locate in God's being greater in size.

It is important to note here, as we have seen in the chapter two detailing the biblical data, there is an appropriate way to talk about incomprehensibility related to size. For example, it is appropriate to say that God's work in the divine economy is incomprehensible in respect to scope and size. This is why John can write, "Now there are also many other things that Jesus did. Were every one of them to be written, I suppose that the world itself could not contain the books that would be written" (Jn 21:25). It is also why Paul can write, "Oh, the depth of the riches and wisdom and knowledge of God! How unsearchable are his judgments and how inscrutable his ways! For who has known the mind of the Lord, or who has been his counselor?" (Rom 11:33-34).

It is appropriate to say that the creature cannot comprehend the scope of God's economic activity because it is simply outside our intellectual capacity to fathom the kind of work that entails this level of cosmic consequence. However, God's work in the economy is still within the realm of creation. So, while the economy is incomprehensible to the creature, the economy is nevertheless also creaturely in its mode of existence. So it is not due to the creation's being a different kind than humankind that we cannot comprehend God's full work in the economy; it is simply because our mode of knowing has finitude entangled within it, and the fullness of God's work *ad extra* is outside the bounds of our finitude's mode of knowing.

Given the reality of God's economy and our inability to fully comprehend the work of his hand, we can discuss incomprehensibility of size and scope. However, this is not the way that we should predicate incomprehensibility to the divine life. For while the product of God's economic activity is a creature—as we are—God is not. Therefore, our inability to comprehend God is not due to his being a larger creature than the creature entangled in finitude but rather that he is Creator, and we are creatures, which is a difference in kind and not merely size.

While there is a large cast to whom we could turn in hopes to see the theological folly of rooting the doctrine of divine incomprehensibility within the notion of size rather than within the divine life, one that might not be obvious is the seventeenth-century Dutch theologian Wilhelmus à Brakel (1635–1711). The reason it is advantageous to inject Brakel at this point in the discussion is due to his understanding of divine infinitude. Brakel writes of infinitude, "When we define God to be infinite, however, we do so in the literal sense of the word, thereby conveying that His Being is truly without any parameters or limitations."

This means, according to Brakel, that it is inappropriate to ascribe any concepts of "quantity, dimension, [or] locality" to God.[10]

Brakel's notion of infinitude is significant, for it is illogical to think of God in terms of "size" if we negate concepts of quantity, dimension, and locality. Negating these concepts seems to have a biblical basis as God is not a man but a spirit (Jn 4:24). The divine life is not a life of corporality, but as he who has life in himself is self-subsistent and that subsistence is incorporeal, there is no quantifying him in any way. The creature cannot measure God, nor count God, nor flee from God, nor locate God, for all of these would entail a predication of quantity, which cannot be said of God. As Job's friend Zophar reminds him, "Can you find out the limit of the Almighty?" (Job 11:7). The rhetorical answer—at least in respect to those who are created—is a resounding "no." The almighty will not be measured, he will not be quantified, and he will not be limited in any predication of sequence or chronology.

Of course, Brakel is not novel in predicating this understanding of infinitude. Yet Brakel's articulation of the doctrine of divine infinitude shows the theological dilemma of attempting to locate the doctrine of divine incomprehensibility in something like size, scale, or scope of the divine life. Size would entail something—or someone—quantifiable. When Brakel works to illustrate his definition of infinitude, he writes:

> Occasionally, when referring to something of which the limits are not known, we refer to infinity in a hypothetical sense, as when we speak of the total number of grains of sand, blades of grass, or stars. We also define as infinite that to which something can always be added, which for instance is true of a number. Regardless of how long one counts, the ultimate sum will either be even or uneven, a reality which changes as soon as one number is added—even if you were to count during your entire lifetime.[11]

---

[10]*CRS* 1:93.

[11]*CRS* 1:93. It should be no surprise, then, that Brakel does this with other divine perfections. For example, he writes of eternity: "[We humans] cannot even begin to comprehend eternity. By way of negation, we seek to comprehend eternity by comparing it with time, stating that it is without

Brakel's point here is the negation of any quantifying predication. This privation makes the comparison of size between the creature and the Creator a difficult one. For to compare any two entities, or beings, by virtue of size is to say that this one occupies this much size, while this other one occupies that much size. Even if the "this" in the previous sentence is "infinite size," we would still be predicating quantity to God, which Brakel argues should be a negation.

If the Christian theologian wishes to affirm the doctrine of divine incomprehensibility, rooting the doctrine in the Creator-creature distinction seems to be the most fitting place for the doctrine. While the noetic effects of the fall indeed impact the theological imagination of God's creatures, it alone is not the reason for the creatures' inability to comprehend God. This can be seen in the fact that created beings who are without sin, like angelic beings, also cannot comprehend God. We also ought not attempt to situate the doctrine of incomprehensibility in God's being merely bigger than his creature. As the distinction between God and his creation is not one of mere size, but of kind.

To foreshadow where this book is going, there will be a few theological implications in rooting the doctrine of divine incomprehensibility in the Creator-creature distinction. Namely, there will be significant implications in the kind of language the creature uses to name God in light of the distinction between the two. This implication of language will be the topic of consideration in the next chapter. Locating incomprehensibility in the Creator-creature distinction will also have implications related to the beatific vision, which we will turn to discuss here.

---

beginning, continuation, and end. If we go beyond this in seeking to comprehend the 'how' and the 'why,' we shall spoil it for ourselves and be in darkness. If we wish to consider the eternity of God within the context of our conception of time, then we will dishonor God and entertain erroneous notions concerning Him" (1:91).

Table 5.1. Possible Locations for Divine Incomprehensibility

Location	Meaning	Appropriate place to locate?
Sin	Locating incomprehensibility in sin argues that God is incomprehensible to the creature due to the noetic effects of the fall. In this model the creature cannot comprehend God because sin has clouded the intellectual ability of the creature.	No. While sin *does* impact the creatures' ability to contemplate God, there are creatures *not* tainted by sin who nevertheless still cannot fully comprehend God's essence such as angelic beings and prelapsarian humans.
Size	Locating incomprehensibility in size argues that God is incomprehensible to the creature due to God's being infinitely bigger than the creature. In this model the creature cannot comprehend God because God is beyond the scope of human intellect.	No. While God is "beyond the scope" of human intellect, it is not due to God's being merely *larger* than the creature. Rather, God's essence is not that it renders God like creatures just infinitely bigger, but instead renders him altogether different. He is not merely larger in size but different in kind.
Creator-creature distinction	Locating incomprehensibility in the Creator-creature distinction argues that the reason God is incomprehensible to the creature is his being altogether different in kind from the creature. In this model the creature cannot comprehend God as the creature cannot bridge the distinction between the one who creates and the ones created.	Yes. The distinction between he who created all things and those who are created is not traversable by the creature. For, the creature's existence is clothed in temporality, finitude, complexity, mutability, and the like.

"MAN SHALL NOT SEE ME AND LIVE": THE CREATOR-CREATURE DISTINCTION, DIVINE INCOMPREHENSIBILITY, AND THE BEATIFIC VISION

When begining his 2018 treatment of the beatific vision, Hans Boersma claims that "seeing God is the purpose of our life."[12] Whether one wants to agree with Boersma's significant claim about the telos of humankind, there should be little debate concerning the emphasis on the *visio Dei* in Scripture. Paul writes that while "now we see in a mirror dimly, *but then face to face. Now I know in part; then I shall*

---

[12]Hans Boersma, *Seeing God: The Beatific Vision in Christian Tradition* (Grand Rapids, MI: Eerdmans, 2018), 1.

know fully, even as I have been fully known" (1 Cor 13:12, emphasis added). Along with Paul, David writes that "One thing have I asked of the LORD, that will I seek after: that I may dwell in the house of the LORD all the days of my life, *to gaze upon the beauty of the LORD* and to inquire in his temple" (Ps 27:4, emphasis added). Moreover, Boersma does seem to have more explicit biblical credence to insist on the beatific vision as the ultimate telos of the human progression. We read in Revelation, "They will see his face, and his name will be on their foreheads. And night will be no more. They will need no light of lamp or sun, for the Lord God will be their light, and they will reign forever and ever" (Rev 22:4-5).

These passages become all the more bewildering—and magnificent—when one considers a passage that has already been discussed in this book, Exodus 33. I opened the book with this mysterious scene between YHWH and Moses upon Sinai as Moses requests of the Lord, "Show me your glory," to which the Lord replies, "Man shall not see me and live" (Ex 33:20). This passage brings together the current and the previous sections well as the declaration of Exodus 33—"man shall not see me and live"—and puts on display the sheer otherness of God. There is not a "bigger" version of the creature such that if one were to lay their eyes on them, it would prove fatal; rather, the otherness of God means that the Creator is beyond the ocular (and intellectual) ability of creatures. Few passages bring out the distinction between the Creator and the creature and therefore demonstrate the incomprehensibility of YHWH quite like Exodus 33.

Balancing the relationship between divine incomprehensibility and the beatific vision calls for careful exegetical and theological work. Just putting together Paul's notion of "seeing God face to face" in 1 Corinthians 13:12 with God's proclamation that "man shall not see me and live" in Exodus 33:20 demonstrates the tension. On one hand, the eschatological telos of all creatures is to behold God. On the other hand, God is the kind of being that if one were to see him, it would prove fatal. So then, in any eschatological discussion of the beatific vision, there are tensions to navigate.

In the tension between the incomprehensibility of God and the beatific vision, the doctrine of the Creator-creature distinction not only comes into focus but becomes a doctrine that might offer something of a solution to the theological tension between these biblical passages. A pertinent question one might ask when thinking about the relationship between incomprehensibility and the beatific vision would be something like, Does the ocular and intellectual deficiency that prohibits creatures from seeing God in the here and now go away with the beatific vision in the hereafter? Moreover, does this beatific vision render the creature now capable of comprehending God? Paul does say that while he knows in "part" now, he will know "fully even as he is fully known" (1 Cor 13:12). Paul's words here seem to indicate a connection between the vision of the blessed and a sort of comprehension in the hereafter. However, given that the proper location of incomprehensibility is the Creator-creature distinction, more can and should be said.

While maybe not obvious at first, this tension demonstrates one of the many significant implications of rooting the doctrine of divine incomprehensibility in the Creator-creature distinction. Allow me to give a rather direct answer to these two questions and then recruit Aquinas for aid in establishing the point: it seems that rooting the doctrine of divine incomprehensibility in the Creator-creature distinction gives the Christian theologian the needed theological and exegetical tools to affirm that in this life, we cannot "see God," while in the eschatological life to come the creature will be able to gaze upon the Lord. However, since the doctrine of divine incomprehensibility is rooted in the Creator-creature distinction and the distinction between the Creator and his creatures is not eliminated in glory—even with the blessed beatific vision—the creature will not be able to exhaustively comprehend God in eternity. In this end, this should be understood as good news since God's perfections are inexhaustible even when explored for an eternity. In the life to come, those in Christ will be granted the blessed sight and will be able to apprehend God with greater clarity than possible on this side of the eschaton; even still, while ever and eternally apprehending God in the beatific vision, the creature will never comprehend the triune God.

This is not a novel position as we can see a similar conclusion in the pages of a few different Christian thinkers. Michael Allen notes, for example, "We know God as finite humans can know an infinite and transcendent LORD. While adequate and even good, such knowledge and talk is neither divine nor perfect." Allen continues, "Even when glorified, we shall still see the glory of the LORD with creaturely, limited eyes. Yet we shall see, and we will praise. God honors such language—so should we."[13]

Moreover, Aquinas proves helpful on this point as well. As we have previously seen, Aquinas notes, "Act is proportional to the nature which possesses it," which is why "he cannot be seen by the sense or the imagination but only by the intellect."[14] This is the prolegomenous affirmation that leads Aquinas to affirm that what can be known is determined by the mode of the knower. Three articles later, Aquinas builds on this thought of what it means to "see God by the intellect," and he answers the objections: (1) "It seems that those who see the divine essence, comprehend God"; and (2) "further, Augustine says that is comprehended which is so seen as a whole, that nothing of it is hidden from the seer." These two objections, put forward in Ia.12.7, are quite pertinent for our discussion of the relationship between incomprehensibility and the beatific vision. For is it not the case with the glorified eyes—both literally ocular and the spiritual intellect—that the creature truly sees God and therefore might comprehend him? Aquinas answers:

---

[13]Michael Allen, *The Knowledge of God: Essays on God, Christ, and the Church* (London: T&T Clark, 2022), 48.

[14]*ST* Ia.12.4.

God is called incomprehensible not because anything of Him is not seen; but because He is not seen as perfectly as He is capable of being seen; thus when any demonstrable proposition is known by a probable reason only, it does not follow that any part of it is unknown, either the subject or the predicate, or the composition; but that it is not as perfectly known as it is capable of being known. Hence Augustine [in the second objection] in his definition of comprehension, says the whole is comprehended when it is seen in such a way that nothing of it is hidden from the seer, or when its boundaries can be completely viewed or traced; for the boundaries of a thing are said to be completely surveyed when the end of the knowledge of it is attained.[15]

Aquinas's articulation of incomprehensibility here would allow for a creature to legitimately *see* God and yet still not comprehend him. It is important to include Aquinas's conclusion to his point here. He writes, "Therefore, he who sees God's essence, sees in Him that He exists infinitely, and is infinitely knowable; nevertheless, this infinite mode does not extend to enable the knower to know infinitely."[16] For Aquinas, divine infinitude means that even in the life to come, the creature will not be able to comprehend God as he is in himself, for he is infinitely knowable as he is infinite. The infinitude of the divine essence becomes the very thing that renders God incomprehensible, even if the creature can now gaze at the infinite.

Returning to Hans Boersma's important work on the beatific vision, Boersma opens and closes his work with a similar observation as Aquinas here. In the opening, Boersma writes:

Theologies of the beatific vision have struggled with the question of how to speak of the object of the Vision. What do we mean when we say we hope to see God? The church fathers typically shied away from saying that in the beatific vision we will see the essence of God. The reason, I think, is their quite appropriate fear that we might end up claiming it

---

[15]*ST* Ia.12.7.
[16]*ST* Ia.12.7.

is possible to comprehend God exhaustively. The divine attribute of invisibility—illustrated by the biblical notion that one cannot see God and live (cf. Exod. 33:20; John 1:18)—prevented the fathers from claiming that we can ever see the divine essence . . . In this book, I am with the church fathers and the Orthodox in emphatically maintaining that we will never comprehend or exhaust the nature of God; there is always more of the infinite God to apprehend and this is why I endorse Gregory of Nyssa's concept of an "eternal progress" (*epektasis*) in the being of God.[17]

Boersma repeats this important point and brings it directly into conversation with the Creator-creature distinction toward the end of his book, writing, again about Aquinas' view of the beatific vision, "This built-in reservation, meant to safeguard God's transcendence or otherness vis-à-vis the creature, seems to me important: regardless of what it means that we will see God 'as he is.' It cannot mean that the creator-creature distinction will disappear."[18]

In conclusion, it seems reasonable to me to think that, in glory with the beatific vision, Moses' request to see God might be met with a majestic approval. This is not to say, however, that while in glory as we see God face to face in Christ (1 Cor 13:12), this glorious sight will lead to our exhaustively knowing God as he knows himself. Or, to put it another way, participating in the beatific vision, the creature will be able to apprehend God in ways never before dreamed of on this side of the resurrection, but univocal comprehension will still be out of the intellectual or visual jurisdiction for the creature.

There is eschatological payoff for the Christian life in rooting the doctrine of divine incomprehensibility in the Creator-creature distinction. Since the telos of humankind is that vision which beatifies, and whereas this vision is a beholding of God's glory, without comprehension the eschatological joy of the Christian is one in which we will ever

---

[17]Boersma, *Seeing God*, 12.
[18]Boersma, *Seeing God*, 415.

apprehend that which is glorious about God without end. In this cul-
mination of conclusions from variegated theological realities, we have
the fruition of Lewis's classic line in *The Last Battle* of "further up and
further in." The fate that awaits those united to the Son is a sight
through the Son in which the redeemed will get to ever apprehend the
beauty of God's essence without comprehension or exhaustion. While
it may seem counterintuitive, not arriving at a state of comprehension—
even while partaking in the beatific vision—is the good news of the
eschaton. For it means that those perfections which we adore most
about God will never run out of material even with everlasting growth
in apprehension.

There are various potential locations to ground the incomprehensibility of God in Christian theology. The most appropriate, however, is
to dogmatically locate the doctrine of divine incomprehensibility in
the Creator-creature distinction. Grounding the inability of creatures
to fully comprehend God in the distinction between God and those he
made means that incomprehensibility should not be understood as a
problem we must surmount. Rather, as "act is proportional to the
nature which possess it,"[19] our act of knowing and naming God will
always—even in the eschaton—be informed by the distinction between him who called all things into existence and those who were
called into existence.

---

[19] *ST* Ia. 12.4.

6

Implications of Language and Knowledge

Accommodation, Analogy, and the Archetype

Let us call upon him, then, as the ineffable God who

is beyond our intelligence, invisible, incomprehensible,

who transcends the power of mortal words. Let us call

on him as the God who is inscrutable to the angels,

unseen by the Seraphim, inconceivable to the Cherubim,

invisible to the principalities, to the powers, and to the

virtues, in fact, to all creatures without qualification,

because he is known only by the Son and the Spirit.

John Chrysostom

GIVEN WHAT HAS BEEN SAID thus far about the doctrine of divine incomprehensibility and its corollary doctrine, divine ineffability, it ought to come as little surprise that the distinction between the Creator and the creature will demand nuance concerning what the creature can say and think about God. It is these very nuances that will provide the material for the methodological implications from the doctrine of divine incomprehensibility. The goal of this chapter is to canvas at least a few of the implications for theological method that result from the primary subject of the theological enterprise—God himself—being out of intellectual and linguistic reach of those who seek after him.

In this chapter I discuss the significant role of divine accommodation for the creature's hope to participate in meaningful knowledge and speech about the divine. Ultimately, my claim is that God's accommodation grounds analogical language and ectypal knowledge within theological method. It is the possibility of knowing God ectypally and naming God analogically that gives the creature hope to have any positive knowledge of God. This positive knowledge of the divine is, of course, disciplined by negative theology and framed by methodological implications flowing from divine incomprehensibility, but it is meaningful knowledge and speech nevertheless. The double blessing of meaningful knowledge and speech about an incomprehensible God is a consequence of God's gracious accommodation.

AN ACCOMMODATING GOD

Divine incomprehensibility is a revealed doctrine. The notion of incomprehensibility's revealed status in Scripture protects the doctrine from a self-defeating struggle. Due to the doctrine's being revealed within Scripture, the idea that admitting an incomprehensibility of essence is itself a predication that requires comprehension will not stand. That God has revealed himself to be incomprehensibility protects the doctrine from such remonstrance. However, there are other consequences of the doctrines being a revealed doctrine than just self-protection.

Since the doctrine of divine incomprehensibility is a revealed doctrine, it is a doctrine not merely deduced from Scripture by good and necessary consequence. Instead, God is quite aware that the distinction between him and his creatures puts him out of the intellectual and verbal capacities of humankind. God's being given to the process of self-disclosure, as seen in the economy, means that the creature can be confident that God wants to be known. In fact, God demands to be known. Therefore, interwoven in the wonder that is the divine economy together with God's desire of being known is the grace that God reveals himself in a way that accommodates the creatures' limitations. Here we come to the doctrine of divine accommodation, which will prove to be one of the more significant imports into theological method from the doctrine of divine incomprehensibility.

Simply put, the doctrine of divine accommodation is the notion while God is incomprehensible and dwells in unapproachable light, he nevertheless reveals himself in a way that creatures might be said to have meaningful knowledge of him. This gracious act of self-accommodation does not make comprehension possible, but it does make apprehension along with meaningful knowledge and trust of God an achievable reality even with all our creaturely limitation in view.

The doctrine of God's condescending to bring himself within intellectual reach of the creature has gone by many names. As we saw in chapter four's section on Calvin, the Reformer referred to it as God's "lisping" to his children. Much earlier in theological antiquity, John Chrysostom discussed the doctrine, calling it God's "considerateness" and "condescension." Another oft-used phrase to describe this same reality throughout theological literature is the notion of a predication "befitting God." In his third homily against the Eunomians, Chrysostom's category of considerateness and condescension is on full display as he writes:

> Yet they did not see the pure light itself nor the pure essence itself. What they saw was a *condescension accommodated to their nature*. What is this condescension? God condescends whenever He is not seen as He is, but in a way one incapable of beholding Him is able to look upon Him. In this way God reveals Himself by accommodating what reveals to the weakness of vision of those who behold Him.[1]

---

[1] *Hom.* III.15, emphasis added.

Mark Sheridan traces this theme in Chrysostom and others. In his book *Language for God in the Patristic Tradition,* Sheridan serves readers well in explicating John Chrysostom's use of the divine accommodation and this divine "considerateness." Sheridan points to Chrysostom's *Homilies on Genesis* to demonstrate his point. Chrysostom writes:

> Notice once again, I ask you, the considerateness of Sacred Scripture: "God was mindful," it says. Let us take what is said, dearly beloved, in a sense befitting God [*theoprepōs*], and not interpret the concreteness of the expressions from the viewpoint of the limitations of our human condition. I mean, as far as the ineffable essence is concerned, the word is improper; but as far as our limitations are concerned, the expression is made appropriately.[2]

Sheridan goes on to explain just how frequent Chrysostom makes this kind of emphasis throughout his homilies, saying, "Chrysostom seems constantly to be concerned that his hearers will take the text too literally, and he frequently (several hundred times) introduces the distinction between God's 'considerateness' in formulating things in a human way and what is 'a sense befitting God.'"[3] Moreover, later in his work, Sheridan shows that this hermeneutical decision is not confined to the pages of Chrysostom either. Sheridan writes, "[Both Greek and Latin writers] use the categories of God's 'considerateness,' that is, his adapting himself to human ways of speaking, as well as the technical terminology of anthropomorphism, anthropopathism and what is fitting to or worthy of divinity."[4]

While the hermeneutical tool of divine accommodation was frequently utilized by the early church, it was not confined to the early church. For example, the Reformers discussed the doctrine as a

---

[2]John Chrysostom, *Homilies on Genesis 18–45*, trans. Robert C. Hill (Washington, DC: Catholic University of America Press, 1986), 149. The word Chrysostom is explaining here, which seems to be an accommodation, is God's being "mindful" of Noah and other animal creatures.
[3]Mark Sheridan, *Language for God in the Patristic Tradition: Wrestling with Biblical Anthropomorphism* (Downers Grove, IL: IVP Academic, 2014), 42.
[4]Sheridan, *Language for God*, 125.

significant tool in the task of biblical exegesis, especially as it relates to more difficult passages. Explaining the nuances of Genesis 6:6, "And the LORD regretted that he had made man on the earth, and it grieved him to his heart," Martin Luther wrote,

> God in His essence is altogether unknowable; nor is it possible to define or put into words what He is, though we burst in the effort. It is for this reason that God lowers Himself to the level of our weak comprehension and presents Himself to us in images, in coverings, as it were, in simplicity adapted to a child, that in some measure it may be possible for Him to be made known to us.[5]

Or, as we have noted previously with Calvin's notion of God's accommodation coming to the creature by way of divine lisping:

> For who even of slight intelligence does not understand that, as nurses commonly do with infants, God is wont in a measure to "lisp" in speaking to us? Thus such forms of speaking do not so much express clearly what God is like as accommodate the knowledge of him to our slight capacity. To do this he must descend far beneath his loftiness.[6]

While a full history of the church's use of accommodation would prove quite lengthy and out of the jurisdiction of what this project hopes to get at, it is important to note that the idea that "Scripture speaks the language of men" is an idea handed from generation to generation.[7]

---

[5]Martin Luther, *Lectures on Genesis: Chapters 6–14*, ed. Jaroslav Pelikan, Luther's Works (St. Louis: Concordia, 1960), 45.

[6]*ICR* I.xiii.1. The idea of Scripture being God's treating us as discipled children shows up in Augustine as well. Augustine writes: "Consequently, in order that the human mind may be cleansed from errors of this kind, Sacred Scripture, *adapting itself to little ones*, has employed words from every class of objects in order that our intellect, as though strengthened by them, might rise as it were gradually to divine and sublime things." Augustine, *On the Trinity*, in *NPNF¹* 1.1.2.

[7]For more on the development and doctrinal evolution of divine accommodation, see Amos Funkenstein, *Theology and the Scientific Imagination: From the Middle Ages to the Seventeenth Century* (Princeton, NJ: Princeton University Press, 1986), 213-70; see also Hoon J. Lee, *The Biblical Accommodation Debate in Germany: Interpretation and the Enlightenment* (Dordrecht: Springer, 2017); Jon Balserak, *Divinity Compromised: A Study of Divine Accommodation in the Thought of John Calvin* (Dordrecht: Springer, 2006). Funkenstein helps demonstrate that while there are distinguishable differences, those who utilized divine accommodation came from broad backgrounds, showing the significance of the doctrine. He writes, "Even those who deny that God can be spoken

One of the most significant implications for theological method from the doctrine of divine incomprehensibility is the divine act of grace that is God's accommodation. Predicated on the double premise that (1) God is incomprehensible, so his essence is out of the intellectual capacity of the creature, and (2) that God desires to be known by the creature, we arrive at the significant conclusion that God's self-disclosure takes into consideration the limitations of the creature. God's self-revelation accommodates these limitations that the creature might meaningfully apprehend and know God.

While the methodological implication of divine accommodation is one of the first fruits of examining divine incomprehensibility in search of finding import for theological method, it is not the last. A natural transition from a discussion of God's gracious act of accommodation is to ask, "How does God accommodate his incomprehensible essence in a way that might permit creaturely knowledge and apprehension?" To answer this question, we turn now to what I've come to call "the anthros."

THE "ANTHROS": ANTHROPOMORPHISM, ANTHROPOPATHISM, AND ANTHROPOCHRONISM

If the object of divine considerateness by way of accommodation is a self-disclosure to which the creature can attain, it proves important to spend a moment reflecting on the creature. To consider the creature, a reminder of Aquinas' notion that "act is in proportion to nature" is helpful. For example, Aquinas can say, in respect to the creature: "It is impossible for any created intellect to see the essence of God by its own natural power. For knowledge is regulated according as the thing known is in the knower. But the thing known is in the knower

---

of with positive attributes could still claim that all scriptural predicates of God are reducible to attributes of action or negations of a privation. Still, the very original presence of *prima facie* anthropomorphism in the Bible was embarrassing and called for a justification. The reason they are employed is to accommodate the lesser capacity for abstraction of the masses. The law was given to all in a language to be understood by all (Maimonides)" He distinguishes between these utilizations of the doctrine as "minimalistic and maximilistic constructions of accommodation" (214).

according to the mode of the knower. Hence the knowledge of every knower is ruled according to its own nature."[8]

The nature of the knower—in our case, the creature—is wrapped up in corporeality and finitude. Men and women live their lives trapped by limitation—we live a corporeal, passionate, and chronological life. Matter, space, emotion, and time confine the creature to live quite a fixed existence. This is not to claim that these notions are *bad*; rather, this is simply to note that if Aquinas is correct that the mode of knowing corresponds to the mode of existence, it is no surprise that the creature (bound by body, space, passion, and time) cannot univocally know or name the Creator (*not* bound by body, space, passion, or time).

To accommodate the limits of human nature, God's revelation is wrapped up in the language of corporeality, passion, and time. These are the tangible realities of the creatures and the dimensions through which creatures can have knowledge of the world. Therefore, we turn to the "anthros" as they relate to divine considerateness and accommodation. As God brings revelation of the divine life and action, he does so in human language accessible to those confined in finitude. Because the creature is corporeal, God accommodates through anthropomorphism; because the creature is passionate, God accommodates through anthropopathism; and because the creature is temporal, God accommodates through anthropochronism. All three kinds of divine accommodation relate to these creaturely imperfections. That is, all three attribute creaturely notions to the divine. Anthropomorphism is the attribution of creaturely-like parts to God. Anthropopathism is the attribution of creaturely-like passions to God. Anthropochronism is the attribution of creaturely-like time to God. We will take each in turn, showing how God accommodates his incomprehensibility through the language of creatures.

---

[8]*ST* Ia12.4.

Anthropomorphism. To demonstrate just how vast the use of anthropomorphism is throughout Scripture is a difficult task. Bavinck has a rather strong statement about the prevalence of anthropomorphism in Scripture that can register as shocking at first read but seems accurate with further reflection. Describing anthropomorphism, Bavinck writes,

> It is God himself who deliberately and freely, both in nature and in grace, reveals himself, who gives us the right to name him on the basis of his self-revelation, and who in his Word has made his own names known to us on that same basis. Now all these names without distinction are characterized by the fact that they have been derived from revelation. Not a single one of them describes God's being as such. The revealed name is the foundation of all the names by which we address him. And inasmuch as the revelation of God in nature and in Scripture is specifically addressed to humanity, it is a human language in which God speaks to us of himself. For that reason the words he employs are human words; for the same reason he manifests himself in human forms. *From this it follows that Scripture does not just contain a few scattered anthropomorphisms but is anthropomorphic through and through.*[9]

The last sentence in this quote can be startling at first glance. The shock subsides when biblical readers turn their attention toward the textual data and see the prevalence of God's accommodation by way of anthropomorphism. John 4:24 informs readers that "God is spirit," and therefore when the scriptural data describes God with any notion of corporeality, the reader can be confident this is God's accommodation by way of anthropomorphism.

For example, the biblical text depicts God as having sight (Deut 11:12; Ps 34:15; Amos 9:4), feet (Gen 3:8; Ex 24:10; Is 66:1), hands (Ex 31:18; Is 5:25; 49:2), ears (2 Kings 19:16; Dan 9:18), a face (Lev 20:6; Num 6:25), arms (Deut 4:34; 5:15; Ps 89:10), and a shadow (Ps 36:7;

---

[9]*RD* 2:99, emphasis added.

57:1; 61:4; 63:7; 91:4; Jer 49:22). It is not just anthropological attribution using human features either. The biblical text also ascribes to God non-human characteristics as well. For example, the Scripture, in varying places, describes God as having wings (Deut 32:11; Ps 17:8; 36:7; 57:1; 61:4; 63:7; 91:4; Jer 49:22).[10]

Returning to Bavinck, the Dutch theologian gives readers a good look at the quantity and types of anthropomorphisms found throughout the biblical data. He notes, like the list above, those passages that seem to indicate creaturely-like features attributed to God, but he takes his list further by adding creaturely-like actions and offices. To see the sheer quantity of texts that speak with anthropomorphic emphasis, his list is worth quoting at length:

> But anthropomorphism in Scripture is even much more extensive. All that pertains to humans and even to creatures in general is also attributed to God. . . . God is said to have a soul (Lev 26:11) and a Spirit (Gen 1:2; Mt 12:28; etc.) . . . There is mention of his face (Ex 33:20, 23; Is 63:9; Ps 16:11; Mt 18:10; Rev 22:4), his eyes (Ps 11:4; Heb 4:13), his eyelids (Ps 11:4), the apple of his eye (Deut 32:10; Ps 17:8; Zech 2:8), his ears (Ps 55:3), his nose (Deut 33:10), his mouth (Deut 8:3); his lips (Job 11:5), his tongue (Is 30:27), his neck (Jer 18:17), his arm (Ex 15:16), his hand (Num 11:23), his right hand (Ex 15:12); his finger (Ex 8:19), his heart (Gen 6:6), his intestines (Is 63:15; Jer 31:20; Luke 1:78); his bosom (Ps 74:11; Jn 1:18), his feet (Is 66:1).[11]

Bavinck continues beyond features to actions, saying:

> All human actions, moreover, are attributed to God: investigating (Gen 18:21), searching minds (Ps 7:9), knowing (Gen 3:5), intending (Gen 50:20), forgetting (1 Sam 1:11), remembering (Gen 8:1; Ex 2:24), speaking (Gen 2:16), calling (Rom 4:17), commanding (Is 5:6), rebuking (Ps 18:15; 104:7); answering (Ps 3:4), witnessing (Mal 2:14), resting (Gen 2:2),

---

[10]These lists come from my work on divine immutability, see Ronni Kurtz, *No Shadow of Turning: Divine Immutability and the Economy of Redemption* (Ross-shire, UK: Mentor, 2022), 142.
[11]*RD* 2:100.

working (Jn 5:17), seeing (Gen 1:10), hearing (Ex 2:24), smelling (Gen 8:21), testing (Ps 11:4-5), sitting (Ps 9:7), arising (Ps 68:1), going (Ex 34:9), coming (Ex 25:22), walking (Lev 26:12), going down (Gen 11:5), meeting (Ex 3:18), visiting (Gen 21:1), passing (Ex 12:13), abandoning (Judg 6:13), writing (Ex 34:1), sealing (Jn 6:27), engraving (Is 49:16), striking (Is 11:4), chastising (Deut 8:5), working (Jn 5:17), binding up (Ps 147:3), healing (Ps 103:3; Deut 32:39), killing and making alive (Deut 32:39), wiping away (Isa 25:8), wiping out (2 Kings 21:13), washing (Ps 51:2), cleansing (Ps 51:2), anointing (Ps 2:2), adorning (Ezek 16:11), clothing (Ps 132:16), crowning (Ps 8:5), girding (Ps 18:32), destroying (Gen 6:7; Lev 26:31), killing (Gen 38:7), inflicting (Gen 12:17), judging (Ps 58:11), condemning (Job 10:2), and so forth.[12]

Finally, Bavinck mentions occupations ascribed to God as well as those anthropomorphisms taken from "organic and inorganic creation." Meaning, Bavinck demonstrates the many names predicated to God that resemble vocational, familial, or simply general titles—all of which would be considered anthropomorphisms:

In addition, God is also very frequently described with names that denote a certain occupation, office, position, or relationship among people. He is a bridegroom (Is 61:10), a man (Is 54:5-6), a father (Deut 32:6), a judge, king, a lawgiver (Is 33:22), a warrior (Ex 15:3), a mighty hero (Ps 78:65-66; Zeph 3:17), an architect and builder (Heb 11:10), a gardener (Jn 15:1), a shepherd (Ps 23:1), a physician (Exo 15:26), and so on. In connection with these occupational descriptions there is mention of his seat, throne, footstool, rod, scepter, weapons, bow, arrow, shield, chariot, banner, book, seal, treasure, inheritance, and so on.

Then, to express what God means to his own, all sorts of expressions are even derived from the organic and inorganic creation. He is compared to a lion (Is 31:4), an eagle (Deut 32:11), a lamb (Is 53:7), a hen (Mt 23:37), the sun (Ps 84:11), the morning star (Rev 22:16), a light (Ps 27:1), a lamp (Rev 21:23), a fire (Heb 12:29), a spring or fountain (Ps 36:9; Jer

---

[12]RD 2:101.

2:13), food, bread, drink, water, ointment (Is 55:1; Jn 4:10; 6:35, 55), a
rock (Deut 32:4), a refuge (Ps 119:114), a tower (Prov 18:10), a stronghold
(Ps 9:9), a shadow (Ps 91:1; 121:5), a shield (Ps 84:11), a road (Jn 14:6), a
temple (Rev 21:22), and so on.[13]

The sheer amount of textual data here can be quite overwhelming.
However, it is vital to consider as it demonstrates a major point in this
project: God's otherness and incomprehensibility has significant
import into our theological method as the doctrine of divine incomprehensibility demands nuance when the creature speaks about the
Creator. The length and number of passages used in these quotes gives
justification to Bavinck's notion that the Scripture does not contain a
few scattered anthropomorphisms throughout but is anthropomorphic
through and through. Inasmuch as Scripture is divine speech in human
words, and inasmuch as the divine life is ineffable to the creature due
to God's incomprehensibility, it makes sense that accommodated language is prevalent throughout God's revelation.

Anthropopathism. God's gracious condescension on behalf of the
creature is not limited to anthropomorphism either; while anthropomorphism enables the creature to apprehend God by way of physical
form and office, there is accommodation on display as well when it
comes to the emotional life of the divine. Like the corporeal creature
may not attend to comprehension of the divine life in so much as God's
essence is simple and incorporeal, while the creature is complex and
corporeal, so too would the creature struggle to apprehend the impassible and immutable essence of God. To accommodate the creature's
emotional and mutable existence, God's accommodation includes
condescension of emotional expression.

Throughout the Scripture, the biblical authors write of God's being
"jealous (Ex 20:5; 34:14; Deut 4:24; 2 Cor 11:2), angry (Ex 15:7; 32:10-11;
Deut 9:8; Job 4:9; Jer 32:29), and regretful (Gen 6:6-7; 1 Sam 15:11;

---

[13]*RD* 2:101.

2 Sam 24:15-16; Jonah 4:2; Ps 106:45; Amos 7:1-6)."[14] Bavinck adds to my list by noting the Scriptures saying, "Every human emotion is also present in God (Is 62:5; 65:19); sorrow (Ps 78:40; Is 63:10), grief (Ps 95:10); provocation (Jer 7:18-19); fear (Deut 32:27)." He continues, "Love in all is variations such as mercy, compassion, grace, long-suffering and so on; also zeal and jealousy (Deut 32:21); repentance (Gen 6:6); hatred (Deut 16:22); wrath (Ps 2:5); and vengeance (Deut 32:35)."[15]

Again, if the mode of knowing is dictated by the mode of the knower, it ought not come as a surprise that God, intending to condescend to those who are passionate and emotional creatures, reveals himself in words laced with emotive connotation. Biblical notions like anger, sorrow, regret, zeal, and jealousy, as mentioned in these previous examples, are used for the sake of the reader, not as univocally describing the revealer. Learning from our early church examples, when we predicate such notions to God as these emotive concepts, we must do so in a way which our predications are "befitting God."

Anthropochronism. There is one more—albeit less known or used—category of accommodation through anthropomorphism.[16] For the category of anthropochronism, I am pulling from British philosopher Paul Helm, who wrote, "It may be alleged that almost any ascription of an action to God, and the Bible is full of such ascriptions indicates that God is in time."[17] Helm asserts this because "actions are events, they are datable, they take time, and so God is portrayed as being an agent in time." However, Helm is not convinced that these descriptions of God's action within time necessitate that the reader must conclude that God is literally in time. He questions this assumption, introducing our category, asking, "But may not such representations of God be

[14]Kurtz, *No Shadow of Turning*, 142
[15]*RD* 2:100.
[16]Inasmuch as anthropopathisms and anthropochronisms can be said to be subcategories of anthropomorphism.
[17]Paul Helm, *Eternal God: A Study of God Without Time* (Oxford: Oxford University Press, 2010), 2.

anthropomorphic (or anthropochronic) in order to render his relations to his creation more intelligible to us?"[18]

Helm serves students of theology well by introducing this category of anthropochronism or ascribing to God a creaturely-like relation to time. The prevalence and significance of a category like anthropochronism shows up when we realize that the opening salvo of Scripture is nothing other than an anthropochronism. The first words of the scriptural testimony are, "In the beginning . . ." (Gen 1:1). What does it mean for this unfolding drama to start "in the beginning" when the psalmist declares, "Before the mountains were brought forth, or ever you had formed the earth and the world, from everlasting to everlasting you are God" (Ps 90:2). It seems this marker of time is to serve the reader in making sense of the story from a creaturely perspective while not intending to mark the divine life with a marker of temporality. There is no beginning for a God who is outside time, so this condescension is to serve the reader of the divine speech. As the divine life is one outside time, not impacted or stuck in successive moments of time, humankind needs this kind of existence condescended in hopes to even apprehend life, as the creature's existence is confined in moment-by-moment chronology.

It is important to note that the "anthros," as I've called them—anthropomorphism, anthropopathism, and anthropochronism—are not mere accommodations to make revelation merely easier. Instead, these accommodations should be thought of as divine speech in human language and concepts such that God is pursuing self-revelation within concepts and language that make sense for the creature. Table 6.1 hopes to demonstrate what is being accommodated and why the creature needs the accommodated language.

---

[18]Helm, *Eternal God*, 2. He pushes the questioning, asking, "References to God being in space are anthropomorphic while references to him being in time, are, apparently, not anthropomorphic. Is there prejudice here?"

Table 6.1. Divine Accommodation in Scripture

	Definition	Form of Accommodation	Examples
Anthropomorphism	Attributing to God creature-like parts and positions.	As an infinite and incorporeal spirit, God condescends to those who dwell in finite corporeal bodies.	Eyes (Deut 11:12) Feet (Gen 3:8) Arms (Ps 89:10) Wings (Jer 49:22) Tongue (Is 30:27)
Anthropopathism	Attributing to God creature-like passions and volition.	As the simple and impassible Creator, God condescends to the passionate and emotive creatures.	Jealous (Ex 20:5) Angry (Job 4:9) Regretful (1 Sam 15:11) Fear (Deut 32:27) Repentance (Gen 6:6)
Anthropochronism	Attributing to God creature-like time and chronology.	As him who is atemporal and does not experience successive moments of time, God condescends to those who dwell within time.	In the beginning (Gen 1:1) First and last (Rev 22:13) One day/1,000 years (2 Pet 3:8)

As God goes about the business of self-disclosure, he is aware that his is an essence his creation cannot comprehend. In his economic activity of revelation, he demonstrates divine considerateness in condescending to the limitations of the creatures. Since creatures are (1) embodied and corporeal, (2) emotive and with wavering volition, and (3) confined to experience life in successive moments of chronological events and time, God condescends his (1) spiritual and incorporeal, (2) impassible, and (3) atemporal and eternal existence using anthropomorphism, anthropopathism, and anthropochronism, respectively.

ANALOGICAL, EQUIVOCAL, AND UNIVOCAL THEOLOGY

The history surrounding the conversation of analogical, equivocal, and univocal predication within theological method is vast and rather nuanced. Therefore, it will not be the goal of this section to present a technical demonstration of analogical theory in conversation with its historical opponents and proponents. However, there are a few voices and nuances withing the conversation of analogical theology that, while bordering on technical theological discussion, are so vital to the theory that it would be a disservice to readers to omit them. So, what is presented here is in line with the thesis of this project—my main hope is to not delve into all the technicalities of this conversation but rather to bring those nuances to the forefront, which will allow us to think through the theological import for methodology arising from the doctrine of divine incomprehensibility.[19] To state why this conversation is relevant at the outset, it should be noted that whereas univocal language leads to a kind of theological idolatry and equivocal language leads to a kind of theological despair, the proper way forward for the Christian theologian is through analogical language.

It will prove most helpful to begin this section by simply defining terms. Working on theology of analogical predication post-Aquinas, Domenic D'Ettore serves readers well with a quick and accessible definition of univocal and equivocal predication. As for univocal language, D'Ettore says: "It is univocal when a single name is said about many according to the same signification. That is, the intellect refers one and the same of its concepts to diverse things through one name." He continues, explaining equivocal language, "By contrast, there is equivocation, when a single name is predicated according to

---

[19]While I will not attempt to bring the many nuances of this conversation to bear, I have been quite helped by the literature on this topic. In hopes to serve readers, even though some of these texts will not show up in the body of this project, here are the major works that impacted my thinking on this topic. Of course, some of these texts are in tension, or even disagreement, yet they each carry the conversation forward. See Tommosa de Vio Cajetan, *The Analogy of Names, and the Concept of Being*, trans. Edward A. Bushinski (Eugene, OR: Wipf & Stock, 2009); Erich Przywara, *Analogia Entis: Metaphysics—Original Structure and Universal Rhythm*, trans. John R. Betz and David Bentley Hart (Grand Rapids, MI: Eerdmans, 2014); Domenic D'Ettore, *Analogy After Aquinas: Logical Problems, Thomistic* Answers (Washington, DC: Catholic University of America Press, 2019); Ralph McInerny, *Aquinas and Analogy* (Washington, DC: Catholic University of America Press, 1996); Archie J. Spencer, *The Analogy of Faith: The Quest for God's Speakability* (Downers Grove, IL: IVP Academic, 2015); Thomas Joseph White, ed., *The Analogy of Being: Invention of the Antichrist or the Wisdom of God?* (Grand Rapids, MI: Eerdmans, 2011); Thomas Joseph White, "*Analogia Entis* within *Analogia Fidei*: Arguments for God's Existence" and "Naming God Analogically" in *The Trinity: On the Nature and Mystery of the One God* (Washington, DC: Catholic University of America Press, 2022).

diverse significations; that is, the intellect uses the same name to refer different concepts to different things."[20]

Perhaps an example would prove helpful in illustrating D'Ettore's definition here. An oft-used illustration to demonstrate equivocal language is the notion of a "bat." Suppose I said, "I have a bat flying around in my attic at night, so I'm going to grab a Louisville Slugger baseball bat and try to chase it out." While this might not be the most effective method of bat removal, it does prove helpful in illustrating equivocal language. As D'Ettore stated in his definition, this sentence uses the "same name" in referring to "different significations." The word *bat* refers both to the nocturnal flying mammal and to the wooden object used in the great game of baseball. While this sentence utilizes the same word—*bat*—the signification of that word is equivocal. Simply put, there is not a relationship between the one kind of bat and the other.[21]

If equivocal language is that kind of predication in which one name can signify two unrelated objects, univocal language is on the other end of the spectrum. To predicate something univocally is, as D'Ettore writes, to use a single name referring to many significations that have a kind of exactness. Again, to assist D'Ettore's definition with an example, thinkers have often made use of colors to demonstrate univocal language. For example, suppose I say, "The St. Louis Cardinal's baseball field is green, and Liverpool Football Club's pitch is green." In this sentence (in which I am admittedly being indulgent using two teams I enjoy as examples) the term *green* is being used univocally. When I call the two fields green, I am using one signification—the color green— to refer to two entities—Busch Stadium in St. Louis and Anfield in Liverpool. When I utilize the color green, even though I am referring

---

[20]D'Ettore, *Analogy After Aquinas*, 3. For history on the development of both the archetype-ectype distinction as well as theological analogy in early Reformed orthodoxy, see *PRRD* 1:222-38.

[21]Aquinas defines it similarly: "Whatever is predicated of various things under the same name but not in the same sense, is predicated equivocally." *ST* Ia.13.5.

to two different locations, I mean to communicate something the same, namely, both share the accidental quality of being green. Another oft-used example to showcase univocal language is that of "human." If I say that Plato and Aristotle are both human beings, the single predication "human" is being used univocally of both Plato and Aristotle.[22]

While the use of equivocal and univocal language might sound like a non-issue or splitting semantical hairs unnecessarily, this linguistic distinction is quite important in the field of Christian theology and has been the impetus for a body of literature so large it is difficult to master all that has been said. The pertinent theological question concerning univocal and equivocal language is, How do we speak about God? When, for example, I say that God is "good," should we categorize this predication— God is good—as univocal or equivocal? If it is an equivocation, then what I mean when I say "God is good" and the actual goodness of God have a dissimilitude that renders the speech rather ineffective. Whereas, if I say, "God is good," and that word has an exactness with God's actual perfection of goodness, then I've implemented univocal language.

Even in this above paragraph, the answer is likely apparent to readers, we ought to denounce both kinds of linguistic predication when it comes to the creatures' speech about God. For in the case of equivocal language, if there is a nonexistent relationship between what we say about God in our worship and the way he exists in himself, it will lead to a kind of theological despair. In other words, theological language reduced to equivocation leaves the creature with no way forward for meaningful speech about God.

Psalm 100 tells readers, "Enter his gates with thanksgiving, and his courts with praise! Give thanks to him; bless his name!" (Ps 100:4). How

---

[22]To hear from a proponent of univocal theory of language, here is how Duns Scotus defines what it means for language to be univocal: "And lest there be a dispute about the name 'univocation,' I designate that concept univocal which possesses sufficient unity in itself, so that to affirm and deny it of one and the same thing would be a contradiction. It also has sufficient unity to serve as the middle term of a syllogism, so that wherever two extremes are united by a middle term that is one in this way, we may conclude to the union of the two extremes among themselves." John Duns Scotus, *Philosophical Writings,* trans. Alan Wolter (Indianapolis: Hackett, 1987), 20.

sad it would be if the creature did not have access to the kind of religious speech that leads to our blessing his name and giving him praise. Moreover, how contrary it would be to the Scriptures' oft-repeated command to praise the Lord. There must be something in the speech of the creature that meaningfully communicates who God is and what he has done such that devotion and praise are rendered possible in the religious life.

On the other side is a different issue. In the case of univocal language, the worry is not theological despair but instead theological idolatry. While Psalm 100 tells us to enter his gates with thanksgiving and praise, Psalm 145 tells us, similarly, "Great is the LORD, and greatly to be praised" but goes on to remind us, "and his greatness is unsearchable" (Ps 145:3). Regardless of how high we intellectually climb or how deep our meditation becomes, no matter how seasoned our speech or wise our tongue, our God is ever a God who dwells in "unapproachable light" whose "greatness is unsearchable" (1 Tim 6:16; Ps 145:3). God can be apprehended with the creatures' mind and tongue, but he will never be comprehended by either. While our speech about God contains meaningful truthfulness—as we will see—they do not contain exactness as if the essence of God and his life *in se* could be captured in the religious thought or speech of the creature.

In sum, we ought to reject the notion that theological speech is so dissimilar from God as to be equivocal while also rejecting that theological speech shares such a similitude to God's essence as to be univocal. Instead, with many in the history of the church, we ought to affirm that the theological speech of the creature is meaningfully true by way of analogical theology.

Juxtaposing the three kinds of theological speech and ultimately showing the superiority of analogical theology, Thomas Joseph White notes:

> This means we cannot speak of God univocally or "essentially," as we do the beings in the world (like substances of various kinds having specific properties). . . . Instead, we can speak of God only analogically, as one

who is the transcendent cause of all creatures, of both substances with their various properties and those transcendental features of being in which they all participate (like existence and goodness). All of these categorical modes of being, together with their transcendental properties, *resemble God in some way* and *all of them fail to resemble him in some way,* because of his incomprehensible perfection and transcendence of all created realties. . . . The purpose of analogy theory, accordingly, is to try to speak rightly of how creatures are like God so that we may truly name him, while at the same time calling our attention to how God is utterly unlike creatures, so that he remains beyond our comprehending grasp.[23]

White's quote above, showing the better way between mere equivocation and pure univocation, is quite similar to what Aquinas seemed to pose for the proper mode of signification. Aquinas uses "wisdom" or "wise" as an example to demonstrate how one might predicate wisdom to creatures compared to how one might predicate wisdom to the Creator. He begins by eliminating univocation, saying, "No name belongs to God in the same sense that it belongs to creatures; for instance, wisdom in creatures is a quality but not in God."[24] This proves important for Aquinas because wisdom, within the creature, is merely an *quality* of that individual whereas in God, it is not distinct from God's essence.[25] Aquinas notes two differences in the way wisdom is predicated to creatures and the way wisdom is predicated to God:

For instance, by this term *wise* applied to a man, we signify some perfection distinct from a man's essence, and distinct from his power and existence, and from all similar things; whereas when we apply it to God,

---

[23]White, *The Trinity*, 229-30, emphasis original. White earlier uses similar categories to the above, saying, "This theory [analogy] is advantageous because it allows us to avoid two unhelpful extremes. We could characterize one extreme as a form of linguistic despair, in which it is said that our ordinary language is incapable of denoting God in himself, as a result of our epistemological limitations and his transcendence. We could characterize the other extreme as a form of linguistic presumption, in which our speech is thought to be capable of denoting God in just the same way that is capable of denoting created realities. The first tendency leads to semantic agnosticism, while the second leads to semantic idolatry" (223-24).

[24]*ST* Ia1.3.5.

[25]Of course, this is said by way of analogy lest I contradict the very argument I'm working to build.

we do not mean to signify anything distinct from His essence, or power, or existence. Thus also this term *wise* applied to man in some degree circumscribes and comprehends the thing signified; whereas this is not the case when it is applied to God; but it leaves the thing signified as incompreheneded, and as exceeding the signification of the name. Hence it is evident that this term *wise* is not applied in the same way to God and man.[26]

We can see in the quote above that the term *wise* when applied to the creature compared to the Creator has two significant differences: first, the term, when applied to the creature, signifies something other than the creatures' essence. Namely, inasmuch as a creature can be said to be wise, they can only be said to have wisdom as a quality, not as a perfection of essence. On the contrary, God does not merely have wisdom as an accidental quality that may increase or decrease. Rather, God is all-wise (omnisapient) by virtue of his undivided and simple essence. Second, the term *wise*, when applied to the creature, is something "circumscribable." Meaning, inasmuch as the creature can be said to be wise, the wisdom of the creature can be comprehended or traversed. We could plumb the depths of the creatures' wisdom and find its bottom. On the contrary, when God is said to be wise, it is an incomprehensible wisdom. Creatures may attempt an apprehension of God's wisdom, but they will never attain a full comprehension of God's wisdom. This truth is echoed in the Prophets, "For my thoughts are not your thoughts, neither are your ways my ways, declares the LORD. For as the heavens are higher than the earth, so are my ways higher than your ways and my thoughts than your thoughts" (Is 55:8-9). So we can rightly use one word, *wise*, to describe two parties—both creatures and God. While we use the one predicate—"wise" in this case— for two parties, we do not mean to communicate that the creature's wisdom is exactly like God's wisdom. We do not mean to communicate

---

[26]*ST* Ia13.5.

that the fullness of what it means for God to be "wise" is contained in what it means for the creature to be "wise." Rather, the creature's wisdom is analogous to God's wisdom.

While we've established a definition for equivocal and univocal language, a final quote from Aquinas will help us land with a definition for analogical predication:

> Thus, whatever is said of God and creatures, is said according to the relation of a creature to God as its principle and cause, wherein all perfections of things pre-exist excellently, now. This mode of community of idea is a mean between pure equivocation and simple univocation. For in analogies the idea is not, as it is in univocal, one and the same, yet it is not totally diverse as in equivocals; but a term which is thus used in a multiple since signifies various proportions some one thing.[27]

As we can see in this quote, there is a participatory element in the Creator-creature distinction in which, according to Aquinas, there is a "relation of a creature to God as its principle and cause, wherein all perfections of things pre-exist excellently." Through doctrines like *imago Dei* and participation, the creature really is like God. However, it is possible to overstress this likeness, which results in univocal predication. For example, describing Dun Scotus's univocal theory of predication, Richard Cross writes, "The difference between God and creatures, at least with regard to God's possession of the pure perfections, is ultimately one of degree."[28] Or, to quote Scotus directly: "Consequently, every inquiry regarding God is based upon the supposition that the intellect has the same univocal concept which it obtained from creatures."[29]

---

[27]*ST* Ia.13.5.

[28]Ricahrd Cross, *Duns Scotus* (Oxford: Oxford University Press, 1999), 39. While this quote comes from Cross, as a secondary commentator, and not Scotus himself, it is a helpful summary of why Scotus might downplay a doctrine like ineffability in comparison to someone like Aquinas. To see more on the Aquinas-Scotus understanding of analogy, see D'Ettore, *Analogy after Aquinas*, 18-33. To hear God cannot be known naturally unless being is univocal to the created and uncreated (5).

[29]Scotus, *Philosophical Writings*, 25.

Yet (as seen in chapter five), any notion of "size" seems to be an improper location for the doctrine of divine incomprehensibility and any correlation of ineffability. God's uniqueness among creatures is not that he is merely "bigger" than we are, even infinitely bigger. This runs the risk of collapsing the Creator-creature distinction and bringing the "unlikeness" of God and man into "likeness."

Andrew Davison uses the language of likeness-in-unlikeness that "belongs to analogy,"[30] which becomes a useful heuristic when considering analogical language. A reason that analogical language is preferable over that of univocal and equivocal language is that the creature is both like and unlike God. On one hand, there is an ontological distinction between the two that the creature cannot traverse. On the other, we are created by God, in his image and for his glory, and are numbered among those who participate in him and his cosmos. As Davison demonstrates, equivocal language collapses the likeness into the unlikeness, whereas univocal language collapses the unlikeness into likeness. Analogy helps us thread the needle in respecting both the Creator-creature distinction and participation. Furthermore, creation and participation become vital categories for meaningful speech about God. It is because God has created the cosmos in a way in which creatures can participate in the divine life that analogical predication has efficacy. Emmanuel Durand captures this concept well, writing of "our ability, on account of the creation of the world by God, to produce analogical significations which pass beyond created limitations without, for all that, overcoming our inability to represent the divine reality."[31]

So then, when the creature speaks of God and seeks to name him according to the biblical data and biblical reasoning, we do so by

---

[30] Andrew Davison, *Participation in God: A Study in Christian Doctrine and Metaphysics* (Cambridge: Cambridge University Press, 2019), 173.

[31] Emmanuel Durand, *Divine Speech in Human Words: Thomistic Engagements with Scripture* (Washington, DC: Catholic University of America Press, 2022), 279.

analogy. Analogical theology allows us to witness the similitude of creatures to God inasmuch as the creature participates in the cause of all things—God himself. At the same time, analogy helps our theological language, while recognizing similitude, remain in a holy silence as it comes to God's preeminence and uniqueness above all. As the Creator of all beings, God will not be merely numbered among those who have being. Analogical language allows us to meaningfully predicate attributes and names while not attempting the fool's errand of trying to traverse God's transcendence.

Table 6.2. Equivocal, Univocal, and Analogical Language in Theology

	Definition	Example	Use in Theological Language
Equivocal	When one term is used to signify two entities which do not share similitude or relationship.	"He used a baseball *bat* to scare the *bat* out of his attic."	*Theological despair*: if none of our vocabulary could meaningfully describe God, it would lead to a theological despair as we could not properly praise or name God.
Univocal	When one term is used to signify two entities which have an exactness of quality or relationship.	"The baseball field and soccer pitch both have *green* grass." "Aristotle and Plato are both *humans*."	*Theological idolatry*: if our words could actually capture the very essence of God, it would lead to a linguistic idolatry.
Analogical	When one term is used to signify two entities in which one signification is an analogy or shadow of the other.	"My biological father is *good* to me, and my Heavenly Father is *good* to me."	*Proper theology*: While our words do not describe God *in himself*, they nevertheless are meaningful and true. Our words analogously signify what God actually is in himself.

ARCHETYPAL AND ECTYPAL
THEOLOGICAL KNOWLEDGE

When considering the implications springing from the doctrine of divine incomprehensibility into linguistic and epistemological realms of Christian theological method, the conversation of archetype and ectype comes into focus. Like the distinctions between univocal,

equivocal, and analogical language are significant for parsing theological *language* in light of divine incomprehensibility, the categories
of archetypal and ectypal theology prove important for working on
theological epistemology in light of divine incomprehensibility.

As for definition, Edward Leigh brings clarity to these terms in his
definition: "Theology of divinity is two-fold, either first, archetypal, of
divinity in God, of God himself, by which God by one individual and
immutable act knows himself in himself, and all other things out of
himself, by himself." He continues by way of contrast, "or second, ectypal
and communicated, expressed in us by divine revelation after the pattern
and idea which is in God."[32] Similarly, Franciscus Junius works toward
a bifurcated understanding of the material that is Christian theology as
well. Junius, asking the question of how many parts theology contains,
begins his treatment of theological analogy. He notes that analogical
language is that kind of theological speech in which "of those things
which are said equivocally, the meaning is the same in one respect or
relatively, and at the same time differs in another respect."[33] Establishing
his understanding of "analogical equivocation" as opposed to "pure
equivocation," Junius roots a notion of archetypal and ectypal theology
in the realm of analogy. Flowing from his conversation of analogy, Junius
arrives at his sixth thesis of true theology, which reads: "Thesis 6: This
theology is either archetypal, undoubtedly the wisdom of God Himself,
or it is ectypal, having been fashioned by God."[34] Finally, John Webster
provides a helpful summarizing definition in a single sentence, writing,
"Archetypal theology is God's self-knowledge; ectypal theology is the
knowledge of God possible for finite rational creatures."[35]

---

[32]*SBD*, 2. This distinction causes Leigh to opine that we ought to approach learning divinity with
"a denial of our wit and carnal reason, not measuring the unsearchable wisdom of God by our
shallow capacities" (4).

[33]*TTT*, 103.

[34]*TTT*, 104.

[35]John Webster, "Principles of Systematic Theology," in *The Domain of the Word: Scripture and
Theological Reason* (New York: T&T Clark, 2014), 139. Webster continues, "The former is God's
simple, eternal intelligence of himself, the latter can be described in its temporal unfolding."

Archetypal knowledge of God and his work is the kind of divine wisdom God, through his line of questioning, suggest Job lacks. In Job 38 God asks, "Where were you when I laid the foundation of the earth? Tell me, if you have understanding. Who determined its measurements—surely you know!" (Job 38:4-5). This line of question has an obvious rhetorical flourish as God knows that this kind of knowledge is inaccessible to a creature like Job. What is more, this is knowledge of God's economic activity, such as creation, let alone wisdom pertaining to God's own essence. Nevertheless, this kind of knowledge of divine matters is available to God alone, which places it in that arena of archetypal knowledge.

There are, of course, variegated trails we could consider when exploring the notions of archetypal and ectypal theology. Junius himself devotes six complete chapters to the topic, three outlining the contours of the distinction and three explaining how creatures might explore the material content of ectypal theology. While exploring all the nuances of the archetypal and ectypal distinction is a valuable theological exercise, in order to remain on topic in this section, I must focus the material on the ways in which archetypal and ectypal theology intersect with the doctrine of divine incomprehensibility.

However, table 6.3 will serve as something of a summary of Junius's and my own doctrine and distinction of archetypal and ectypal theology. Following the table, I will attempt to make plain the connection to the doctrine of divine incomprehensibility. In this simple chart, I attempt to systematize and summarize Junius's distinction between the two forms of theology by utilizing the categories of definitions, discerning the epistemological range of each, working through whether either category is communicable or incommunicable, and finally exploring the leftover prevailing attributes of each category.[36]

---

[36]This table is a combination of my own thought paired with that of Franciscus Junius. To differentiate between the two, I've put quotations and summaries of Junius in italics while my own words are standard. I attempted to summarize and categorize major points of emphasis from Junius's doctrine of archetypal and ectypal theology found in three chapters, or five total theses, of his *Treatise on True Theology*. See *TTT*, 103-20. It is important here to note that since the goal

Table 6.3. Franciscus Junius on Archetypal and Ectypal Theology

	Archetypal Theology	Ectypal Theology
Definition	*"Archetypal Theology is the divine wisdom of divine matters. Indeed, we stand in awe before this and do not seek to trace it out."*	*"Ectypal theology, whether taken in itself, as they say, or relatively in relation to something else, is the wisdom of divine matters, fashioned by God from the archetype of Himself, through the communication of grace for His own glory."*
Epistemological Range	Available only to God as the fullness of wisdom and knowledge of himself and those in relation to himself. *"The former [Archetypal] is the very same thing as unbounded wisdom, which God possesses concerning His own person and all other things, as they have been set in order with respect to Him necessarily, individually, and by an uninterrupted relation among themselves."*	Available to the creature, by the grace of accommodation. *"God has fashioned the second kind of theology on the model of the divine and immutable exemplar, proportionally to the creatures' capacity."* *"The second theology is that wisdom which the creatures have concerning God according to their own manner and concerning those things that are oriented toward God through His communication of Himself."*
Essential or Relative	Essential: Exists in God himself and is therefore prototypical. *"For that essential, archetypal theology is a characteristic of the nature of God, and part (as we would put it) of that infinite knowledge which in God is essential. Whatever is essential, moreover, is agreed that this is properly assigned to the same genus, together with the actual essence of which that this is essential."*	Relative: Exists as a grace and is therefore not prototypical. *"Nonessential and created, or dispositional; this you might also conveniently call ectypal, as a certain copy and, rather, shadowy image of the formal, divine, and essential theological image."*
Incommunicable or Communicable	Incommunicable: Archetypal theology is the wisdom of God in himself which is wholly inaccessible to creatures and therefore creatures participate in the imprint of the archetypal through the analogical ectypal theology.	Communicable: Ectypal theology is the revealed imprint of archetypal theology in which God takes into account the limitations of the creatures and accommodates their finitude in self-revelation.

was not merely to give Junius's doctrine in its entirety but to show how the conversation of archetypal and ectypal theology connect to the doctrine of divine incomprehensibility I've left off Junius's understanding of the threefold exploration of ectypal theology. Using his next three chapters, Junius shows that the creature can explore the material content of ectypal theology through (1) union with Christ, (2) visions in the heavens, and (3) revelation in this life. *TTT*, 121-40.

Attributes	Uncreated wisdom Essential Absolute Infinite In all aspects simultaneously present Incommunicable Lacking nothing Containing no variation Devoid of all defects including parts, change, or motion.	Created revelation Transmitted as an imprint The "emanation" of the prototype "Fashioned by God" "Wisdom of divine matters communi- cated to things created, according to the capacity of the created things themselves."

The "first theology," or archetypal theology, is—as Junius says—*divine wisdom of divine matters*.[37] Inasmuch as archetypal theology is God's knowledge *of God*, it is an impenetrable realm of religious epistemology. Archetypal theology exists alone in the mind of God and is out of the epistemological jurisdiction of creatures. To demonstrate, Junius ends his treatment of archetypal theology quite abruptly, saying:

> About this infinite and amazing wisdom of God, what more shall we say? We said it before with one assertion: that we should not seek to trace it out but rather stand in awe. Whatever we can say about this wisdom is nothing in comparison to it. Whatever it is, it is infinite; it cannot be expressed. It is in itself amazing, and we ought to behold it with the highest reverence . . . the apostle, consequently, caught up in the wonder of this wisdom, exclaimed very enthusiastically: "O the depth of the riches of the wisdom and recognition or knowledge of God" (Rom 11:33). And we also halt our advance here, overcome with holy fear. For because that abyss is one of wisdom, it is better that we should not come to the rivers that are communicated through it and flow from it [ectypal theology], lest its magnitude should swallow up our weakness if we should plunge ourselves into that ocean.[38]

While it could be said that this divine wisdom of divine matters is the truest form of theological contemplation, God did not leave his creatures without the ability to nevertheless contemplate true theology.

---

[37]*TTT*, 107.
[38]*TTT*, 111-12.

It is for this reason that the words *grace* and *gracious* must not be missed in the definitions and charts above. While archetypal theology is the true wisdom of the true God, ectypal theology is still a meaningful imprint of those archetypal realities. Therefore through the grace of God's accommodating revelation, creatures can participate in archetypal theology by means of analogical ectypal theology. While analogical and ectypal theology is a shadow or imprint of archetypal theology, it is nevertheless meaningful and true.

CATAPHATIC/APOPHATIC THEOLOGY AND THE ROLE OF THE ECONOMY IN RELIGIOUS EPISTEMOLOGY

Given the work done on apophasis, cataphasis, and supereminence in the historical survey on Pseudo-Dionysius in this project, we will not spend much time here. Nevertheless, no chapter seeking to explore the linguistic and epistemological implications of divine incomprehensibility for theological method would be quite complete without discussing the role the economy plays in religious epistemology, along with the distinction of cataphatic and apophatic language in theology.

Dionysius writes that since God is the cause of all beings, we should "posit and ascribe [to him] all the affirmations we make in regard to beings." However, he qualifies this statement by continuing, "And, more appropriately, we should negate all these affirmations, since [he] surpasses all being."[39] The anonymous mystic here is getting at the notion of "apophatic" and "cataphatic" theology. In their most simple form, apophatic and cataphatic are concerned with predications by way of negation or by way of affirmation. Apophatic theology emphasizes the likeness-in-unlikeness distinction between the Creator and the creature by insisting that the best and most proper way of speaking about God is to suggest what he is not, rather than what he is. On the contrary,

---

[39] *MT* 1.2. Moreover, the legacy of apophatic and cataphatic theology has largely been attributed to Dionysius. For example, Paul Van Geest writes, "Pseudo-Dionysius was the first to make a systematic distinction between negative (apophatic) theology and positive (cataphatic) theology." Van Geest, *Incomprehensibility of God: Augustine as a Negative Theologian in Late Antique History and Religion* (Leuven: Peeters, 2011), 35.

cataphatic theology stresses the similitude between God as the cause of all things and creatures as his effect and insist that—at least through analogical predication—there really is a possibility of denoting what and who God is in the positive, not merely the negative.

Examples of apophatic predication would be those negations we make of God to protect his perfection. When, for example, creatures say, along with Malachi 3:6, that God is immutable, we are in reality predicating something God is not—God is not changeable. This is an example of predication by negation, or apophatic speech. On the contrary, a passage like 1 John 4:7, which says that God is love, exemplifies cataphatic language inasmuch as it denotes, in the positive, what God is rather than what he is not.

Both apophatic and cataphatic predications are present in the biblical texts. Theologian Gregory Rocca serves readers well as he demonstrates the prevalence of negative theology even within Scripture. While it is true that the theological tradition makes use of negative names through the alpha privative by phrases such as *atheotos* ("invisible"), *agenētos* ("uncreated"), *anarchos* ("without beginning"), *aphthartos* ("incorruptible"), *akatalēptos* and *aperienoētos* ("incomprehensible"), and the like. It is also true that there is a precedent for negative names, using the alpha privative even in the Scriptures. For example *aoratos* ("invisible") in Romans 1:20, *arrētos* ("ineffable") in 2 Corinthians 12:4, *anekdiēgētos* ("indescribable") in 2 Corinthians 9:15, *anexereunētos* ("unsearchable") from Romans 11:33, *anexichniastos* ("untraceable") from Romans 11:33, *athanasia* ("immortality") from 1 Timothy 6:16, and *aprositos* ("inaccessible") from 1 Timothy 6:16.[40]

It is my contention that these two processes and strategies of theological language ought not to be too heavily pitted against one another. While it might be proper to say that the creature is on the steadiest of grounds in

---

[40]These two lists come from Gregory P. Rocca, *Speaking the Incomprehensible God: Thomas Aquinas on the Interplay of Positive and Negative Theology* (Washington, DC: Catholic University of America Press, 2004), 5-8. Rocca includes more uses of the alpha privative than are listed here as well.

utilizing negative language given the severe distinction between God and his creation, it should nevertheless also be affirmed that the student of theology ought not let apophatic theology be their only tool within theological method. While there is apparent tension between these two quotes, it seems the best relationship between positive and negative names within theological predication would be to affirm both of the following quotes from Aquinas and Peter Van Geest. On the one side, Aquinas writes, "We cannot know what God is, but rather what He is not, we have no means for considering how God is, but rather how He is not."[41] Van Geest, commenting on the development of negative theology in the early church with a focus on its reception in the theology of Augustine, writes,

> Whereas Dionysius made the distinction between kataphatic and apophatic theology precisely in order to emphasize their mutual implication and complementarity, gradually the impression arose in the West that apophatic discourse about God was nothing more than negation of God. *And "negation" alone was believed to be unacceptable for a religion that was based on revelation.*[42]

While there is tension between what Aquinas and Van Geest postulate here, I believe there is no final conflict when all things are considered. Furthermore, it is in the tension of these two statements that the student of theology can find the proper balance between cataphatic and apophatic language. As God is altogether different in kind from the creature, there can be no knowledge of an incomprehensible God nor any naming of an ineffable God—that is, if the only way to obtain knowledge of God or the ability to name God is archetypal knowledge or univocal naming. Yet through divine accommodation with biblical anthropomorphism, anthropopathism, and anthropochronism, the

---

[41] *ST* Ia.3.

[42] Van Geest, *Incomprehensibility of God*, 37, emphasis added. Van Geest continues, saying, "Exactly because it was insufficiently recognized that cataphatic theology is rooted in apophatic theology, too little attention was paid to the fact that the language of the theologian is not only explanatory but also laudatory: it expresses a joyful celebration of an incomprehensible God, who has revealed himself to humankind, in creation and in revelation."

creature can obtain ectypal knowledge of God and participate in analogical speech about God. So Aquinas is correct to postulate that, in the end, there is no univocal knowledge or univocal language that is accessible to the creature. God is altogether outside the bounds of the creaturely mind and language. At the same time, Van Geest is correct to assert that an exclusively negative theology is inappropriate for a religion based on revelation, as if the revelation was not actually efficacious in anyway. While the divine revelation of Scripture is *not* efficacious to bring about archetypal knowledge—as it seems Scripture never *intended* to bring about this kind of knowledge—it *is* nevertheless efficacious in providing the creature with the opportunity to apprehend, not comprehend, God. Consequently, as creatures attempt to participate in theological speech, we do so balancing negative and positive names. With nuance and attempted precision, we know and name God—using the example of Holy Scripture and theologians before us—with a mixture of apophatic and cataphatic predications.

It is further important to note that the use of *both* negative and positive names is only possible due to God's gracious self-disclosure within his economic activity.[43] In creation and revelation the creature learns that God *is*, yet through biblical reasoning and dogmatic reasoning on the revealed word, the creature must also come to the conclusion that whatever God *is*, it is removed from what the creature *is*. The economic activity of creation serves a pedagogical role in instructing, from the effects to their cause, the creature's regenerate imagination of God. The pedagogy of creation is further and more authoritatively established by the divine instruction that comes through sacred Scripture. God did not leave humankind to wonder in

---

[43]By way of definition, John Webster provides readers with a helpful working definition of the divine economy: "It is both the work of the triune God in which he administers the temporal order of creaturely being and activity in accordance with his eternal purpose, and also the sphere of creaturely reality so administered by him: both God's act of *dispensation* and that which he disposes." Webster, *Domain of the Word*, 116.

half-formed reason at the effects only; his creation not only proclaims his handiwork, but his Word tells us directly, "I am the Creator."

We, therefore, ought to affirm with the history of the church that God's economic activity, from creation, revelation, and salvation, serve to teach his children what proper theological speech might look like. With negative and positive names in our mouth we work to negate the imperfect and attribute the perfect. I will conclude this section returning to Basil of Caesarea, who summarizes much of what has been communicated in this section well:

> For he who says that he does not know the substance has not confessed that he does not know God, since the concept of God is gathered by us from the many attributes which we have enumerated. . . . But if they say substance is something else, let them not mislead us by citing its simplicity. For they themselves have confessed that substance is one thing and each of what was enumerated was another. "Nay, the activities are varied and the substance is simple." *But we say that from His activities we know our God, but His substance itself we do not profess to approach.* For His activities descend to us, but His substance remains inaccessible.[44]

A final point must be made concerning God's economy: while God's economic activity serves as a divine instructor on his person and work, it should still be affirmed that in some ways even the economy of God is incomprehensible. John 21:25 tells readers concerning the work of Jesus, "Now there are also many other things that Jesus did. Were every one of them to be written, I suppose that the world itself could not contain the books that would be written." Romans 11:33 reminds readers that the economic works of God are inscrutable: "Oh, the depth of the riches and wisdom and knowledge of God! How

---

[44]Basil of Caesarea, *Collected Letters of Saint Basil*, vol. 3, *Letters 186-248*, Loeb Classical Library (Cambridge, MA: Harvard University Press, 1930), 373, emphasis added. This particular letter of Basil's was brought to my attention in reading Tomasz Stępień and Krolina Kochańczyk-Bonińska, *Unknown God, Known in His Activities: Incomprehensibility of God During the Trinitarian Controversy of the 4th Century*, European Studies in Theology, Philosophy and History of Religion 18 (Berlin: Peter Lang, 2018), 102. Their work proves erudite when considering the relationship between the doctrine of divine incomprehensibility and God's economic work.

unsearchable are his judgments and how inscrutable his ways!" Finally, even the results of God's economic action are incomprehensible. Those united to Christ through the gospel of grace are said to possess a "peace" that "surpasses all understanding" (Phil 4:6-7).

A distinction could and should be made here though differentiating the kind of incomprehensibility that is proper of God's being and the kind of incomprehensibility that is proper of God's work. In chapter five, I argued that neither the noetic effects of sin nor any predication of size are sturdy enough foundations to root the doctrine of divine incomprehensibility. Rather, God is incomprehensible to humankind because he is altogether different from creatures. It does seem that we can talk of an incomprehensibility of size, however, when it comes to the economy of creation, revelation, and salvation. These pedagogical elements of God's work among his people are not God himself and exist within the created cosmos. It would be improper to ascribe to them the same kind of incomprehensibility of kind we would denote God with as the eternal, infinite, and incorporeal Spirit. It is helpful then to bring about a new distinction within the realm of incomprehensibility: an incomprehensibility of being that is proper to predicate of God, and an incomprehensibility of size and scope we could properly predicate of God's economic activity.

Basil captures much of the previous themes in his work against Eunomius as he makes the very point that if even the economy is incomprehensible, so too is the substance behind and responsible for the divine economy—God himself. Basil writes:

> Let's ask him from which source he claims to have comprehended it. So, then, from a common notion? But this tells us that God exists, not what God is. Perhaps from the Spirits' teaching? Which one? Where is it located? Isn't it clear that the great David, to whom God manifested the secret and hidden things of his own wisdom, confessed that such knowledge is inaccessible? For he said: *I regard knowledge of you as a marvel, as too strong—I am not able to attain it* [Ps. 138.6]. And when Isaiah came to contemplate the glory of God, what did he reveal to us

about the divine substance? He is the one who testified in the prophecy about Christ, saying: *Who shall tell of his begetting* [Is. 53.8] Then there's Paul, *the vessel of election* [Acts 9.15], who had *Christ speaking in him* [2 Cor. 13.3] and *was snatched away up to the third heaven and heard ineffable words which are impossible for a person to utter* [2 Cor. 12.2-4] What teaching did he bequeath to us about the substance of God? He is the one who peered into the particular reasons for the economy and cried out with this voice, as if the vastness of what he contemplated made him dizzy: *O the depth of the riches and wisdom and knowledge of God! How inscrutable are his judgements, and how unsearchable are his ways!* [Rom. 11.33] If these things are beyond the understanding of those who have attained the measure of the knowledge of Paul, how great is the conceit of those who profess to know the substance of God?[45]

There are variegated methodological implications springing from the doctrine of divine incomprehensibility that chasten what we say and know about him who dwells in light unapproachable. As God is incomprehensible, it is the jurisdiction of the divine to permit creatures to have meaningful knowledge of him. This kind of meaningful knowledge is possible only because God has condescended toward the creature's limitations and has accommodated revelation such that the creature might apprehend, not comprehend, him. For our apprehension of God's accommodated glory, God speaks to creatures in his Word through anthropomorphism, anthropopathism, and anthropochronism. These varying types of anthropomorphism allow the creature to participate in the archetypal divine self-knowledge of God through ectypal creaturely knowledge. In turn, the creature expresses theology through language fitting for those distinct from the Creator, which is through analogical language. As God is distinct from the creatures, he pursues the economy of revelation with gracious accommodation and condescends to our weakness, so the creature is left in a posture of receiving wisdom of God himself from God himself.

---

[45] *AE* 1.12, emphasis original.

7

IMPLICATIONS OF POSTURE

The Necessity of Theological Humility

> *The teachableness which characterizes properly ordered*
>
> *reading involves a certain passivity: respect, receptivity,*
>
> *readiness to be confronted, and, above all, humility.*
>
> **John Webster**

IF WHAT I HAVE SAID up to this point is found true, one implication is that theological humility is not a just virtue. Or rather, theological humility cannot be properly categorized as a mere virtue. Instead, if the preceding chapters be found true, theological humility runs deeper than mere virtue and should be understood as an ontological necessity of creatureliness. In the end, any accurate contemplation of God will be found only possible due to God's gracious and efficacious self-disclosure. Therefore, those of us who wish to spend our days with a Godward gaze in hopes to see him and all things in relation to him will act most in line with our vocation when we assume the posture of receivers of accommodated glory and forsake any notion of prideful creators of theological truth.

It is toward that end I hope to argue in this final chapter: due to God's incomprehensibility and his response therein, theological humility is not an optional virtue but an ontological necessity. This incomprehensibility-informed humility recognizes the impossibility of the theological enterprise had God not accommodated the weakness of us creatures and at the same time delights in the truth that God has condescended to our limitations that we might know, love, and follow him. Given what has been said thus far in these pages, it may be the case that the premises needed to arrive at this conclusion are already coming into focus. However, this chapter seeks to make plain what is hiding beneath the varying points of emphasis and will do so in three sections: (1) discussing the difference between theological humility and theological hopelessness; (2) working to demonstrate the role of prayer in the task of Christian theology; and finally, (3) developing the idea that on this side of the beatific vision, we labor toward contemplation of God as pilgrims using the idea of *theologia viatorum*.

HUMBLE, NOT HOPELESS

As anyone whose had the chance to do so knows, there is a joy in teaching university students at the outset of their theological journey. Often, freshman university students interested in the theological life show up to campus not only lacking theological conclusions but also lacking the proper kind of questions needed to establish a holy curiosity. To help kindle the kind of good question asking that might lead to fruitful theological exploration, I will sometimes start my introductory theology classes giving my students two propositions that, on the surface, seem to be at odds with one another.

> Proposition one: Theology is best understood as the study of God and all things in relation to God.

> Proposition two: God is the kind of being such that creature's cannot see him. As Exodus instructs us, the sight of God would prove fatal for humankind; in fact, God is the kind of being who dwells in light unapproachable according to 1 Timothy 6.

With these two propositions in hand, students work on wrestling toward resolve. Given that the students I am blessed to teach are often bright and the resolution between these two propositions is not overly brilliant, students will typically come to sound remedies to the problem. Yet we do not obtain the joy of the proper resolution of these two propositions without first asking the question, at least for a moment, Is this whole thing hopeless? Is it something of a fool's errand for finite creatures to attempt contemplating God in any meaningful way? If theology is studying God, and God dwells in unapproachable light, is this a hopeless endeavor? Moreover, given God's otherness, is the task of knowing or naming God riddled with arrogance such that we act out of line with our intellectual and linguistic jurisdiction in trying? Barth captures the tension between the two propositions well when he writes, "As ministers we ought to speak of God. We are human, however, and so cannot speak of God. We ought therefore to recognize both our obligation and our inability and by that very recognition give God the glory."[1]

It is in wrestling with these two propositions that my students come to recognize just how significant a role of divine accommodation plays in the task of Christian theology. To state it rather frankly, it is due to God's gracious act of accommodation that we creatures are not theologically hopeless. Even our best attempts of theological contemplation would be chasing the wind had God not spoken with a speech befitting our faculties. Yet the story of a God speaking with a speech outside the intellectual jurisdiction of his creatures is not our story, for God, in his grace, has accommodated his glory with a condescension we might apprehend. It is in this realization that the thesis of this chapter comes to fruition: given that God has accommodated his glory with a speech befitting creaturely faculties, we are not hopeless; however, given that theological contemplation is only possible for the very reason that God

---

[1]Karl Barth, "The Word of God and the Task of the Ministry," in *The Word of God and the Word of Man* (London: Hodder & Stoughton, 1928), 186.

has condescended to our limitations means that we receive from God and are therefore necessarily humble. Humility is not a mere virtue we put on as if we had deviating options; rather, humility becomes a necessity given our ontological limitation due to our doing theology as creatures.

To state it plainly, there is an important connection between a robust understanding of divine accommodation and theological humility. Divine accommodation is the answer for much of this book. Beyond the resolution of the tension above, the methodological import of divine accommodation becomes clear when revisiting the ghost of Dionysius that runs throughout this project and in the conversation pertaining to God's incomprehensibility at large. I argued in chapter four that students of the Word ought to be eager to embrace a Dionysian understanding of incomprehensibility's definition; however, we should be a touch slower to affirm a Dionysian resolution to God's inaccessible essence—that of mystical ascent into the cloud of unknowing. So, it could be said, we ought to accept a Dionysian diagnosis of the doctrine while possibly rejecting the remedy Dionysius called us toward. Now, with the categories of archetype and ectype more substantially defined, we can revisit this opinion with the help of John Webster and in so doing see the significant role of accommodated revelation. Webster writes, on the relationship between archetype and ectypal theology:

> [The term] "theology" is not a term used univocally of archetype and ectype; that is because the distinction between the two duplicates the distinction between uncreated and created. Unlike uncreated knowledge, finite theology is unoriginal, communicated, non-essential, discrete, mutable and so forth. Yet the discontinuity is not absolute— this, indeed, is the force of the category of "type." It would be an abuse of the distinction to press it in such a way that the archetype became a blank abyss, entirely inaccessible to creatures; uncreated intelligence is incommensurate with, but not wholly alien to, created intelligence. The

connection, however, of type to archetype is not established by analogical ascent from creaturely forms, nor by participation in God, but
by God's communicate acts in which he gives himself to be known
through the service of creatures to created reason.[2]

There is wisdom in what Webster says here. Contra Dionysius, the
way creatures "overcome" the notion of God's incomprehensibility is
not through either ascent, even analogical ascent, or an overrealized
category of participation.[3] Both—theological ascent and a robust
understanding of participation—are needed categories for theological method (both of which have been advocated for in this very
book). Neither methodological turn is going to prove strong enough
to establish a kind of archetypal or univocal knowledge or predication in relation of the creature to God. For creatures cannot anal-
ogize their way out of creatureliness, nor can they participate outside
of human limitation.

On the contrary, the "remedy" to divine incomprehensibility is not
a creaturely ascent out of creatureliness but an act of divine love and
plenitude. There is a death to the notion of our helplessness to know
and name God not because we ascend but because God condescends,
and out of the fullness of his own goodness he communicates to us in
accommodated language. It is the gracious accommodation of God,
through revelation, that any kind of analogy or participation is possible. As Michael Allen says, "Though humans cannot analogously
work upward to knowledge of God, God's revelation in the Scriptural
stories can be analogously received."[4]

---

[2]John Webster, *Domain of the Word: Scripture and Theological Reason* (London: T&T Clark, 2012),
140. This has a significant implication for theological *movement* as it were. Webster summarizes:
"Thinking of theological activity in such terms requires us to envisage creaturely reason as within
the economy of divine grace rather than as a capacity to transcend that economy."

[3]I put quotation marks around the word *overcome* to signify that there is, properly speaking, no
overcoming God's incomprehensibility in this life or the next. Rather, this gets at truthful theological speech given our inability to comprehend God.

[4]Michael Allen, *The Knowledge of God: Essays on God, Christ, and the Church* (London: T&T Clark,
2022), 27.

In his seminal work *Divine Speech in Human Words*, Emmanuel Durand is correct in establishing the connection of possibility between "discursive elaboration" within theological speech and God's accommodating himself to human speech via the textual revelation. Durand writes:

> Christian theology is the discursive elaboration of our human knowledge concerning God, founded on revelation and developed in accord with our capacities. . . . What does God offer us in order that we may know him precisely as he gives himself to us? His communication to us is not presented by way of pure intuitions, direct significations, and immediate experiences. Rather, he speaks in human language through the words of scripture. In order to know him in accord with his self-revelation, we have at our disposal an ensemble of origin tales, histories, prescriptive texts, prophetic oracles, the maxims of Wisdom literature, evangelical parables and discourses, narratives telling us of interpersonal encounters, letters to the churches, and so forth. These words are associated with actions, sign, situations, events, and salvific realities.[5]

Durand points to oracles, histories, letters, maxims of wisdom, and the like as the arsenal creatures have to pursue "discursive elaboration" toward theological articulation. It is in these rather mundane concursive tools in which God condescends and "lisps" to us with a lisping fit for our ears. It is for this reason that any hope toward accurate reflection on the person and work of God must pay excruciating attention and account for the details of the textual data that is God's self-revelation. A robust doctrine of divine accommodation will help readers of the biblical data see that not only do we find *in the text* a story of the miraculous, but the very existence and ontology *of the text itself* is a story of the miraculous. The Christian Scriptures are nothing less than the cleft of the rock found in the Exodus narrative. Whereas God graciously accommodated his glory before Moses by placing him

---

[5]Emmanuel Durand, *Divine Speech in Human Words: Thomistic Engagements with Scripture* (Washington, DC: Catholic University of America Press, 2022), 258.

in the safety of the cleft of the rock, God has graciously accommodated his glory before our own eyes by a miraculous condescension of a written text composed of human speech. We are right, therefore, to say along with John Webster, "In the history of revelation, tempered to creatures by divine benevolence, and unfolding as a movement from life *in via* to life *in patria*, God is known, theology is possible."[6]

Junius, pointing out the connection between the definitional realities of theology and the humility needed to pursue the task with any measure of faithfulness, writes: "True theology, therefore, because it is the highest wisdom and marked by the greatest importance and value in itself, and the greatest usefulness for us *if only we would receive it from the Lord with humility of mind and acknowledgment of our weakness*."[7] As this chapter seeks to establish, Junius notes the significance of theology as a *received* endeavor. We are those who have received, with much grace, God's accommodated glory, and with redeemed intellect we seek to make sense of God's speech and his world. Consequently, while intellectual ability proves a significant help in the task of theology, it is humility that will characterize those who pursue theology in the proper posture.

ON THE ROLE OF PRAYER IN CHRISTIAN THEOLOGY

The conclusion that ought to become clear from the above work on divine accommodation is that theology is possible because God has willed it so. There are simultaneously true realities that God, at the same time, is incomprehensible and yet wants to be known. Out of the

---

[6]Webster, *Domain of the Word*, 140. Webster says earlier in the essay, "Revelation is an act of accommodation, by which of his charity God tempers knowledge of himself to finite modes of knowing" (138). Junius calls this kind of accommodation which moves the archetype toward the ectype the work of a "craftsman." He writes: "Therefore, a very serious topic remains concerning its form and manner. These two concepts in our definition we touched upon separately in a few words when we said that this theology was fashioned from the archetypal one through the communication of grace. For form, from whatever craftsman it arises, is properly constituted as twofold: the one exists in the mind of the craftsman, while the other is in his work." *TTT*, 115. Theology is therefore possible because the craftsman is effective.

[7]*TTT*, 99, emphasis added.

plenitude of his goodness, God not only wants to be known but makes himself known through revealing himself in human speech. Indeed, prayer is the mode of humility through which we enter proper contemplation of the incomprehensible God.

The notion that theology is possible if and only if God wills it is not merely a conclusion based upon theological reasoning alone. On the contrary, God's allowing for theological development is an idea found in the biblical data as well. Given the soteriological complexities found within the sixth chapter of Hebrews, it might be easy to miss, but this chapter contains a three-worded caveat that is significant for this final chapter.

Beginning the chapter, the anonymous author of Hebrews begins by discussing what he considers to be "the elementary doctrines of Christ." The author suggests that for the sake of Christian maturity, the audience ought to be moving past the elementary doctrines and pressing into those doctrines which are of deeper spiritual truths. Of the elementary doctrines, the author lists, "Let us leave the elementary doctrine of Christ and go on to maturity, not laying again a foundation of repentance from dead works and of faith toward God, and of instruction about washings, the laying on of hands, the resurrection of the dead, and eternal judgement" (Heb 6:1-2). These five doctrines comprise the elementary doctrines the audience is called to "leave" that they might "go on to maturity." However, the author of Hebrews includes an important caveat about the possibility of pushing beyond the elementary doctrines into more doctrinal maturity. The author writes, in the third verse, "And this we will do *if God permits*" (emphasis added).

It seems that a product of God's plenitude is the conclusion that he was under no obligation to make himself known and knowable to his creation. Yet the fullness of beatitude God enjoys notwithstanding, the Lord still went about the economic activity of self-disclosure. Pulling together the notion of God's eternal plenitude and his activity of revelation, it seems to indicate that God's gracious act of accommodation is not in any way a gain for him or a fulfillment of a lack in the revealer. On the contrary, the one who sits in the seat of benefit from God's revelation is the one who receives the revelation, not the revealer. The simple yet profound truth to Christian revelation is that God *wants* to be known; moreover, we see in the biblical text that since the revelation has a *telos*—the knowing, naming, and enjoyment of God—he has tied the mode of revelation to himself. Consider the prerequisite conditions of doing successful Christian theology. First, the entire enterprise would be one of hopelessness without divine accommodation. Second, as John Webster notes, theology is the work of the "regenerate intellect" and therefore is a spiritual act; this act can be imitated within a secular framework yet will remain unfulfilled without the illuminating and regenerative work of the Holy Spirit.[8] Christian theology and spiritually are inseparable. Third, and finally, Christian theology calls for the permission of the Lord. If we are to take seriously the claims of Hebrews 6, the student of the divine will not see progress into doctrinal maturity apart from God's permission to gain such progress. These three prerequisites within the task of theology come together to create a rather strong argumentation that within Christian prolegomena the antecedent condition of any successful contemplation or discourse about God is none other than prayer.

As the God we consider is incomprehensible to our minds and ineffable with our language, and as the possibility of our studying him is predicated on his accommodating his own glory, we will move from the elementary doctrines of Christ into maturity *if God permits.*

Theology in the second person. If one spends time with some of the theological texts of antiquity, it is not uncommon to see the intermingling of doctrinal exposition and explicit prayers or the beseeching of

---

[8]Webster writes, "Christian theology is biblical reasoning. It is the redeemed intellect's reflective apprehension of God's gospel address through the embassy of Scripture, enabled and corrected by God's presence, and having fellowship with him as its end." Webster, *Domain of the Word,* 128.

the Lord's guidance. Theological antiquity is quite full of examples of high-level theological discourse situated between prayers and pleas. Insisting that prayer be the proper first step in Christian theological method might come across as unacademic. One may opine that beginning the theological enterprise in prayer is substandard within the theological academia today. While possibly failing to meet certain contemporary criteria of academic method, weaving prayer throughout the unfolding of theology seems to be the norm for much of theological antiquity. For example, Augustine opens his influential work *De Trinitate* by stating, "Therefore, with the help of the Lord our God and as far as lies in our power, we shall endeavor to give an explanation of that very thing which they demand, namely, that the Trinity is the one, only, and true God, and that one rightly says, believes, and understands that the Father, the Son, and the Holy Spirit are of one and the same substance or essence." He goes on to say that he will achieve this operation through the aid of Scripture and God himself, saying, "But we must first find out by an appeal to the authority of the Sacred Scriptures whether faith is in a position to do so. Next, if God is willing and grants us His help, we shall perhaps render such a service to these garrulous disputants." In the same vein, Anselm's *Proslogion* is an exemplary work in seamlessly shifting from erudite exposition within theology proper and Christian proclamation and prayer. The medieval theologian begins the work writing, "Come then, Lord my God, teach my heart where and how to seek you, where and how to find You . . . I was made in order to see You, and I have not yet accomplished what I was made for."[9]

Augustine and Anselm, in this way, become exemplary in what Helmut Thielicke briefly discusses as doing theology in the second person rather than the third. Given that the enterprise of theology is

---

[9]Anselm, *The Major Works: Monologion, Proslogion, and Why God Became Man* (Oxford: Oxford University Press, 1998), 85. Ellen Charry shows numerically the significant role prayer plays in *Proslogion*: "Only three of the twenty-three chapters of the *Proslogion* are philosophical, while the remainder constitute a prayer to God." Ellen Charry, *By the Renewing of Your Minds: The Pastoral Function of Christian Doctrine* (Oxford: Oxford University Press, 1999), 162.

only possible due to divine accommodation in which God allows the creature to apprehend his being and action though he be incomprehensible, theology is situated in *personal* revelation. God reveals *himself.* Moreover, God self-discloses to a people. Thielicke points out, therefore, when we shift from considering theological endeavors from pursual of a personal and ecclesial relationship to one of mere technical reference, we have begun to misstep in the task of theology. In other words, the theologian moves into dangerous territory if the task of Christian theology moves exclusively into exposition of data and not exaltation of the redeemer.

To further illustrate his point, Thielicke reminds readers the difference between what examining God in the third person, or merely talking *about* God sounds like compared to considering God in the first or second person, that is, talking *to* God through prayer. Thielicke reminds us that the first ever recorded incident of speech about God from the third person is when the serpent asks, "Did God actually say?" (Gen 3:1).[10] Compare this to Christ's piercing cry of dereliction in which he declares, "*My* God, *my* God, why have *you* forsaken me?" (Mt 27:46, emphasis added). Thielicke calls the subtle shift most obvious in those who have moved toward the "phenomena called the history-of-religion-school."[11]

While the shift from second person to third person may feel subtle, it has significant methodological implications. The Augustine-Anselm methodology of beginning, mixing, and ending the theological enterprise with prayer keeps in focus the notion of the *telos* of God's revelation—self-disclosure toward a relationship with creatures. Working to keep prayer in theological method prevents the student of theology from treating the biblical text in a way it was never meant to be treated—like a mere set of data points to be scrutinized.

---

[10]Helmut Thielicke, *A Little Exercise for Young Theologians*, trans. Charles Taylor (Grand Rapids, MI: Eerdmans, 1962), 63-64.

[11]Thielicke, *Little Exercise*, 63.

The limp of Jacob, the awe of Moses. A final idea is important in developing prayer's role in theological method in hopes to work toward a theologically informed humility. The final point, bringing variegated emphasis of this chapter together, is that (1) since theology is only possible because God has accommodated his glory, and (2) we therefore ought to treat the theological enterprise as imminently relational which necessitates prayer, we will therefore (3) often have to *work* toward theological clarity and nuance as God permits doctrinal maturity and our theological and biblical reasoning allow. In his work detailing the metaphysical context of divine revelation, Matthew Levering has a passing quote that captures what I am after here with memorable strength. Levering writes, "For this earlier theological tradition, the Church's mode of contemplating the triune God in Scripture requires a difficult metaphysical *ascesis—the limp of Jacob, the awe of Moses*—because her God is salvifically and radically strange."[12]

Levering's phrase "the limp of Jacob, the awe of Moses" serves as something like a summary for the kind of personal piety and prayer called for in Christian theological method this chapter is after. He is, of course, alluding to two different scriptural pericopes. As for the "limp of Jacob," Levering is referring to the scene recorded in Genesis 32:22-32 in which Jacob wrestles with the Lord leading to his dislocated hip. As for the "awe of Moses," Levering is referring to the Sinai scene in which Moses converses with the Lord and comes back with a radiance such that his fellow Israelite are fearful to even look at him (Ex 34:29-35). Together, these two passages show something of the "ascesis" needed to do proper Christian theology. Given that God is incomprehensible, there will be a "wrestling" as the task of finite creature's contemplating the infinite God will call for a lifetime of prayer and pursual of the intellectual life. Yet while the infinite God is incomprehensible, due to the grace of divine accommodation, he *is*

---

[12]Matthew Levering, *Scripture and Metaphysics: Aquinas and the Renewal of Trinitarian Theology* (Malden, MA: Blackwell, 2004), 3, emphasis added.

knowable. So when the creature does lay hold of God through wrestling with the Lord, it ought to lead to a vision of God in which the creature leaves radiating the glory of him whom they have seen. The limp of Jacob and the awe of Moses is something of a clarifying call toward what the Christian theological life will look like. Like Jacob, we grab hold of the Lord and say, "I will not let you go unless you bless me" (Gen 32:26). Also, like Moses, because we know God to be a gracious God who actually *wants to be known* and has taken the pains *to be known*, we will boldly request, "show me your glory" and intellectually gaze at the glory of the Lord until we radiate to others the goodness we have seen in looking at him (Ex 33:18). In conclusion, as Scripture is God's accommodation to humankind, whom he wishes to know him, and as theological maturity is predicated on his "permitting it," part of what it means to possess true theological humility is to recognize our position as *receivers* of theology and therefore have a robust category of prayer in our theological method.

THEOLOGIA VIATORUM

A final implication of divine incomprehensibility, which roots humility in the soul of the doctrinal participant, is the difficult-but-blessed realization that the task of Christian contemplation is not a completable task. Especially on this side of beatific vision, humankind participates in the theological enterprise with a strong category of *theologia viatorum*—a theology of pilgrims.[13] We again return to the pen of John Webster who writes of the *theologia viatorum* when making use of the archetypal-ectypal distinction. Webster notes, "Archetypal theology is God's self-knowledge; ectypal theology is the knowledge of God possible for finite rational creatures. The former is God's simple, eternal intelligence of himself, the latter can be described in its temporal

---

[13]Muller's definition of the term: "a term applied to the incomplete or imperfect theology of believers in the world, in contrast to the theology of those who have reached their end in God." *Dictionary of Latin and Greek Theological Terms: Drawn Principally from Protestant Scholastic Theology* (Grand Rapids, MI: Baker Academic, 2017), 366.

unfolding—before the defection of Adam as *theologia ante lapsum*, after the fall as *theologia viatorum*, in paradise as *theologia beatorum*."[14]

Our theological context is situated between the fall and the beatific vision and is therefore a theology of pilgrims. As revelation progresses, so too does the theological accuracy and contemplation of humankind. There is a teleological end to both theological revelation and theological contemplation—an ever-increasing knowledge and relationship between the Creator and the creature, which will culminate in the *theologia beatorum*. Knowing the limitations due to incomprehensibility and the telos due the *theologian beatorum* allows the creature to know that God is simultaneously unknowable and knowable—unknowable univocally and knowable analogically—and so there ought to be a deep-rooted humility knowing that our theological wisdom and language takes place in the intersection of the already/not yet. "The eschatological orientation of theological discourse, whose complexity will, in the end, be brought back to unity in the beatific vision" says Emmanuel Durand. He continues, "This enables us to accept the imperfections and complexity of our knowledge of God and to maintain an authentic hope for the believer's understanding."[15] As creatures, we will experience many instances of theological stumbling given that we do theology as wayfarers on the way home; yet, stumble as we may, the beatific vision gives us hope that God's incomprehensibility will be an eternal delight to our mind's eye on our arrival across the Jordan.

Theology as pilgrims is best done in the covenantal family of Christ's body—the church. Given the contextual situation of our theological contemplation between the fall and the beatific vision, we know that

---

[14]Webster, *Domain of the Word*, 139. He continues toward the *telos* of theological contemplation: "In so far as it takes its Christian confession seriously, theology has the resources to interpret its pathos as embraced by the divine *ordination*. Theology does not measure its situation in terms of an ideal of rational perfection and security, but in terms of the way in which God conducts the redeemed through time to their homeland, supplying them with what is necessary to bring them to the knowledge of the blessed" (141).

[15]Durand, *Divine Speech*, 279.

we are prone to fail, even failure of mind, and therefore need other regenerate minds holding us accountable to the biblical text. The Christian is in the greatest place of theological health when their doctrinal contemplation is covenantally bound to a people who will watch both their soul and their confession. Divine incomprehensibility renders confessional fidelity difficult, and therefore those of us who wish to have an active intellectual imagination ought have the humility to bring others into our thought life so we might watch our life and our doctrine closely (see 1 Tim 4:16).

CONCLUSION

Theological humility is something greater than mere virtue. Given the contextual situation that springs forth from the doctrine of divine incomprehensibility, theological humility is an ontological necessity that recognizes that the possibility of theology is a direct result of God's gracious act of accommodation. The Creator-creature distinction renders God incomprehensible and ineffable such that it would be hopeless to do the theological task apart from God's gracious communication. However, given that God has gone about the economic activity of self-disclosure, we creatures sit not in a place of hopelessness, but humility. Given the theological task's reliance on accommodated divine revelation, we do not pursue Christian theology as those who are creators of intellectual brilliance but instead as those who are radical receivers of divine speech in human words and of the person of Christ incarnate.

We ought to be eager to affirm, then, that due to incomprehensibility there is no hope for theological ascending beyond our faculties. Indeed, we need not ascend, as our God has done the work of condescending. In his work on the Trinity, Thomas Joseph White argues this when he suggests that the life of the Trinity is accessible only by means of God's gracious gift. It is revelation that cannot be arrived at through human contemplation alone, but received from elsewhere. He writes:

This kind of epistemic humility is entirely reasonable and warranted, but also complementary to our simultaneous acknowledgement in faith of the gratuity and fittingness of God's unveiling of the Trinity. Just as we know God in a limited way in his natural unity, so too we are able to be receptive to the gift of knowledge of God's inner life as Trinity, which is given to us from 'above and beyond' all our natural capacities. This is a truth acknowledged not only outside or before Christian theology but also from within, in our very way of studying the mystery of the Holy Trinity.[16]

This is why creatures must pursue the theological vocation with humility, knowing no intellectual or linguistic power could have bridged the distinction between the Creator and the creature. So we recognize our place as receivers of theological truth by way of divine accommodation and therefore have a vigorous understanding of prayer's role in Christian theology as we will only move from theological infancy into maturity on the basis of God's own permission (Heb 6:1-3). We wrestle like Jacob, laying hold of God through prayer in hopes that he will permit us to obtain the awe of Moses. All the while, humility remains at the heart of our enterprise, knowing we do theology as pilgrims—*theologia viatorum*—on the way home.

---

[16]White, *The Trinity*, 225.

Working Theses on Incomprehensibility and Theological Method

Principles for Knowing and Naming the Incomprehensible God

> *Whatever you do anyway, remember that these things*
>
> *are mysteries and that if they were such that we could*
>
> *understand them, they wouldn't be worth understanding.*
>
> *A God you understood would be less than yourself.*
>
> **Flannery O'Connor**

IT IS MY HOPE THAT the emphases of this book have become rather clear: my hope is that it is God who is incomprehensible, not the conclusions or emphases of this work. In line with this hope, and out of a desire to serve the reader, I offer an appendix by way of ten "working theses" concerning the doctrine of incomprehensibility. Of course, these ten points do not represent all the conclusions through the book in its entirety, as I have labored to say more than these ten theses. Also, the full nuance for each of these ten theses comes by way of the preceding chapters. Yet my goal for this appendix is to bring together the many variegated nuances worked on throughout these pages and provide the reader with something of a summary of the previous seven chapters by way of ten working theses.

Thesis one: The doctrine of divine incomprehensibility is a revealed doctrine that has exegetical justification as well as support from theological reasoning. The Scriptures declare, demonstrate, and demand the doctrine of divine incomprehensibility.

Thesis two: The proper dogmatic location for the doctrine of divine incomprehensibility is the Creator-creature distinction. It is due to the distinction between God and his creation that he is out of the intellectual jurisdiction of humankind.

Thesis three: As the proper dogmatic location for the doctrine of divine incomprehensibility is the Creator-creature distinction, we negate alternative locations. While notions of "the size of God" or the "noetic effects of sin" may impact the creature's ability to comprehend God, God is first and foremost incomprehensible not because he is merely bigger than sinful creatures but because he is altogether different from created beings.

Thesis four: Due to God's being incomprehensible, he is out of both the intellectual and linguistic comprehension of creatures. Divine incomprehensibility and divine ineffability are therefore distinct but related theological affirmations.

Thesis five: Since God is outside the intellectual and linguistic jurisdiction of creatures, we cannot possess archetypal knowledge of God, nor can we name God univocally.

Thesis six: While naming God univocally is not obtainable for creatures, we can hope for more than theological equivocation. Due to God's accommodation, the Spirit's illumination, and creaturely participation, we can meaningfully name God using analogical language.

Thesis seven: While archetypal knowledge of God is not obtainable for creatures, we can still hope to possess meaningful ectypal knowledge as God has condescended and revealed himself in correspondence to our faculties allowing creatures to participate in divine wisdom.

Thesis eight: Ectypal knowledge and analogical language are meaningful and true. These are not "lesser" forms of knowledge and language for God, rather these are the forms of knowledge and language fitting for the creature.

Thesis nine: Given that theological contemplation is only possible because of God's gracious act of accommodation, Christian theologians ought to see theological humility not only as virtuous but ontological necessary since the task of theology would be impossible unless God permits (Heb 6:3).

Thesis ten: Divine incomprehensibility brings into focus the eschatological telos of theological contemplation as we currently work as pilgrims, *theologia viatorum*, on our way toward the *theologia beatorum*. As we do theology in the crosshairs of the already/not yet, between the fall and the beatific vision, we continue to apprehend, but never comprehend, God.

TABLES AND FIGURES

THROUGHOUT THIS BOOK, I have attempted to make a few conversations which can feel complex and unruly accessible for readers. One method of doing this is to provide summaries of differing positions or ideas through navigable charts. In hopes to serve the reader, the varying charts used throughout this book are brought here in one place.

Table 1.1. Possible Misconceptions About Divine Incomprehensibility

Possible Misconception	Potential Brief Answer
Incomprehensibility is synonymous with God being un-comprehended.	Divine incomprehensibility is not asserting that God is *yet to be comprehended*. It is not the case that with enough theological evolution and contemplation, the creature will arrive one day at a full and complete comprehension of God's essence. God is not only *currently* "un-comprehended"; he is the ever-incomprehensible one who dwells in unapproachable light (1 Tim 6:16).
Incomprehensibility is part of the noetic effects of the fall.	The doctrine of divine incomprehensibility is not rooted in the intellectual capacity of the creature *alone*. Rather, the doctrine is rooted in God's otherness. We cannot comprehend God not *just* because we are fallen, but because we are the creature, and he is the Creator.
Incomprehensibility means that we can have *no* positive knowledge of God.	The doctrine of divine incomprehensibility does not entail *mere apophasis*. Instead, *cataphatic* knowledge of God is possible due to his gracious accommodation. Yet theologians must still be nuanced about the nature of positive names and theology.
The incarnation of Jesus Christ as the fullest revelation of God nullifies the need to affirm divine incomprehensibility.	While the economic act of Jesus' incarnation is a real and even the *best* self-revelation of God, it is nevertheless itself a form of accommodated glory. While we can say, with Jesus, that those who have seen Jesus have seen the

Possible Misconception	Potential Brief Answer
	Father (Jn 14:9), we must affirm still, also with Jesus, that no one has truly seen the Father but the one begotten Son (Jn 6:46).
While the incarnation might not nullify the doctrine of divine incomprehensibility, the full concept of the economy does.	The church has, throughout its long history, affirmed that God is best known through his works in the economy of redemption. Nevertheless, God *in se* cannot be made synonymous with *what God does* in the economy. Moreover, according to Ps 139:5-6 and John 21:25, even the fullness of the economy is incomprehensible.
Affirming incomprehensibility will diminish Christian's zeal to contemplate their Lord.	The doctrine of divine incomprehensibility is a *revealed* doctrine. Meaning, the God who dwells in unapproachable light (1 Tim 6:16) has *told* us he is incomprehensible and yet still invites us to contemplate his glory through his gracious acts of accommodation. Instead of demotivating the Christian in theological reflection in the lifelong process of Christian contemplation, we are invited to explore the incomprehensible one in whom we move and live and have our being (Acts 17:28).
The doctrine of divine incomprehensibility and divine ineffability is self-defeating because such an affirmation is itself a kind of comprehension and articulation.	Again, a vital point in a healthy understanding of divine incomprehensibility and its corollary doctrine, divine ineffability, is that God has *revealed* himself as such. In affirming the apophatic concepts of incomprehensibility and ineffability we stand on the epistemic ground of God's self-disclosure; from that ground do we draw the authority to affirm these two negations of the divine.

Table 2.1. Incomprehensibility in the Biblical Data

Declare	These passages can be exegeted to show an explicit declaration of God's incomprehensibility.
Psalm 139:1-6	"O LORD, you have searched me and known me! You know when I sit down and when I rise up; you discern my thoughts from afar. You search out my path and my lying down and are acquainted with all my ways. Even before a word is on my tongue, behold, O LORD, you know it altogether. You hem me in, behind and before, and lay your hand upon me. *Such knowledge is too wonderful for me; it is high; I cannot attain it*" (emphasis added).
Psalm 145:1-3	"I will extol you, my God and King, and bless your name forever and ever. Every day I will bless you and praise your name forever and ever. *Great is the LORD, and greatly to be praised, and his greatness is unsearchable*" (emphasis added).
Isaiah 55:8-9	"For my thoughts are not your thoughts, neither are your ways my ways, declares the LORD. For as the heavens are higher than the earth, so are my ways higher than your ways and my thoughts than your thoughts."
Romans 11:33-34	"Oh, the depth of the riches and wisdom and knowledge of God! How unsearchable are his judgments and how inscrutable his ways! For who has known the mind of the Lord, or who has been his counselor."

1 Corinthians 2:9-11	"But, as it is written, 'What no eye has seen, nor ear heard, nor the heart of man imagined, what God has prepared for those who love him'—these things God has revealed to us through the Spirit. . . . For who knows a person's thoughts except the spirit of that person, which is in him? So also no one comprehends the thoughts of God except the Spirit of God."
1 Timothy 6:15b-16	"He who is the blessed and only Sovereign, the King of kings and Lord of lords, who alone has immortality, who dwells in unapproachable light, whom no one has ever seen or can see. To him be honor and eternal dominion. Amen."
Demonstrate	**These passages *implicitly demonstrate* God's incomprehensibility by virtue of his majesty and mystery.**
Exodus 33:18-20	"Moses said, 'Please show me your glory.' And he said, 'I will make all my goodness pass before you and will proclaim before you my name "the LORD" . . . but,' he said, 'you cannot see my face, for man shall not see me and live.'"
Job 11:7-8	"Can you find out the deep things of God? Can you find out the limit of the Almighty? It is higher than heaven—what can you do? Deeper than Sheol—what can you know?"
Job 38-40	"Where were you when I laid the foundation of the earth? Tell me, if you have understanding. Who determined its measurements—surely you know! Or who stretched the line upon it? On what were its bases sunk, or who laid its cornerstone, when the morning stars sang together and all the sons of God shouted for joy?"
John 1:17-18	"For the law was given through Moses; grace and truth came through Jesus Christ. *No one has ever seen God*; the only God, who is at the Father's side, he has made him known" (emphasis added).
1 Corinthians 13:12	"For now we see in a mirror dimly, but then face to face. Now I know in part; then I shall know fully, even as I have been fully known."
Demand	**These passages *demand* the doctrine of God's incomprehensibility by being held together with corollary passages and doctrines in constructive biblical and theological reasoning.**
Exodus 3:13-15	"Then Moses said to God, 'If I come to the people of Israel and say to them, "The God of your fathers has sent me to you," and they ask me, "What is his name?" what shall I say to them?' God said to Moses, 'I AM WHO I AM.' And he said, 'Say this to the people of Israel: "I AM has sent me to you."' God also said to Moses, 'Say this to the people of Israel: "The LORD, the God of your fathers, the God of Abraham, the God of Isaac, and the God of Jacob, has sent me to you." This is my name forever, and thus I am to be remembered throughout all generations.'"
Psalm 90:2	"Before the mountains were brought forth, or ever you had formed the earth and the world, from everlasting to everlasting you are God."
Malachi 3:6	"For I the LORD do not change; therefore you, O children of Jacob, are not consumed."
Job 11:7-9	"Can you find out the deep things of God? Can you find out the limit of the Almighty? It is higher than heaven—what can you do? Deeper than Sheol—what can you know."

Passages on negative and positive names of God.	Readers could turn to doctrines within theology proper like simplicity, infinitude, incorporeality, aseity, pure act, and the like to see how God's essence and existence is *wholly other* than the existence of the creatures. These passages, taken together, seem to *demand* the doctrine of divine incomprehensibility.

Table 3.1. Ascent and ineffability in *Oration* 28

Person	Ascent as Illustration	Emphasis on Ineffability
First, Gregory himself as a consecrated theologian.	Ascends the mountain of the divine: "I eagerly ascend the mount—or, to speak truer, ascend in eager hope matched with anxiety for my frailty—that I may enter the cloud and company with God" (OR 28.2).	Even atop the mountain as a consecrated theologian: "But when I directed my gaze I scarcely saw the averted figure of God . . . peering in I saw not the nature prime, self-apprehended, the nature as it abides within the first veil and is hidden by the Cherubim . . . but as it reaches us at its furthest removed from God, being, so far as I can understand . . . Thus and thus only can you speak of God" (OR 28.3).
Second, the apostle Paul.	Paul's ascent to the third heaven: "Had Paul been able to express the experienced gained from the third heaven, and his progress, ascent, or assumption to it" (OR 28.20).	Paul doesn't attempt to describe or articulate his experience: "Since they were ineffable, let them have the tribute of our silence" (OR 28.20).
Third, and finally, the hearer of Gregory's oration.	From OR 28.21-28.30, Gregory takes his listeners on their own "ascent" from considering themselves in 28.21 to the highest heaven in 28.30. In order, Gregory calls to mind: 28.22 = Human beings themselves 28.23 = The animal kingdom on land 28.24 = The animal kingdom in the sea 28.25 = The animal kingdom in the air 28.26 = The plants and their fruit 28.27 = All the seas and waters of the earth 28.28 = The air, clouds, and all things in the sky 28.29 = The entire cosmos, planets, and stars 28.30-31 = The angelic hosts of heaven	In considering this hypothetical ascent from humans themselves up to the heavenly hosts: "Even the nature of beings on the second level is too much for our minds, let alone God's primal and unique, not to say all-transcending, nature" (OR 28.31).

Table 5.1. Possible Locations for Divine Incomprehensibility

Location	Meaning	Appropriate place to locate?
Sin	Locating incomprehensibility in sin argues that God is incomprehensible to the creature due to the noetic effects of the fall. In this model the creature cannot comprehend God because sin has clouded the intellectual ability of the creature.	No. While sin *does* impact the creatures' ability to contemplate God, there are creatures *not* tainted by sin who nevertheless still cannot fully comprehend God's essence such as angelic beings and prelapsarian humans.
Size	Locating incomprehensibility in size argues that God is incomprehensible to the creature due to God's being infinitely bigger than the creature. In this model the creature cannot comprehend God because God is beyond the scope of human intellect.	No. While God is "beyond the scope" of human intellect, it is not due to God's being merely *larger* than the creature. Rather, God's essence is not that it renders God like creatures, just infinitely bigger, but instead renders him altogether different. He is not merely larger in size but different in kind.
Creator-creature distinction	Locating incomprehensibility in the Creator-creature distinction argues that the reason God is incomprehensible to the creature is his being altogether different in kind than the creature. In this model the creature cannot comprehend God as the creature cannot bridge the distinction between the one who creates and the ones created.	Yes. The distinction between he who created all things and those who are created is not traversable by the creature. For, the creature's existence is clothed in temporality, finitude, complexity, mutability, and the like.

Table 6.1. Divine Accommodation in Scripture

	Definition	Form of Accommodation	Examples
Anthropomorphism	Attributing to God creature-like parts and positions.	As an infinite and incorporeal spirit, God condescends to those who dwell in finite corporeal bodies.	Sight (Deut 11:12) Feet (Gen 3:8) Arms (Ps 89:10) Wings (Jer 49:22) Tongue (Is 30:27)
Anthropopathism	Attributing to God creature-like passions and volition.	As the simple and impassible Creator, God condescends to the passionate and emotive creatures.	Jealous (Ex 20:5) Angry (Job 4:9) Regretful (1 Sam 15:11) Fear (Deut 32:27) Repentance (Gen 6:6)

Anthropochronism	Attributing to God creature-like time and chronology.	As him who is atemporal and does not experience successive moments of time, God condescends to those who dwell within time.	In the beginning (Gen 1:1) First and last (Rev 22:13) One day/1,000 years (2 Pet 3:8)

Table 6.2. Equivocal, Univocal, and Analogical Language in Theology

	Definition	Example	Use in Theological Language
Equivocal	When one term is used to signify two entities which do not share similitude or relationship.	"He used a baseball *bat* to scare the *bat* out of his attic."	*Theological despair*: if none of our vocabulary could meaningfully describe God, it would lead to a theological despair as we could not properly praise or name God.
Univocal	When one term is used to signify two entities which have an exactness of quality or rela-tionship.	"The baseball field and soccer pitch both have *green* grass." "Aristotle and Plato are both *humans*."	*Theological idolatry*: if our words could actually capture the very essence of God, it would lead to a linguistic idolatry.
Analogical	When one term is used to signify two entities in which one signification is an analogy or shadow of the other.	"My biological father is *good* to me, and my Heavenly Father is *good* to me."	*Proper theology*: While our words do not describe God *in himself*, they nevertheless are meaningful and true. Our words analogously signify what God actually is in *himself*.

Table 6.3. Franciscus Junius on Archetypal and Ectypal Theology

	Archetypal Theology	Ectypal Theology
Definition	*"Archetypal Theology is the divine wisdom of divine matters. Indeed, we stand in awe before this and do not seek to trace it out."*	*"Ectypal theology, whether taken in itself, as they say, or relatively in relation to something else, is the wisdom of divine matters, fashioned by God from the archetype of Himself, through the communi-cation of grace for His own glory."*

	Archetypal Theology	Ectypal Theology
Epistemological Range	Available only to God as the fullness of wisdom and knowledge of himself and those in relation to himself. *"The former [Archetypal] is the very same thing as unbounded wisdom, which God possesses concerning His own person and all other things, as they have been set in order with respect to Him necessarily, individually, and by an uninterrupted relation among themselves."*	Available to the creature, by the grace of accommodation. *"God has fashioned the second kind of theology on the model of the divine and immutable exemplar, proportionally to the creatures' capacity."* *"The second theology is that wisdom which the creatures have concerning God according to their own manner and concerning those things that are oriented toward God through His communication of Himself."*
Essential or Relative	Essential: Exists in God himself and is therefore prototypical. *"For that essential, archetypal theology is a characteristic of the nature of God, and part (as we would put it) of that infinite knowledge which in God is essential. Whatever is essential, moreover, is agreed that this is properly assigned to the same genus, together with the actual essence of which that this is essential."*	Relative: Exists as a grace and is therefore not prototypical. *"Nonessential and created, or dispositional; this you might also conveniently call ectypal, as a certain copy and, rather, shadowy image of the formal, divine, and essential theological image."*
Incommunicable or Communicable	Incommunicable: Archetypal theology is the wisdom of God in himself which is wholly inaccessible to creatures and therefore creatures participate in the imprint of the archetypal through the analogical ectypal theology.	Communicable: Ectypal theology is the revealed imprint of archetypal theology in which God takes into account the limitations of the creatures and accommodates their finitude in self-revelation.
Attributes	*Uncreated wisdom* *Essential* *Absolute* *Infinite* *In all aspects simultaneously present* *Incommunicable* *Lacking nothing* *Containing no variation* *Devoid of all defects including parts, change, or motion.*	Created revelation Transmitted as an imprint The "emanation" of the prototype *"Fashioned by God"* *"Wisdom of divine matters communicated to things created, according to the capacity of the created things themselves."*

BIBLIOGRAPHY

Adams, Marilyn McCord. "Praying the Proslogion." In *The Rationality of Belief and the Plurality of Faith*, edited by Thomas Senor. Ithaca, NY: Cornell University Press, 1995.

Alexander, T. Desmond, and Brian S. Rosner, eds. *New Dictionary of Biblical Theology*. Downers Grove, IL: InterVarsity Press, 2000.

Alfsvåg, Knut. "'With God All Things Are Possible'—Luther and Kierkegaard on the Relation Between Immutability, Necessity and Possibility." *Neue Zeitschrift für Systematische Theologie und Religionsphilosophie* 60, no. 1 (2018): 2-26.

Allen, Michael. *Grounded in Heaven: Recentering Christian Hope and Life on God*. Grand Rapids, MI: Eerdmans, 2018.

———. *Sanctification*. Grand Rapids, MI: Zondervan, 2017.

———. *The Knowledge of God: Essays on God, Christ, and the Church*. London: T&T Clark, 2022.

Allen, Michael, and Scott R. Swain, eds. *Christian Dogmatics: Reformed Theology for the Church Catholic*. Grand Rapids, MI: Baker Academic, 2016.

———. *Reformed Catholicity: The Promise of Retrieval for Theology and Biblical Interpretation*. Grand Rapids, MI: Baker, 2015.

Allen, R. Michael, ed. *Theological Commentary: Evangelical Perspectives*. New York: T&T Clark, 2011.

Anatolios, Khaled. *Retrieving Nicaea: The Development and Meaning of Trinitarian Doctrine*. Grand Rapids, MI: Baker Academic, 2018.

Anonymous. *The Cloud of Unknowing and Other Works*. London: Penguin, 2001.

Anselm. *The Major Works: Monologion, Proslogion, and Why God Became Man*. Edited by Brian Davies and G. R. Evans. Oxford: Oxford University Press, 1998.

Ayres, Lewis. *Nicaea and Its Legacy: An Approach to Fourth-Century Trinitarian Theology*. Oxford: Oxford University Press, 2009.

Asbill, Brian D. *The Freedom of God for Us: Karl Barth's Doctrine of Divine Aseity*. London: T&T Clark, 2015.

Athanasius. *Against the Arians*. In *Nicene and Post-Nicene Fathers*, second series. Edited by Philip Schaff and Henry Wace. Peabody, MA: Hendrickson, 2012.

————. *On the Incarnation*. In *Nicene and Post-Nicene Fathers*, second series. Edited by Philip Schaff and Henry Wace. Peabody, MA: Hendrickson, 2012.

Augustine. *Confessions*. Translated by Henry Chadwick. Oxford: Oxford University Press, 1991.

————. *Letter to Dioscorus*. In *Nicene and Post-Nicene Fathers*, first series, vol. 1. Peabody, MA: Hendrickson, 2012.

————. *On Christian Doctrine*. In *Nicene and Post-Nicene Fathers*, first series. Edited by Philip Schaff. Peabody, MA: Hendrickson, 2012.

————. *On the Trinity*. In *Nicene and Post-Nicene Fathers: First Series*, vol. 3. Edited by Philip Schaff. Peabody, MA: Hendrickson, 2012.

Baines, Ronald S., et al. *Confessing the Impassible God: The Biblical, Classical, and Confessional Doctrine of Divine Impassibility*. Palmdale, CA: RBAP, 2015.

Balserak, Jon. *Divinity Compromised: A Study of Divine Accommodation in the Thought of John Calvin*. Dordrecht: Springer, 2006.

Barrett, Matthew. *Canon, Covenant and Christology: Rethinking Jesus and the Scriptures of Israel*. Downers Grove, IL: IVP Academic, 2020.

————. *None Greater: The Undomesticated Attributes of God*. Grand Rapids, MI: Baker Books, 2019.

————. *Simply Trinity: The Unmanipulated Father, Son, and Spirit*. Grand Rapids, MI: Baker Books, 2021.

Barth, Karl. *Church Dogmatics*. Edited by G. W. Bromiley and T. F. Torrance. Translated by T. H. L. Parker, W. B. Johnston, Harold Knight, and J. L. M. Haire. Edinburgh: T&T Clark, 1957.

————. "The Word of God and the Task of the Ministry." In *The Word of God and the Word of Man*. London: Hodder & Stoughton, 1928.

Basil of Caesarea. *Collected Letters of Saint Basil*. Vol. 3, *Letters 186-248*. Loeb Classical Library. Cambridge, MA: Harvard University Press, 1930.

Bavinck, Herman. *The Doctrine of God*. Edinburgh: Banner of Truth, 1977.

Baxter, Jason. *The Medieval Mind of C. S. Lewis: How Great Books Shaped a Great Mind*. Downers Grove, IL: InterVarsity Press, 2022.

Beeke, Joel R., and Paul M. Smalley. *Reformed Systematic Theology*. Vols. 1-2. Wheaton, IL: Crossway, 2019.

Beeley, Christopher A. *Gregory of Nazianzus on the Trinity and the Knowledge of God: In Your Light We Shall See Light*. Oxford: Oxford University Press, 2008.

Behr, John. *The Case Against Diodore and Theodore: Texts and Their Contexts*. Oxford: Oxford University Press, 2011.

Berkhof, Louis. *Systematic Theology*. Edinburgh: Banner of Truth, 1998.

Betz, John R. "After Heidegger and Marion: The Task of Christian Metaphysics Today." *Modern Theology* 34, no. 4 (2015): 565-97.

————. *Christ, the Logos of Creation: An Essay in Analogical Metaphysics*. Steubenville, OH: Emmaus Academic, 2023.

———. "Theology Without Metaphysics? A Reply to Kevin Hector." *Modern Theology* 31, no. 3 (2015): 488-500.

Billings, J. Todd. *Calvin, Participation, and the Gift: The Activity of Believers in Union with Christ*. New York: Oxford University Press, 2007.

———. *Union with Christ: Reframing Theology and Ministry for the Church*. Grand Rapids, MI: Baker Academic, 2011.

Bird, Michael F., and Scott Harrower, eds. *Trinity Without Hierarchy: Reclaiming Nicene Orthodoxy in Evangelical Theology*. Grand Rapids, MI: Kregel Publications, 2019.

Boersma, Hans. *Heavenly Participation: The Weaving of a Sacramental Tapestry*. Grand Rapids, MI: Eerdmans, 2011.

———. *Scripture as Real Presence: Sacramental Exegesis in the Early Church*. Grand Rapids, MI: Baker Academic, 2017.

———. *Seeing God: The Beatific Vision in Christian Tradition*. Grand Rapids, MI: Eerdmans, 2018.

Boyer, Steven D., and Christopher Hall. *The Mystery of God: Theology for Knowing the Unknowable*. Grand Rapids, MI: Baker Academic, 2012.

Bray, Gerald L. *The Doctrine of God*. Downers Grove, IL: IVP Academic, 1993.

———. *Documents of the English Reformation*. 3rd ed. Cambridge: James Clarke, 2020.

Brueggemann, Walter. *Theology of the Old Testament: Testimony, Dispute, Advocacy*. Minneapolis: Fortress, 2012.

Cajetan, Tommosa de Vio. *The Analogy of Names, and the Concept of Being*. Translated by Edward A. Bushinski. Eugene, OR: Wipf & Stock, 2009.

Calvin, John. *Daniel 7-12 and Hosea*. Grand Rapids, MI: Baker Books, 2009.

Campbell, Constantine R. *Paul and Union with Christ: An Exegetical and Theological Study*. Grand Rapids, MI: Zondervan, 2012.

Carabine, Deirdre. *The Unknown God: Negative Theology in the Platonic Tradition: Plato to Eriugena*. Lueven: Peeters, 2015.

Carter, Craig A. *Interpreting Scripture with the Great Tradition: Recovering the Genius of Premodern Exegesis*. Grand Rapids, MI: Baker Academic, 2018.

———. *Contemplating God with the Great Tradition: Recovering Classical Trinitarian Theism*. Grand Rapids, MI: Baker Academic, 2021.

Carson, D. A. *The Gospel According to John*. Pillar New Testament Commentary. Grand Rapids, MI: Eerdmans, 1991.

Charnock, Steven. *Works of Stephen Charnock*. Edinburgh: Banner of Truth, 2010.

Charry, Ellen. *By the Renewing of Your Minds: The Pastoral Function of Christian Doctrine*. Oxford: Oxford University Press, 1999.

Childs, Brevard S. *Biblical Theology of the Old and New Testaments: Theological Reflection on the Christian Bible*. Minneapolis: Fortress, 1993.

———. *The Struggle to Understand Isaiah as Christian Scripture*. Grand Rapids, MI: Eerdmans, 2004.

Clark, John C., and Marcus Peter Johnson. *The Incarnation of God: The Mystery of the Gospel as the Foundation of Evangelical Theology*. Wheaton, IL: Crossway, 2015.

Cole, R. A. *Exodus: An Introduction and Commentary*. Downers Grove, IL: InterVarsity Press, 1973.

Craig, William Lane. *God Over All: Divine Aseity and the Challenge of Platonism*. Oxford: Oxford University Press, 2016.

———. *Time and Eternity: Exploring God's Relationship to Time*. Wheaton, IL: Crossway, 2001.

Crisp, Oliver D. *Divinity and Humanity: The Incarnation Reconsidered*. Cambridge: Cambridge University Press, 2007.

———. *The Word Enfleshed: Exploring the Person and Work of Christ*. Grand Rapids, MI: Baker Academic, 2016.

Crisp, Oliver, and Fred Sanders, eds. *Advancing Trinitarian Theology: Explorations in Constructive Dogmatics*. Grand Rapids, MI: Zondervan, 2014.

———. *The Task of Dogmatics: Explorations in Theological Method*. Grand Rapids, MI: Zondervan, 2017.

Cross, Richard. *Duns Scotus*. Oxford: Oxford University Press, 1999.

Crowe, Brandon D. *The Last Adam: A Theology of the Obedient Life of Jesus in the Gospels*. Grand Rapids, MI: Baker Academic, 2017.

Cumming, Nicholas A. *Francis Turretin (1623–1687) and the Reformed Tradition*. Leiden: Brill, 2020.

Cyril of Alexandria. *Doctrinal Questions and Answers*. In *Select Letters*, edited by Lionel R. Wickham. Oxford: Oxford University Press.

———. *On the Unity of Christ*. Popular Patristics Series 13. Crestwood, NY: St. Vladimir's Seminary Press, 1995.

Cyril of Jerusalem. *Catechesis Six*. In *Cyril of Jerusalem*, translated by Edward Yarnell. London: Routledge, 2000.

Davies, Brian. *An Introduction to Philosophy of Religion*. 3rd ed. Oxford: Oxford University Press, 2004.

———. *Thomas Aquinas'* Summa Theologiae: *A Guide and Commentary*. Oxford: Oxford University Press, 2014.

Davies, Brian, and Brian Leftow. *The Cambridge Companion to Anselm*. Cambridge: Cambridge University Press, 2005.

Davidson, Ivor, and Murray A Rae, eds. *God of Salvation: Soteriology in Theological Perspective*. London: Routledge, 2011.

Davison, Andrew. *Participation in God: A Study in Christian Doctrine and Metaphysics*. Cambridge: Cambridge University Press, 2019.

DelCogliano, Mark. *Basil of Caesarea's Anti-Eunomian Theory of Names: Christian Theology and Late-Antique Philosophy in the Fourth-Century Trinitarian Controversy*. Leiden: Brill, 2010.

D'Ettore, Domenic. *Analogy After Aquinas: Logical Problems, Thomistic Answers*. Washington, DC: Catholic University of America Press, 2019.

Dennison, James T. *Reformed Confessions of the 16th and 17th Centuries in English Translation.* 4 vols. Grand Rapids, MI: Reformation Heritage, 2008.

Dodds, Michael J. *The Unchanging God of Love: Thomas Aquinas and Contemporary Theology on Divine Immutability.* 2nd ed. Washington, DC: Catholic University of America Press, 2008.

Dolezal, James E. *All That Is in God: Evangelical Theology and the Challenge of Classical Christian Theism.* Grand Rapids, MI: Reformation Heritage, 2017.

———. *God Without Parts: Divine Simplicity and the Metaphysics of God's Absoluteness.* Eugene, OR: Pickwick, 2011.

Duby, Steven J. *Divine Simplicity: A Dogmatic Account.* London: T&T Clark, 2016.

———. *God in Himself: Scripture, Metaphysics, and the Task of Christian Theology.* Downers Grove, IL: IVP Academic, 2019.

Durand, Emmanuel. *Divine Speech in Human Words: Thomistic Engagements with Scripture.* Washington, DC: Catholic University of America Press, 2022.

Emery, Giles. *The Trinity: An Introduction to Catholic Doctrine on the Triune God.* Translated by Matthew Levering. Washington, DC: Catholic University of America Press, 2011.

Emery, Gilles, and Matthew Levering, eds. *The Oxford Handbook of the Trinity.* New York: Oxford University Press, 2011.

Eunomius. *The Extant Works.* Translated by Richael Paul Vaggione. Oxford: Oxford University Press, 2002.

Fairbairn, Donald, and Ryan M. Reeves. *The Story of Creeds and Confessions: Tracing the Development of the Christian Faith.* Grand Rapids, MI: Baker Academic, 2019.

Feinberg, John S. *No One like Him.* Wheaton, IL: Crossway, 2006.

Ferguson, Sinclair B. *The Holy Spirit.* Contours of Christian Theology. Downers Grove, IL: InterVarsity Press, 1996.

Feser, Edward. *Scholastic Metaphysics: A Contemporary Introduction.* Lancaster: Editions Scholasticae, 2014.

Fesko, J. V. *Beyond Calvin: Union with Christ and Justification in Early Modern Reformed Theology.* Göttingen: Vandenhoeck & Ruprecht, 2012.

———. *Death in Adam, Life in Christ: The Doctrine of Imputation.* Ross-shire, UK: Christian Focus, 2016.

———. *The Trinity and the Covenant of Redemption.* Ross-shire, UK: Christian Focus, 2016.

Fishbane, Michael. "Through the Looking Glass: Reflections on Ezekiel 43:3, Numbers 12:8 and 1 Corinthians 13:8." *Hebrew Annual Review* 10 (1986): 63-75.

Frame, John M. *The Doctrine of God.* Phillipsburg, NJ: P&R, 2002.

———. *Systematic Theology: An Introduction to Christian Belief.* Phillipsburg, NJ: P&R, 2013.

Frei, Hans W. *The Eclipse of Biblical Narrative: A Study in Eighteenth and Nineteenth Century Hermeneutics.* New Haven, CT: Yale University Press, 1980.

Funkenstein, Amos. *Theology and the Scientific Imagination: From the Middle Ages to the Seventeenth Century.* Princeton, NJ: Princeton University Press, 1986.

Gavrilyuk, Paul. *The Suffering of an Impassible God: Dialectics of Patristic Thought*. Oxford: Oxford University Press, 2004.

Gill, John. *A Complete Body of Doctrinal and Practical Divinity*. Paris, AR: The Baptist Standard Bearer, 2007.

Gregory of Nazianzus. *On God and Christ: The Five Theological Orations and Two Letters to Cledonius*. Crestwood, NY: St Vladimir's Seminary Press, 2002.

Gregory of Nyssa. *Homilies on the Beatitudes*. Supplements to Vigiliae Christianae 52. Leiden: Brill, 2000.

Gunton, Colin E. *Act and Being: Toward a Theology of the Divine Attributes*. Grand Rapids, MI: Eerdmans, 2002.

Hanson, R. P. C. *The Search for the Christian Doctrine of God: The Arian Controversy, 318–381*. Grand Rapids, MI: Baker Academic, 2006.

———. *The Promise of Trinitarian Theology*. 2nd ed. New York: T&T Clark, 2003.

Hart, David Bentley. *The Beauty of the Infinite: The Aesthetics of Christian Truth*. Grand Rapids, MI: Eerdmans, 2005.

———. *The Experience of God: Being, Consciousness, Bliss*. New Haven, CT: Yale University Press, 2013.

———. *The Hidden and the Manifest: Essays in Theology and Metaphysics*. Grand Rapids, MI: Eerdmans, 2017.

Hartshorne, Charles. *Creative Synthesis and Philosophic Method*. London: Open Court, 1970.

———. *The Logic of Perfection: Neoclassical Metaphysics*. Lasalle, IL: Open Court, 1962.

Hector, Kevin. *Theology Without Metaphysics: God, Language, and the Spirit of Recognition*. Cambridge: Cambridge University Press, 2011.

Helm, Paul. *Eternal God: A Study of God Without Time*. Oxford: Oxford University Press, 2010.

———. *John Calvin's Ideas*. Oxford: Oxford University Press, 2004.

Henry, Carl F. H. *God, Revelation, and Authority*. 6 vols. Waco, TX: Word, 1979.

Hewitt, Simon. *Negative Theology and Philosophical Analysis: Only the Splendor of Light*. London: Palgrave Macmillan, 2020.

Hilary of Poitiers. *De Trinitate*. Translated by Stephen McKenna. Washington, DC: Catholic University of America Press, 1954.

Hill, Wesley. *Paul and the Trinity: Persons, Relations, and the Pauline Letters*. Grand Rapids, MI: Eerdmans, 2015.

Hinlicky, Paul R. *Divine Simplicity: Christ the Crisis of Metaphysics*. Grand Rapids, MI: Baker Academic, 2016.

Holmes, Christopher R. J. *The Lord Is Good: Seeking the God of the Psalter*. Downers Grove, IL: IVP Academic, 2018.

Holmes, Stephen. *The Quest for the Trinity: The Doctrine of God in Scripture, History and Modernity*. Downers Grove, IL: InterVarsity Press, 2012.

Irenaeus. *Against Heresies*. In *The Faith of the Early Fathers, Volume 1*. Translated by William Jurgens. Collegeville, MN: Liturgical Press, 1970.

———. *Fragments from the Lost Writings of Irenaeus*. In *Ante-Nicene Fathers*, vol. 1. Peabody, MA: Hendrickson, 2012.

Jamieson, R. B., and Tyler R. Wittman. *Biblical Reasoning: Christological and Trinitarian Rules of Exegesis*. Grand Rapids, MI: Baker Academic, 2022.

Jenson, Matt. *Theology in the Democracy of the Dead: A Dialogue with the Living Tradition*. Grand Rapids, MI: Baker Academic, 2019.

John Chrysostom. *Homilies on Genesis 18–45*. Translated by Robert C. Hill. Washington, DC: Catholic University of America, 1986.

John of Damascus. *Exposition of the Orthodox Faith*. In *Nicene and Post-Nicene Fathers*, vol. 9. Peabody, MA: Hendrickson, 2012.

Kapic, Kelly M., and Bruce L. McCormack, eds. *Mapping Modern Theology: A Thematic and Historical Introduction*. Grand Rapids, MI: Baker Academic, 2012.

Kärkkäinen, Veli-Matti. *Christology: A Global Introduction*, 2nd ed. Grand Rapids, MI: Baker Academic, 2016.

———. *The Doctrine of God: A Global Introduction*. Grand Rapids, MI: Baker Academic, 2017.

Knepper, Timothy D. "Pseudo-Dionysius and Paul's Sermon to the Unknown God." In *Ineffability: An Exercise in Comparative Religion*. Dordrecht: Springer, 2017.

Kurtz, Ronni. *No Shadow of Turning: Divine Immutability and the Economy of Redemption*. Ross-shire, UK: Mentor, 2022.

Laird, Martin. *Gregory of Nyssa and the Grasp of Faith: Union, Knowledge, and Divine Presence*. Oxford: Oxford University Press, 2004.

Le Poidevin, Robin, Peter Simons, Andrew McGonigal, and Ross P. Cameron. *The Routledge Companion to Metaphysics*. New York: Routledge. 2012.

Lee, Hoon J. *The Biblical Accommodation Debate in Germany: Interpretation and the Enlightenment*. Dordrecht: Springer, 2017.

Legaspi, Michael C. *The Death of Scripture and the Rise of Biblical Studies*. New York: Oxford University Press, 2010.

Legge, Dominic. *The Trinitarian Christology of St. Thomas Aquinas*. Oxford: Oxford University Press, 2017.

Levering, Matthew. *Engaging the Doctrine of Creation: Cosmos, Creatures, and the Wise and Good Creator*. Grand Rapids, MI: Baker Academic, 2017.

———. "The Holy Spirit in the Trinitarian Communion: 'Love' and 'Gift'?" *IJST* 16, no. 2 (2014): 126-42.

———. *Scripture and Metaphysics: Aquinas and the Renewal of Trinitarian Theology*. Malden, MA: Blackwell, 2004.

Littlejohn, Bradford. *God of Our Fathers: Classical Theism for the Contemporary Church*. Landrum, SC: Davenant Institute, 2018.

Loux, Michael J., and Thomas M. Crisp. *Metaphysics: A Contemporary Introduction*. New York: Routledge, 2017.

Luther, Martin. *Lectures on Genesis: Chapters 6–14.* Edited by Jaroslav Pelikan. Luther's Works. St. Louis: Concordia, 1960.

Macdonald, Paul. *Knowledge and the Transcendent: An Inquiry into the Mind's Relationship to God.* Washington, DC: Catholic University of America Press, 2009.

Manoussakis, John Panteleimon. *God After Metaphysics.* Bloomington: Indiana University Press, 2007.

Marion, Jean-Luc. *God Without Being.* Translated by Thomas A Carlson. Chicago: University of Chicago Press, 2012.

———. "Metaphysics and Phenomenology: A Summary for Theologians." In *The Postmodern God: A Theological Reader,* edited by Graham Ward. Oxford: Blackwell, 1997.

Maximus the Confessor. *Two Hundred Chapters on Theology.* Crestwood, NY: St. Vladimir's Seminary Press, 2015.

McCall, Thomas H. *Which Trinity? Whose Monotheism? Philosophical and Systematic Theologians on the Metaphysics of Trinitarian Theology.* Grand Rapids, MI: Eerdmans, 2010.

McCormack, Bruce L., ed. *Engaging the Doctrine of God: Contemporary Protestant Perspectives.* Grand Rapids, MI: Baker Academic, 2008.

McInerny, Ralph. *Aquinas and Analogy.* Washington, DC: Catholic University of America Press, 1996.

Mercer, Jarred A. *Divine Perfection and Human Potentiality: The Trinitarian Anthropology of Hilary of Poitiers.* New York: Oxford University Press, 2019.

Molnar, Paul D. *Divine Freedom and the Doctrine of the Immanent Trinity.* New York: T&T Clark, 2017.

Moltmann, Jürgen. *History and the Triune God: Contributions to Trinitarian Theology.* Translated by John Bowden. New York: Crossroad, 1992.

———. *The Crucified God.* Minneapolis: Fortress, 2015.

———. *The Trinity and the Kingdom: The Doctrine of God.* Minneapolis: Fortress, 1993.

Muller, Richard. *Dictionary of Latin and Greek Theological Terms: Drawn Principally from Protestant Scholastic Theology.* Grand Rapids, MI: Baker Academic, 2017.

———. *Divine Will and Human Choice: Freedom, Contingency, and Necessity in Early Modern Reformed Thought.* Grand Rapids, MI: Baker Academic, 2017.

———. "Incarnation, Immutability, and the Case for Classical Theism." *Westminster Journal of Theology* 45 (1983): 22-40.

Nelson, R. David., Darren Sarisky, and Justin Stratis. *Theological Theology: Essays in Honour of John Webster.* London: T&T Clark, 2018.

Niewenhove, Rik van. *An Introduction to Medieval Theology.* Cambridge: Cambridge University Press, 2012.

Ortlund, Gavin. *Anslem's Pursuit of Joy: A Commentary on the Proslogion.* Washington, DC: Catholic University of America Press, 2020.

———. *Theological Retrieval for Evangelicals: Why We Need Our Past to Have a Future.* Wheaton, IL: Crossway, 2019.

Owen, John. *Biblical Theology.* 5th ed. Morgan, PA: Soli Deo Gloria, 2012.

———. *The Works of John Owen*. Edited by William H. Goold. Vol. 1. Edinburgh: Banner of Truth Trust, 2000.

Palmer, D. W. "Atheism, Apologetic, and Negative Theology in the Greek Apologists of the Second Century." In *Vigiliae Christianae: A Review of Early Christian Life and Language* 37, no. 3 (1983): 234-59.

Pannenberg, Wolfhart. *Systematic Theology*. Translated by G. W. Bromiley. 4 vols. Grand Rapids, MI: Eerdmans, 1991.

Pasnau, Robert. *Metaphysical Themes: 1274–1671*. Oxford: Oxford University Press, 2013.

Pattison, George. *God and Being: An Enquiry*. Oxford: Oxford University Press, 2011.

Pelikan, Jaroslav. *Credo: Historical and Theological Guide to Creeds and Confessions of Faith in the Christian Tradition*. New Haven, CT: Yale University Press, 2003.

Pinnock, Clark. *The Most Moved Mover: A Theology of God's Openness*. Grand Rapids, MI: Baker, 2001.

Plantinga, Alvin. *Warranted Christian Belief*. Oxford: Oxford University Press, 2000.

Przywara, Erich. *Analogia Entis: Metaphysics—Original Structure and Universal Rhythm*. Translated by John R. Betz and David Bentley Hart. Grand Rapids, MI: Eerdmans, 2014.

Radde-Gallwitz, Andrew. *Basil of Caesarea, Gregory of Nyssa, and the Transformation of Divine Simplicity*. New York: Oxford University Press, 2009.

Rahner, Karl. *The Trinity*. 3rd ed. London: Burns & Oates, 1986.

Richards, Jay Wesley. *The Untamed God: A Philosophical Exploration of Divine Perfections, Simplicity, and Immutability*. Downers Grove, IL: InterVarsity Press, 2003.

Riches, Aaron. *Ecce Homo: On the Divine Unity of Christ*. Grand Rapids, MI: Eerdmans, 2016.

Rocca, Gregory P. *Speaking the Incomprehensible God: Thomas Aquinas on the Interplay of Positive and Negative Theology*. Washington, DC: Catholic University of America, 2004.

Rorem, Paul. *Pseudo-Dionysius: A Commentary on the Texts and an Introduction to Their Influence*. Oxford: Oxford University Press, 1993.

Rousseau, Philip. *Basil of Caesarea*. Berkely: University of California Press, 1994.

Sailhamer, John H. *Introduction to Old Testament Theology: A Canonical Approach*. Grand Rapids, MI: Zondervan, 1995.

Sanders, Fred. *The Triune God*. Grand Rapids, MI: Zondervan, 2016.

Sanders, Fred, and Oliver D. Crisp, eds. *Advancing Trinitarian Theology: Explorations in Constructive Dogmatics*. Grand Rapids, MI: Zondervan, 2014.

———. *The Task of Dogmatics: Explorations in Theological Method*. Grand Rapids, MI: Zondervan, 2017.

Sanders, Fred, and Scott Swain, eds. *Retrieving Eternal Generation*. Grand Rapids, MI: Zondervan, 2017.

Schaff, Philip. *The Creeds of Christendom*. 3 vols. Grand Rapids, MI: Baker, 1983.

Schleiermacher, Friedrich. *The Christian Faith*. London: T&T Clark, 2016.

Scotus, John Duns. *Philosophical Writings*. Translated by Alan Wolter. Indianapolis: Hackett, 1987.

Sheridan, Mark. *Language for God in the Patristic Tradition: Wrestling with Biblical Anthropomorphism*. Downers Grove, IL: IVP Academic, 2014.

Sonderegger, Katherine. *Systematic Theology*, vol. 1, *The Doctrine of God*. Minneapolis: Fortress, 2015.

Soskice, Janet. *Naming God: Addressing the Divine in Philosophy, Theology and Scripture*. Cambridge: Cambridge University Press, 2023.

Spencer, Archie J. *The Analogy of Faith: The Quest for God's Speakability*. Downers Grove, IL: IVP Academic, 2015.

Stang, Charles M. *Apophasis and Pseudonymity in Dionysius the Areopagite: "No Longer I."* Oxford: Oxford University Press, 2012.

Stępień, Tomasz, and Krolina Kochańczyk-Bonińska. *Unknown God, Known in His Activities: Incomprehensibility of God During the Trinitarian Controversy of the 4th Century*. European Studies in Theology, Philosophy and History of Religion 18. Berlin: Peter Lang, 2018.

Stump, Eleonore. *The God of the Bible and the God of the Philosophers*. Milwaukee: Marquette University Press, 2016.

Swain, Scott R. *Trinity, Revelation, and Reading: A Theological Introduction to the Bible and Its Interpretation*. London: T&T Clark, 2011.

Swinburne, Richard. *The Christian God*. Oxford: Oxford University Press, 1994.

———. *The Coherence of Theism*. Oxford: Oxford University Press, 1993.

Tertullian. *A Treatise on the Soul*. In *Ante-Nicene Fathers*, vol. 3. Peabody, MA: Hendrickson, 2012.

Thielicke, Helmut. *A Little Exercise for Young Theologians*. Translated by Charles Taylor. Grand Rapids, MI: Eerdmans, 1962.

Thomas Aquinas. *Commentary on the Gospel of John: Chapters 1–5*. Translated by Fabian Larcher and James A. Weisheipl. Washington, DC: Catholic University of America Press, 2010.

———. *Commentary on the Gospel of John: Chapters 13–21*. Translated by Fabian Larcher and James A. Weisheipl. Washington, DC: Catholic University of America Press, 2010.

———. *Thomas Aquinas' Earliest Treatment of the Divine Essence: Scriptum Super libros Sententiarum*. Book 1, Distinction 8. Translated by E. M. Macierowski. New York: New York University Press, 1997.

Torrance, T. F. *The Christian Doctrine of God: One Being, Three Persons*. New York: T&T Clark, 2016.

———. *Incarnation: The Person and Life of Christ*. Edited by Robert T Walker. Downers Grove, IL: IVP Academic, 2015.

Turner, Denys. *The Darkness of God: Negativity in Christian Mysticism*. Cambridge: Cambridge University Press, 1995.

Vaggione, Richard. *Aspects of Faith in the Eunomian Controversy: Gregory of Nyssa Against Eunomius*. Oxford: Oxford University Press, 1976.

Van den Brink, Gijsbert, and C. Van der Kooi. *Christian Dogmatics: An Introduction*. Grand Rapids, MI: Eerdmans, 2017.

Van den Brink, Gijsbert, and Marcel Sarot, eds. *Understanding the Attributes of God.* Frankfurt: Europäischer Verlag der Wissenschaften, 1999.

Van Geest, Paul. *Incomprehensibility of God: Augustine as a Negative Theologian in Late Antique History and Religion.* Leuven: Peeters, 2011.

Vanhoozer, Kevin. *First Theology: God, Scripture, and Hermeneutics.* Downers Grove, IL: IVP Academic, 2002.

———. *Is There a Meaning in This Text? The Bible, the Reader, and the Morality of Literary Knowledge.* Grand Rapids, MI: Zondervan, 2009.

———. *Remythologizing Theology: Divine Action, Passion, and Authorship.* Cambridge: Cambridge University Press, 2012.

Vanhoozer, Kevin J., Craig G. Bartholomew, Daniel J. Treier, and N. T. Wright, eds. *Dictionary for Theological Interpretation of the Bible.* Grand Rapids, MI: Baker Academic, 2005.

Vidu, Adonis. *The Same God Who Works All Things: Inseperable Operations in Trinitarian Theology.* Grand Rapids, MI: Eerdmans, 2021.

Visser, Sandra, and Thomas Williams. *Anselm.* Oxford: Oxford University Press, 2005.

Voetius, Gisbertus. *God's Single, Absolutely Simple Essence.* Translated by R. M. Hurd. *The Confessional Presbyterian* 15 (2019): 9-40.

Vos, Geerhardus. *Reformed Dogmatics: Theology Proper.* Translated by Richard B Gaffin Jr. Bellingham, WA: Lexham, 2014.

Warfield, Benjamin B. *Biblical Doctrines.* Rev. ed. Carlisle, PA: Banner of Truth, 1988.

———. *Selected Shorter Writings.* 2 vols. Edited by John E. Meeter. Phillipsburg, NJ: P&R, 2001.

Webster, John. *Confessing God: Essays in Christian Dogmatics II.* New York: T&T Clark, 2005.

———. *The Culture of Theology.* Grand Rapids, MI: Baker Academic, 2019.

———. *The Domain of the Word: Scripture and Theological Reason.* New York: T&T Clark, 2012.

———. *Holy Scripture: A Dogmatic Sketch.* Cambridge: Cambridge University Press, 2003.

———. "ὑπὸ πνεύματος ἁγίου φερόμενοι ἐλάλησαν ἀπὸ θεοῦ ἄνθρωποι: On the Inspiration of Holy Scripture." In *Conception, Reception, and the Spirit: Essays in Honor of Andrew T. Lincoln,* edited by J. G. McConville and L. K. Pietersen. Eugene, OR: Cascade, 2015.

———. *Word and Church: Essays in Christian Dogmatics.* New York: T&T Clark, 2016.

Weinandy, Thomas G. *Athanasius: A Theological Introduction.* Burlington, VT: Ashgate, 2007.

———. *Does God Change? The Word's Becoming in the Incarnation.* Still River, MA: St. Bede's, 1985.

———. *Does God Suffer?* Notre Dame, IN: University of Notre Dame Press, 2000.

Wellum, Stephen J. *Christ Alone: The Uniqueness of Jesus as Savior.* Grand Rapids, MI: Zondervan, 2017.

———. *God the Son Incarnate: The Doctrine of Christ*. Wheaton, IL: Crossway, 2016.

———. "Jesus as Lord and Son: Two Complementary Truths of Biblical Christology." *Criswell Theological Review* 13, no. 1 (2015): 23-45.

White, Thomas Joseph. "Divine Simplicity and the Holy Trinity." *IJST* 18, no. 1 (2016): 66-93.

———. *Exodus*. Brazos Theological Commentary on the Bible. Grand Rapids, MI: Brazos, 2016.

———. "Intra-Trinitarian Obedience and Nicene-Chalcedonian Christology." *Nova et Vetera* 6 (2008): 377-402.

———, ed. *The Analogy of Being: Invention of the Antichrist or the Wisdom of God?* Grand Rapids, MI: Eerdmans, 2011.

———. *The Trinity: On the Nature and Mystery of the One God*. Washington, DC: Catholic University of America Press, 2022.

Whitehead, Alfred North. *Process and Reality*. New York: Harper & Row, 1929.

Wisse, Maarten. *Trinitarian Theology Beyond Participation: Augustine's De Trinitate and Contemporary Theology*. New York: T&T Clark, 2011.

Wittmann, Tyler R. *God and Creation in the Theology of Thomas Aquinas and Karl Barth*. Cambridge: Cambridge University Press, 2019.

Wrathall, Mark. *Religion After Metaphysics*. Cambridge: Cambridge University Press, 2003.

Wright, David F. "Accommodation and Barbarity in John Calvin's Old Testament Commentaries." In *Understanding Poets and Prophets: Essays in Honour of George Wishart Anderson*, ed. A. G. Auld. Sheffield: Sheffield Academic, 1993. 413-27.

———. "Calvin's Pentateuchal Criticism: Equity, Hardness of Heart, and Divine Accommodation in the Mosaic Harmony Commentary." *Calvin Theological Journal* 21 (1986): 33-50.

General Index

Scripture Index